Current Thinking on Fiscal Policy

Current Thinking on Fiscal Policy

Edited by

Jérôme Creel

and

Malcolm Sawyer

Selection and editorial matter © Jérôme Creel and Malcolm Sawyer 2009
Individual chapters © contributors 2009

First published 2009 by
PALGRAVE MACMILLAN

Palgrave Macmillan in the UK is an imprint of Macmillan Publishers Limited,
registered in England, company number 785998, of Houndmills, Basingstoke,
Hampshire RG21 6XS.

Palgrave Macmillan in the US is a division of St Martin's Press LLC,
175 Fifth Avenue, New York, NY 10010.

Palgrave Macmillan is the global academic imprint of the above companies
and has companies and representatives throughout the world.

Palgrave®and Macmillan®are registered trademarks in the United States,
the United Kingdom, Europe and other countries.

ISBN-13: 978–0–230–20249–8
ISBN-10: 0–230–20249–7

This book is printed on paper suitable for recycling and made from fully
managed and sustained forest sources. Logging, pulping and manufacturing
processes are expected to conform to the environmental regulations of the
country of origin.

A catalogue record for this book is available from the British Library.

Library of Congress Cataloging-in-Publication Data
Current thinking on fiscal policy / edited by Jérôme Creel and Malcolm
    Sawyer.
      p. cm.
    Includes bibliographical references and index.
    ISBN 978–0–230–20249–8 (alk. paper)
    1. Fiscal policy. I. Creel, Jérôme   II. Sawyer, Malcolm C.
  HJ192.5.C87 2009
    339.5′2—dc22   2008029921

10   9   8   7   6   5   4   3   2   1
18   17   16   15   14   13   12   11   10   09

Printed and bound in Great Britain by
CPI Antony Rowe, Chippenham and Eastbourne

Contents

List of Tables and Figures

Tables

Figures

Acknowledgements

The chapters in this volume on fiscal policy were presented as papers at the Fourth International Conference on Developments in Economic Theory and Policy at the Universidad del País Vasco, Bilbao, Spain, on 5–6 July 2007. Some of them had been first presented during a Workshop at OFCE/Sciences Po dedicated to 'Current Thinking on Fiscal Policy', Paris on 15 June 2007. We express our thanks to the organizers of the conference and workshop and to the authors of the chapters for enabling this volume to be completed.

JÉRÔME CREEL
MALCOLM SAWYER

Notes on the Contributors

Philip Arestis is University Director of Research, Cambridge Centre for Economics and Public Policy, Department of Land Economy, University of Cambridge, UK; Adjunct Professor of Economics, University of Utah, US; Visiting Professor, University of Leeds, UK, and School of Oriental and African Studies (SOAS), University of London, UK. He was a member of the Economics and Econometrics RAE panel in 1996 and in 2001, and Quality Assessor for the Quality Assessment Exercise in Economics of the Scottish Higher Education Funding Council, the Welsh Funding Councils and of the Higher Education Funding Council in England. He was a member of the Council of the Royal Economic Society (RES), Secretary of the RES Standing Conference of Heads of Department in Economics (CHUDE), and an elected member of the Executive Board of the Eastern Economic Association (EEA), USA. He is Chief Academic Adviser to the UK Government Economic Service (GES) on Professional Development in Economics, and Vice-Chair of the ESRC-funded Macroeconomics, Money and Finance Research Group.

Jérôme Creel is Professor of Economics at ESCP–EAP European School of Management, Paris, and Deputy Director at the Research Department of OFCE/Sciences Po, Paris, France. He is also the Academic Dean of the European Studies Program at Sciences Po, a joint programme with four Japanese universities. He holds a PhD from University Paris–Dauphine in economics (*summa cum laude*). He is a member of the Editorial Board of *Revue de l'OFCE*. He is the author of a book on the European Union and has published more than 40 papers in journals and books. His works have dealt with monetary and fiscal policies, including coordination issues in the EMU, the economics of EU enlargement and institutional economics, notably related to the Constitutional Treaty and delegation issues.

Elisabetta De Antoni is Associate Professor at the University of Trento in Italy. She did her studies at the University of Bologna and at the London School of Economics and Political Science. From 2004 to 2006 she was again in the UK as a Visiting Fellow at the University of Cambridge. Her research and teaching fields are macroeconomics and monetary theory. At present, her main research project concerns post-Keynes heterodox monetary economists. In this context, she has published articles on

Robert Clower, on Axel Leijonhufvud and several articles on Hyman Minsky. The project's basic idea is that heterodox approaches offer a better understanding of European and Italian economic sluggishness and of American financial instability than does mainstream economics.

Giuseppe Fontana is Professor of Monetary Economics at the University of Leeds (UK) and Associate Professor at the Università del Sannio (Italy). He was awarded the 2008 L.S. Shackle Prize, St Edmund's College, Cambridge (UK). He is a Life Member Fellow at Clare Hall (University of Cambridge, UK), and a Visiting Research Professor at the Center for Full Employment and Price Stability (University of Missouri Kansas City, USA), and the Cambridge Centre for Economic and Public Policy (University of Cambridge, UK). He has published several journal articles and is the editor of several books on related topics. He has recently published *Money, Time, and Uncertainty*.

Edwin Le Heron is Maître de Conférences in Economics at the Institut d'Etudes Politiques in Bordeaux, France, and researcher at SPIRIT (Science du politique, Relations Internationales et Territoire) there. He is also the President of the ADEK (the French Association for the Development of Keynesian Studies), which gathers French economists interested in Keynes and in post-Keynesian works. The topics of his research are monetary policy, post-Keynesian monetary theory and the history of thought. His recent papers include (with Tarik Mouakil) 'A Post Keynesian Stock-Flow Consistent Model for the Dynamic Analysis of Monetary Policy Shock on Banking Behaviour', *Metroeconomica*, vol. 59(4).

Francesco Saraceno obtained his PhD from Columbia University, New York, USA. He work at the Observatoire Français des Conjonctures Economiques and teaches at Sciences Po in Paris. He is on leave from the Council of Economic Advisers of the Italian Prime Minister's Office. He specializes in macroeconomics and international economics.

Malcolm Sawyer is Professor of Economics, University of Leeds, UK, and Pro-Dean for Learning and Teaching for the Faculty of Business there. He is managing editor of the *International Review of Applied Economics* and the editor of the series *New Directions in Modern Economics* published by Edward Elgar. He is the author of numerous books, has edited many more and published over 70 papers in journals and contributed chapters to nearly 100 books. His research interests are in macroeconomics, fiscal and monetary policy, the political economy of the European Monetary Union, the nature of money, causes and concepts of unemployment and the economics of Michał Kalecki.

1
Introduction: Current Thinking on Fiscal Policy

Jérôme Creel and Malcolm Sawyer

The central purpose of this book, as the title suggests, is to develop current thinking on fiscal policy and to emphasize the role that fiscal policy can play in macroeconomic policy. At first sight, such emphasis may seem to be at odds with current thinking: as Benjamin Friedman has recently stated: 'For the most part, fiscal *policy* has mostly disappeared from discussion at both the popular and the academic levels' (Friedman, 2007). Friedman is right, but in a specific context: in the past few years, a 'new consensus in macroeconomics' has emerged.[1] This 'consensus' was a reflection of the rise to dominance of monetary policy, whether considered as a 'science' or an 'art'. Monetary policy was viewed as the use of the policy interest rate to almost exclusively target the rate of inflation. The 'consensus' incorporates an endogenous view of money, but most significantly for this volume relegates fiscal policy to the sidelines. Indeed in many presentations of the 'new consensus in macroeconomics', fiscal policy is absent under the implicit assumption that fiscal policy can have no effect.

Such a pessimistic view of the role of fiscal policy is challenged in this volume, and the different contributions all deliver theoretical insights to defend fiscal policy as a valid macroeconomic instrument in the hands of governments, whether through its discretionary or its automatic role. The 'new current thinking' on fiscal policy that this book conveys is in line with the actual evolutions of debts and deficits in the world economy. Many empirical facts question the relevance of disregarding fiscal policy. Let us mention a few: very active fiscal reactions to past recessions or looming ones – they have helped to dampen the crises; the great swings in US public finances since the 1980s which have occurred at the same time as the 'great moderation' – these swings did not produce volatility *per se*; or the slow growth process of European countries during

1

the booming years, which was achieved with limited fiscal deficits – fiscal contractions had depressive effects.

At first sight, the latter regularity appears incompatible with the 'new consensus in macroeconomics'; therefore, it is necessary to analyse fiscal policy in other conceptual frameworks. Such frameworks already exist and we can refer to the 'functional finance' approach or to the 'Minsky analysis'. Some chapters of this book are devoted to emphasizing the role of fiscal policy in these alternative frameworks. Contributions in this book also make a point in proposing modifications in the 'new consensus in macroeconomics' framework so that it also embeds fiscal rules, automatic stabilization device or discretionary policies. It is argued that the provision of sustainable public finances is not irrelevant in the context of stabilizing and growth-improving fiscal policies.

In Chapter 2, 'Fiscal Policy within the "New Consensus Macroeconomics" Framework', Philip Arestis aims to consider this upgrading of monetary policy and downgrading of fiscal policy by focusing on fiscal policy and the proposition that fiscal policy is ineffective. He reviews and appraises recent and not so recent theoretical and empirical developments on the fiscal policy front. The question is posed as to whether fiscal policy rules should replace monetary policy rules, especially when it is noted that both monetary and fiscal policies impact on the level of demand. The possibility of fiscal and monetary policy coordination is also discussed to conclude that it deserves careful consideration. The overall conclusion is that even within the confines of the 'New Consensus in Macroeconomics' framework, fiscal policy as a tool of macroeconomic policy deserves a great deal more attention paid to it than hitherto.

Giuseppe Fontana in Chapter 3, 'Fiscal Policy in Today's Endogenous Money World', continues on this theme with a challenge to the rare mention of the macroeconomic role of discretionary fiscal policy. The challenge is undertaken along three main avenues. First, it argues that there is nothing inherently monetary about the nature of stabilization policy in the new consensus view. Second, it lends support to the view that ideology, policy mistakes and particular historical circumstances played a role at least as important as economic theory in the rejection of post-war Keynesianism, and the consequent downgrading of fiscal policy. Finally, the existence of partial or complete crowding-out in the modern new consensus/endogenous money framework is decided by the central bank rather than by the 'market'. Also, in this framework the different forms of financing real government spending are endogenously decided by private agents rather than exogenously set by policy makers.

In Chapter 4, 'Minsky's Financial Instability Hypothesis: The Crucial Role of Fiscal Policy', Philip Arestis and Elisabetta De Antoni contrast the views of Hyman Minsky with the dominant view in macroeconomics in recent years. Rather than seeking to place limits on budget deficits and fiscal variables like in the new consensus's applied extensions to European countries, Minsky viewed fiscal policies as the most powerful economic control weapon. Minsky placed uncertainty, the financing of capital accumulation and capitalism's financial instability at the centre of his analysis. In his view, government intervention is not only necessary to reach and maintain full employment; it is also indispensable to contain capitalism's instability, avoiding financial crises followed by debt deflations and deep depressions. The effects of fiscal policy do not work themselves out in the goods market, but also concern the financial sector. The unprecedented growth of the financial dimension of the economy and of international financial transactions makes Minsky's analysis extremely modern.

Malcolm Sawyer in Chapter 5, 'The Continuing Relevance of Fiscal Policy', reviews a range of arguments that have been advanced against the use of fiscal policy on the grounds that variations in the government budget position have no impact on the level of demand. It draws the distinction between a 'functional finance' approach and one based on asking about the effects of fiscal policy often in a context where full utilization of resources is assumed. The 'functional finance' approach is outlined. Arguments which have been raised against the use of fiscal policy, like 'Ricardian equivalence' and then the notion of a 'supply-side equilibrium' which acts as a strong attractor for the level of economic activity, are critically appraised. The two final sections before some brief conclusions relate to some empirical considerations and the difference between fine and coarse tuning, promoting a better consideration of the latter in the fiscal policy debate.

Chapter 6, by Philip Arestis and Malcolm Sawyer, 'The Intertemporal Budget Constraint and the Sustainability of Budget Deficits', examines in detail the arguments advanced against the use of fiscal policy and of budget deficits that come under the general heading of the unsustainability of budget deficits. In this chapter they investigate two related objections that have been raised against the use of budget deficits. The first arises from the idea that the government faces an intertemporal budget constraint such that, in effect, the net wealth position of the government is constrained to be zero, and hence that the sum of initial outstanding debt plus discounted future budget positions sum to zero. For a government with outstanding debt, this requires that at some stage (primary) budget surpluses would have to be run. The second is that a continuing budget deficit would be unsustainable, as the borrowing adds to the government debt with debt and interest payments rising over time without limit. It is argued that the objections are themselves unsustainable.

It is well-known that fiscal policy has some in-built automatic stabilization features. In Chapter 7, 'Automatic Stabilization, Discretionary Policy and the Stability Pact', Jérôme Creel and Francesco Saraceno describe recent trends on the efficiency of stabilizers in the European Union. Using both macro evidence on the cyclical sensitivity of budget deficit to economic activity, and micro evidence on the tax and expenditure profiles, they conclude, in agreement with the recent literature, that the importance of automatic stabilization has decreased. After remarking that this trend is contradictory with the current economic institutions of Europe relying exclusively on automatic stabilization for the conduct of fiscal policy, as applied extensions to the new consensus view acknowledge, it is argued that increasing flexibility, one alternative way to reduce cyclical fluctuations, does not seem a viable path. The chapter concludes by defending the appropriateness of discretionary fiscal policy. It is argued by means of a simple model that the theoretical arguments against its use are not conclusive, and a recent stream of literature is described, based on structural VAR models, that conclude rather robustly for the effectiveness of discretionary fiscal policy in the short and long run.

Edwin Le Heron undertakes to analyse the effects of 'Fiscal and Monetary Policies in a Keynesian Stock-Flow Consistent Model' in Chapter 8. Following the New Classical Macroeconomics (NCM) and the New Keynesian Macroeconomics (NKM), the independence of central banks significantly increased after 1990, which could preclude coordination between the fiscal and the monetary policies. The purpose of this chapter is to consider the stabilizing effects of fiscal policy within the framework of the new monetary policies implemented by independent central banks. A rule on public expenditures is contrasted with a rule on public deficits, and for this a two-country model is developed. In the first country, the government implements a fiscal policy with automatic stabilizers and a central bank, like the Fed, has a dual mandate: inflation and growth. There is coordination between fiscal and monetary policies. The second country respects the Maastricht treaty of the European Union. The government implements an orthodox fiscal policy (balanced budget) and a fully independent central bank, like the ECB, has a unique objective: inflation. A Post-Keynesian stock-flow consistent (SFC) model is built with a private banks sector deriving from a Minskian approach.

Within this original framework the consequences of a supply shock are analysed and contrasted between the two countries with two distinct fiscal and monetary regimes. If the society seeks three aims: stability of prices, full employment and stability on the financial markets, the welfare performance of the different policy mixes are computed and a comparison performed between the two countries.

These seven contributions were motivated by a kind of urgency to restate fiscal policy. They showed that fiscal policy could be a stabilizing instrument, whether after a real shock or a financial shock has occurred, as well as a growth-enhancing device. Thinking about fiscal policy as an efficient tool in the toolbox of policymakers is the motto of this volume.

Note

1. See, for example, Meyer (2001); for elaboration see Arestis (2007), and for a critical appraisal Arestis and Sawyer (2008).

References

Arestis, P. (2007) 'What is the new consensus in macroeconomics?', in P. Arestis (ed.), *Is There a New Consensus in Macroeconomics?*, Basingstoke: Palgrave Macmillan.

Arestis, P. and Sawyer, M. (2008) 'A critical reconsideration of the foundations of monetary policy in the new consensus macroeconomics framework', *Cambridge Journal of Economics*, forthcoming.

Friedman, B.M. (2007) 'What we still don't know about monetary and fiscal policy', *Brookings Papers on Economic Activity*, 2, 49–71.

Meyer, L.H. (2001) 'Does money matter?', *Federal Reserve Bank of St. Louis Review*, 83(5), 1–15, online at: http://research.stlouisfed.org/publications/review/past/2001.

2
Fiscal Policy within the 'New Consensus Macroeconomics' Framework

Philip Arestis

Introduction[1]

The purpose of this chapter is to examine the role of fiscal policy within the 'New Consensus Macroeconomics' (NCM). In Arestis (2007) we put forward the NCM theoretical framework in the case of an open economy, and discussed at length the implications for monetary policy. Utilizing this framework we will explore in this contribution the role of fiscal policy within the NCM, and its potential impact on the economy.

While net government spending adds an equal quantity of net financial assets to the combined non-government sectors by identity, the impact of fiscal policy on aggregate demand and economic activity depends heavily on the theoretical model and its assumptions about the real world where the policy is implemented. In the old macroeconomic models with sluggish prices, fiscal policy has positive demand implications. Expansionary fiscal policy adds to aggregate spending, and allows demand-constrained firms to sell more output, thereby increasing income and employment. The inflexibility of prices due to mark-up pricing makes output demand determined. Prices adjust gradually and they follow cost-push increases in wages as captured in some versions of the Phillips-curve type of specifications. The fiscal policy multiplier is positive, although its size can be affected by a number of factors, of which the main ones are as follows: productive capacity close to full use; higher interest rates from anticipated central bank interest rate changes that may crowd out private demand; fiscal policies that may cause the central bank to implement higher interest rates, reflecting higher risk premia; currency depreciation in a flexible exchange rate open economy; composition of the fiscal measure, where government spending is thought to be more effective than tax changes.

These factors are likely to produce a positive, but small, fiscal policy multiplier.

The NCM view of fiscal policy is rather different. Those factors, which produce weak Keynesian results, are given more prominence in a way that weakens fiscal policy substantially. Furthermore, fiscal policy is thought to have further implications in view of the emphasis given to the expectations of economic agents concerning their future income and wealth, thereby producing demand-side, as well as supply-side effects. All these effects so weaken fiscal policy that it is rendered ineffective as a macroeconomic stabilization instrument of policy. Recent contributions, though, begin to question a number of the assumptions adopted for the purposes of deriving these results. In addition, empirical evidence appears to support the basis of these concerns. In what follows we elaborate on these propositions and look at the available empirical evidence.

We begin by sketching the 'new consensus' theoretical model in the following section, followed by a discussion of the role and effectiveness of fiscal policy within this theoretical framework. Recent theoretical developments and empirical findings on the fiscal policy front are then appraised. This is followed by a discussion that poses the question of whether replacing monetary policy rules by fiscal policy rules might make any difference to the NCM theoretical framework and its policy implications. This leads neatly into the question of 'What role for fiscal policy?' The final section summarizes the argument and concludes.

An open economy NCM

We present NCM when extended to an open economy (see, also, Agénor, 2002), although it is fair to suggest that the model is normally portrayed in a closed economy context. We utilize a six-equation open-economy model, which has been used in the context of a similar exercise to highlight NCM and monetary policy (Arestis, 2007). This model can be described as follows:

$$Y_t^g = a_0 + a_1 Y_{t-1}^g + a_2 E_t(Y_{t+1}^g) + a_3[R_t - E_t(p_{t+1})] + a_4(rer)_t + s_1 \quad (2.1)$$

$$p_t = b_1 Y_t^g + b_2 p_{t-1} + b_3 E_t(p_{t+1}) + b_4[E_t(p_{wt+1}) - E_t \Delta(er)_t] + s_2 \quad (2.2)$$

$$R_t = (1 - c_3)[RR^* + E_t(p_{t+1}) + c_1 Y_{t-1}^g + c_2(p_{t-1} - p^T)] + c_3 R_{t-1} + s_3 \quad (2.3)$$

$$(rer_t) = d_0 + d_1[[(R_t - E_t(p_{t+1})] - [(R_{wt}) - E(p_{wt+1})]]$$
$$+ d_2(CA)_t + d_3E(rer)_{t+1} + s_4 \tag{2.4}$$

$$(CA)_t = e_0 + e_1(rer)_t + e_2Y_t^g + e_3Y_{wt}^g + s_5 \tag{2.5}$$

$$er_t = rer_t + P_{wt} - P_t \tag{2.6}$$

with $b_2 + b_3 + b_4 = 1$ in equation (2.2). The symbols have the following meaning: Y^g is the domestic output gap and Y_w^g is world output gap, R is nominal rate of interest (and R_w is the world nominal interest rate), p is rate of inflation (and p_w is the world inflation rate), p^T is inflation rate target, RR^* is the 'equilibrium' real rate of interest, that is the rate of interest consistent with zero output gap, which implies from equation (2.2) a constant rate of inflation; (rer) stands for the real exchange rate, and (er) for the nominal exchange rate, defined as in equation (2.6) and expressed as foreign currency units per domestic currency unit, P_w and P (in logarithms) are world and domestic price levels respectively, CA is the current account of the balance of payments, and s_i (with $i = 1$, 2, 3, 4, 5) represents stochastic shocks, and E_t refers to expectations held at time t. The coefficient a_0 is often treated as a constant, but could reflect, inter alia, the fiscal stance. The change in the nominal exchange rate appearing in equation 2.2 can be derived from equation (2.6) as $\Delta er = \Delta rer + p_{wt} - p_t$.

Equation (2.1) is the aggregate demand equation with the current output gap determined by past and expected future output gap, the real rate of interest and the real exchange rate (through effects of demand for exports and imports). It emanates from intertemporal optimization of a utility function that reflects optimal consumption smoothing. It is, thus, a forward-looking expectational aggregate demand relationship. There is, however, an acute potential problem with the formulation of equation (2.1), and this relates to the size of the coefficient a_3. To the extent that this coefficient is 'too small' (and empirically it is, as suggested by, for example, Chirinko *et al.*, 1999), it implies that effective interest-rate stabilization would require changes in the rate of interest that are implausibly large.

Equation (2.2) is a Phillips curve with inflation based on current output gap, past and future inflation, expected changes in the nominal exchange rate, and expected world prices (with the latter pointing towards imported inflation). Equation (2.3) is a monetary-policy rule, where the nominal interest rate is based on expected inflation, output gap, deviation of inflation from target (or 'inflation gap'), and the 'equilibrium' real rate of interest. The lagged interest rate represents interest rate 'smoothing' undertaken by the monetary authorities. The 'equilibrium' real rate of interest (RR^*) in equation (2.3) is of some importance that relates closely to this chapter – see section titled 'Should fiscal policy rules replace monetary policy rules? Equation (2.3) stipulates that the central bank should set the rate of interest by reference to RR^* (the Wicksellian natural rate of interest), among other variables as stipulated in the same equation. The problem with this formulation is that there is a great deal of uncertainty in terms of its imprecise nature when it comes to empirically verifying RR^*. Weber (2006), the President of the Deutsche Bundesbank, is very categorical on this problem: 'within the very active theoretical literature on optimal monetary policy under uncertainty the question remains prevalent what to do with the – up to now very imprecise – estimates of the natural rate of interest' (p. 18). Under these circumstances, the stability properties of the model are compromised.

Equation (2.4) determines the real exchange rate as a function of the real interest rate differential, the current account position, and expectations of future exchange rates. It is actually a reduced-form of equations that represent a number of theories, most important of which are the uncovered interest rate parity and forward-looking expectations. Equation (2.5) determines the current account position as a function of the real exchange rate, domestic and world output gap. Finally, equation (2.6) expresses the nominal exchange rate in terms of the real exchange rate. There are six equations and six unknowns: output, interest rate, inflation, real exchange rate, current account, and nominal exchange rate as defined in (2.6).

In terms of fiscal policy, equation (2.1) is of particular significance. There is no explicit mention of fiscal policy, though changes in the fiscal stance could be seen as reflected in a change in a_0. A number of arguments have been produced to support the proposition that the use of discretionary fiscal policy should be seen as the exception rather than the rule. The norm for fiscal policy should be to let automatic stabilizers operate in an environment of balanced budgets over the business cycle, and the operation of those stabilizers may be reflected in the coefficients a_1 and a_2.[2] A number of arguments have been put forward to make the case against the use of discretionary fiscal policy and of long-term budget deficits. The most important, and more widely accepted, are those of crowding out, the Ricardian Equivalence Theorem (RET) and what has been labelled as 'institutional aspects of fiscal policy' (Hemming, Kell and Mahfouz, 2002). The latter arguments can be briefly summarized: model uncertainty, in that longer and more uncertain lags prevail than was thought previously; there is the risk of pro-cyclical behaviour in view of cumbersome parliamentary approval and implementation; increasing taxes or decreasing government expenditure during upswings may be politically unrealistic, and this may very well generate a deficit bias; spending decisions may be subjected to irreversibility, which can lead to a public expenditure ratcheting effect; and there may be supply-side inefficiencies associated with tax-rate volatility.

Arestis and Sawyer (2003) deal with these issues and conclude that the case for fiscal policy as in the NCM theoretical framework is not supported by the available evidence and theoretical arguments. Even if the institutional factors just alluded to were shown to be theoretically and empirically pertinent, should not detract from the fact that fiscal policy is still effective. Wren-Lewis (2000) makes this point and proceeds to utilize a simple calibrated model and a more complex econometric macroeconomic model to conclude that 'changes in government spending, income transfers, and indirect taxes can still have an important impact on demand in the short run' (p. 104). Three related studies strengthen the argument. Hemming, Kell and Mahfouz (2002), when reviewing the literature on the issue, conclude that 'There is little evidence of direct crowding out or crowding out through interest rates and the exchange rate. Nor does full Ricardian equivalence or a significant partial Ricardian offset get much support from the evidence' (p. 36). Another relevant study (Hemming, Mahfouz and Schimmelpfennig, 2002, p. 4) summarizes the argument along similar lines:

> Estimates of fiscal multipliers are overwhelmingly positive but small. Short-term multipliers average around a half for taxes and one for spending, with only modest variation across countries and models (albeit with some outliers). There are hardly any instances of negative fiscal multipliers, the exception being that they can be generated in some macroeconomic models with strong credibility effects.

A more recent study (Briotti, 2005, p. 21) is also supportive of these results; it actually concludes that:

> Although many empirical studies strongly reject the full Ricardian Equivalence, the behaviour of private consumption may still be consistent with a partial Ricardian effect. However, empirical evidence is somewhat mixed and no clear conclusions can be reached about

the existence and size of the Ricardian effect. A major difficulty stems from measurement problems and methodological issues that greatly affect the estimation of parameters.

Interestingly enough, Arestis and Sawyer (2006) argue that the appearance of a partial Ricardian effect may come from the operation of stabilizing fiscal policy. Still more important are the recent developments on the role of fiscal policy within the NCM. We discuss these issues in this chapter, but we first examine further the theoretical premises of the NCM fiscal policy.

The theoretical premise of NCM fiscal policy

The NCM approach combines the optimizing general equilibrium framework with short-run nominal price stickiness. Fiscal Policy can have demand implications if it affects the expectations of economic agents concerning their future income and wealth (demand-side effects). It could also have supply-side effects to the extent that it helps to enhance labour market efficiency and labour supply along with the competitiveness of the economy. The latter effects, in their turn, affect the non-accelerating inflation rate of unemployment (NAIRU). Agents in this theoretical framework are expected to be forward looking and not be liquidity constrained; they are assumed to form expectations in terms of how future developments in government budgetary policies and public finances will affect their lifetime income and wealth.

The introduction of expectations as we have just highlighted, along with the acceptance of the RET,[3] implies that expectational and wealth effects might outweigh the Keynesian type of multiplier effects. An increase in government deficit, for example, which is perceived as permanent by agents, would imply an increase in the future tax burden and a permanent decrease in their expected income and wealth. Agents would decrease their current consumption and save more in anticipation of lower future income. Higher lump-sum taxes would decrease household and worker wealth. It is the case that the initial increase in public spending generates a larger decrease in current consumption. Labour supply would decrease as a consequence of the negative wealth effects and so would production. The latter comes about in view of the expected increase in future taxes, which induces expectations of lower production as a result of the distorting effects of higher taxation. There are also other supply-side effects in that the increase in public employment reduces private sector labour supply, exerting an upward pressure on wages, which decreases the present discounted value of the future stream of profits. This affects investment adversely. The latter is also affected by higher interest rates in view of the increased deficit (the usual crowding-out effect).

In effect, the NCM model downgrades fiscal policy, but it upgrades monetary policy. We further discuss this role of fiscal policy in what follows in this chapter. We focus on recent developments, and show that this theoretical construct entails a number of assumptions, which may or may not be validated in the real world. This makes it imperative that we also look at the extent of these assumptions being empirically validated.

Recent theoretical and empirical developments

In general terms, the early empirical studies on the effectiveness of fiscal policy within the confines of the NCM concluded that it was ineffective. The rationalization of this proposition relied essentially on three assumptions: that households optimized intertemporally, that households were not subject to any liquidity constraints, and that households were able to anticipate intertemporal financial constraints (Hemming, Kell and Mahfouz, 2002, survey the theoretical arguments along with the empirical findings of the literature on this approach). However, more recently that unfavourable empirical evidence on fiscal policy has been questioned (see, for example, Van Aarle and Garretsen, 2003), and, in addition, studies have shown results that are contrary to the NCM propositions on the issue of the effectiveness of fiscal policy (Hjelm, 2002). There have also been studies that advocate greater emphasis on fiscal policy as a key economic policy tool in macroeconomic stabilization and that fiscal policy is more effective than previously thought (Wren-Lewis, 2000). We explore these more recent contributions in what follows.

A further aspect we discuss in this section is the importance of distinguishing between developed and developing countries in the study of the role of fiscal policy. One aspect of this distinction is the difference in the evidence adduced from developed and that from developing economies. This is necessary, we maintain, for reasons that have to do with data deficiencies in developing countries. This explains to a large extent why there is rather less evidence on the short-run impact of fiscal policy for developing rather than for developed countries (Hemming, Kell and Mahfouz, 2002). An important observation in this context is that significant differences between developed and developing countries may arise from the nature of the tax systems in the two sets of countries.

A progressive tax system, which may be more typical of the developed country case, would generate counter-cyclical behaviour, whereas a regressive one, most likely to prevail in developing countries, would generate pro-cyclical behaviour. A further important distinction is the extent to which the level and degree of economic development affects the effectiveness of fiscal policy. Unfortunately, it is true that most of the literature on the effectiveness of fiscal policy has focused on developed countries. But then it is not difficult to come up with arguments that show that fiscal policy could be more effective in developing countries. For example, a factor that enhances the effectiveness of fiscal policy in developing countries is the possibility of a relatively high marginal propensity to consume identified for these countries. Such a result would, of course, increase the size of the impact of fiscal policy significantly.

At the same time, though, there are arguments that suggest the existence of serious constraints in the use of fiscal policy in the developing world. Agénor *et al.* (1999) argue that because the developing world is more likely to be influenced by supply shocks, fiscal policy as a tool of demand management is most likely to be used far less frequently and intensely there than in developed countries. Furthermore, there is the argument that suggests that a possible deficit bias may be relatively higher in developing countries. In fact, Hemming, Kell and Mahfouz (2002, p. 12) argue that governance, as it relates to poor tax administration and expenditure management, is probably the most important and significant factor that affects this bias. A further major constraint on fiscal policy in developing countries is the unavailability and high cost of domestic and external finance. It follows that access to finance should determine to a large extent the size of the fiscal deficit. An increase in the fiscal deficit beyond a level that can only be financed on unacceptable terms may be associated with severe crowding-out effects. Relaxing these constraints, therefore, enables fiscal policy to have significant stimulative effects (Lane *et al.*, 1999).

Consequently, it is paramount to distinguish between the developed-country case and the developing-country case in what follows in our discussion of the role of fiscal policy. We begin with the developed-country case.

The developed-country case

An interesting recent study on the possible effects of government spending on private consumption within the confines of a similar model postulated in equations (2.1) to (2.6), and in the case of the euro area, is Coenen and Straub (2005). The novelty of this study is that it attempts to resolve the typical prediction of the NCM type of theoretical models that government expenditure has a strong negative effect on consumption, while the empirical literature concludes on a positive, or at least, not significant negative effect on consumption.[4] It would appear that the evidence does not validate the assumptions of the theoretical model. In view of the latter finding, Coenen and Straub (2005) rely on the Mankiw (2000) study where the argument is advanced that models that attempt to study the effects of fiscal policy should allow for two types of households. One type of households (the 'Ricardian' households) are those that behave in an optimizing, fully forward manner, by trading in asset and other markets and are, thus, able to smooth consumption over time; these households hold expectations about the future, which are essentially consistent with a full-employment situation. Another type of households (the 'non-Ricardian' households) follow non-optimizing simple rules of thumb (they do not optimize intertemporally or intratemporally), cannot and do not participate in asset markets, and they merely consume their net-of-tax disposable income; their expectations of the future, therefore, need not be consistent with a full-employment situation. There is actually empirical evidence that supports the contention that a significant proportion of consumers and firms are actually non-Ricardian in that they are not especially forward-looking or their behaviour is constrained (for example, evidence suggests that many households have little wealth, or are financially constrained, to be able to undertake intertemporal consumption smoothing); this is also supported by survey-based evidence (Campbell and Mankiw, 1989; HM Treasury, 2003; Mankiw, 2000).

Coenen and Straub (2005) also rely on a study by Galí *et al.* (2004), where a model is put forward that allows for the coexistence of non-Ricardian and Ricardian households and their interaction with firms that change prices infrequently and a fiscal authority that issues debt to finance part of its expenditure. This study concludes that calibrating such a model can explain the available evidence on the impact of government expenditure shocks on consumption. The study by Coenen and Straub (2005) proceeds to include both Ricardian and non-Ricardian households in an extended version of the euro area stochastic dynamic general equilibrium model developed by Smets and Wouters (2003),[5] and also employs Bayesian inference methods.[6] The presence of non-Ricardian households is crucial. The quantitative impact of government spending on consumption is higher as compared to the benchmark case without non-Ricardian households.

Nonetheless, the chance of government expenditure crowding-in consumption is rather small in view of the relatively low share of non-Ricardian households assumed in the study. However, the possibility of crowding-in is strengthened once it is recognized that the presence of non-Ricardian households and their behaviour can have significant effects on that of the Ricardian households. To the extent that the increase in consumption of non-Ricardian households following a budget deficit, impacts on the income stream of the Ricardian households, then crowding-in becomes a distinct possibility. Further possibilities suggest themselves. Different fiscal policy rules, of the type discussed later may very well enhance crowding-in. Also allowing for an endogenous response of the long-run government debt-to-GDP ratio to persistent government spending may enhance our understanding of the empirical dimension of the problem. Indeed, modifying the assumption of government expenditure evolving exogenously over time, so that agents would form expectations about government spending shocks, would give the model more realism and could produce results that strengthen the impact of government spending shocks.

Blanchard and Perotti (2002) employ the Structural VAR (SVAR) approach in studying the quantitative impact of fiscal policy. They argue that this approach is superior to those that utilize large-scale econometric models or reduced-forms. Large-scale econometric models 'largely postulate rather than document an effect of fiscal policy on activity' (p. 1), while the reduced-form approach registers the effect of a summary statistic of fiscal policy, and yet no theory suggests this is pertinent. The SVAR approach is argued to be more appropriate in the study of fiscal policy simply because, unlike monetary policy for example, decision and implementation lags imply that there is no response of fiscal policy to economic activity. So that fiscal shocks can be identified and their dynamic effects on economic activity can be traced through the SVAR approach. Blanchard and Perotti (2002) employ post-war US data along with SVAR to conclude that spending multipliers for consumption and output are anything between one-third and unity. However, Perotti (2005) and Mihov (2003), using VAR-based evidence, argue that after 1980 the effectiveness of fiscal policy weakened substantially in the US. Three possible explanations of this change have been put forward. One relates to the financial liberalization era, which took place at the time. The increasing asset market participation has enabled households to smooth consumption in the desired way, thereby influencing the impact of fiscal policy. Another explanation refers to the increasing use of monetary policy since the 1980s in relation to the pre-1980s. It is true that a considerable change has taken place in the way the nominal interest rate is adjusted in response to expected inflation; monetary policy has been more hawkish ever since the 1980s. A third explanation emphasizes the change in the degree of deficit financing, which has assumed more persistence post-1980. These explanations imply that while fiscal policy has a strong and persistent effect on economic activity, this is less significant and persistent post-1980. Bilbiie *et al.* (2006) attempt to throw light on the empirical support of the three explanations just summarized. They conclude that increased asset market participation accounts for some of the change, while the degree of deficit financing is crucial. But the key quantitative factor is, in their empirical findings, monetary policy. But complementarity of the three factors is also very important.

Of equal, if not more, importance for fiscal policy is public investment, which assumes particular significance in view of the emphasis placed upon it in the UK over the recent past. 'Golden rule' is the term used by the UK Treasury in its approach to public investment. Government deficit should only be undertaken for public investment but the current account should be balanced over the cycle, implying a balanced current account. This 'golden rule' is associated with a 'sustainable investment rule', which limits net public debt to a 'stable and prudent level' of no more than 40 per cent of GDP. Such a golden rule implies public investment of 2 per cent of GDP with a 5 per cent nominal growth rate (applying the well-known formula of $g = pi_g/b$, where g is the nominal growth rate, pi_g is public investment as a percentage of GDP, and b is the debt to GDP ratio). A question in this context is whether the 'golden rule' can ensure a sufficient level of public investment without hurting the sustainability of public finances. Recent research appears to be supportive of assigning a significant role to public investment. In their attempt to test for these propositions, Creel *et al.* (2006) elaborate on the Blanchard and Perotti (2002) approach, which, as implied above, popularized the VAR technique in a short-run analysis to account for the long-run properties of fiscal policies. Creel *et al.* (2006) account for debt dynamics in the case of a closed economy, and by utilizing the SVAR approach, they conclude that public investment, and current outlays, in the UK have positive and permanent effects on real GDP.

The developing-country case

The experience of a number of developing countries suggests that fiscal policy is in practice pro-cyclical rather than counter-cyclical in these cases. This means that budget deficit, as percentage of GDP, increases in booms, but decreases in recessions. This is contrary to the counter-cyclical case where the budget deficit, as a share of GDP, decreases during booms but increases in recessions (Alesina and Tabellini, 2005; Kaminski *et al.*, 2004). The pro-cyclical argument applies particularly to the discretionary changes in fiscal policy, but would not apply in the case of the operation of the automatic stabilizers, which provide a counter-cyclical component of fiscal policy. Persson and Tabellini (2000) and Alesina and Tabellini (2005) resort to a political agency problem to explain it. In countries where voters lack significant information, and are faced with corrupt governments that use parts of government revenue for unproductive public consumption, pro-cyclical fiscal behaviour is possible. Voters demand higher utilities for themselves, especially so under booming conditions. They are not irrational; they merely lack full information of the ability of the government to satisfy their demands without creating budget deficits. The government is forced to borrow to satisfy voter demands, for otherwise there is the fear of future electoral losses. The more corrupt the country is, the more pro-cyclicality may be observed. In fact, pro-cyclical behaviour is mainly observed in countries with widespread corruption. Where governments are subject to 'check and balances', voters would not impart pro-cyclicality to fiscal policy.[7] In fact, under conditions of recession corrupt governments are assumed to be able to reduce public deficits in the absence of voter pressure.

Alesina and Tabellini (2005) employ data on 87 countries over the period 1960 to 1999 to test the counter-cyclicality and the pro-cyclicality assumptions just discussed. They conclude that in the OECD countries fiscal policy is counter-cyclical, while in 36 out of 64 non-OECD countries pro-cyclicality is confirmed. The 36 countries are essentially Sub-Saharan African and Latin American countries, thereby supporting the political agency phenomenon in the case of these countries. They also depend on the nature of the tax system and on the expenditure system – a progressive tax and social security system would aid counter-cyclical budgets while a regressive system would point in the other direction. It is also shown that credit constraints impose obstacles to developing country governments to borrow the desired amounts, but it does not appear to be as a significant variable of pro-cyclicality as the political agency variable.

Turning next to the developing-country case, we may note that in terms of the evidence produced on the impact of fiscal policy, this is not dissimilar to that obtained for developed economies. If anything actually fiscal multipliers tend to be rather higher in the case of developing rather than developed economies (see, for example, Hemming, Kell and Mah-fouz, 2002, p. 33). This is due to the relatively high marginal propensity to consume, which can increase the size of the impact of fiscal policy significantly, a possibility discussed earlier in the chapter.

A point that relates to both developed and developing cases is the extent to which budget deficits are measured appropriately in the studies referred to above. Eisner (1989) was very persistent on the importance of proper definitions. In another contribution, Eisner and Pieper (1984, p. 23), suggest that 'an appropriately adjusted high-employment budget turns out to have been not in deficit in recent years, as usually supposed, but in considerable surplus. The view that fiscal policy has generally been too easy and overstimulatory is contradicted.' In the same study it is also argued that:

> official measures of the federal debt and budget deficits are mislead-ing by any of several reasonable standards. Gross public debt figures ignore financial asset accumulation as well as the real assets, which have contributed to a growing government net worth. Budget flows have failed to distinguish between current and capital accounts, and measures of surplus and deficit have been inconsistent with changes in the real value of net debt. (Eisner and Pieper, 1984, p. 23)

It is clear from the discussion in this section that fiscal policy does have a significant role to play in macroeconomic stabilization, provided fiscal measures are appropriately measured. Should one then conclude that fiscal policy rules might be better than monetary rules? This is the question dealt with in the following section.

Should fiscal policy rules replace monetary policy rules?[8]

A strong and growing interest in fiscal policy rules has been evident over the recent past. Fiscal Policy rules aim at containing public sec-tor deficits and at reducing public sector debts by specifying targets for government deficits, debts or spending. As such, they can potentially ameliorate the time-inconsistency and deficit-bias problems, through anchoring expectations about the sustainable course of future policies.[9] Interestingly enough, a fiscal policy rule that replaces the monetary pol-icy rule embedded in equations (2.1) to (2.6) could potentially tackle these problems. More important from the point of view of this chapter is that such replacement could have further interesting implications. We explore this possibility in the rest of this section.

We may, then, proceed to replace equation (2.1) with (2.1)′ and (2.3) with (2.3)′ as shown immediately below (Setterfield, 2006; Taylor, 2000):

$$Y_t^g = (a_0' + \text{PSBR}_t) + a_1 Y_{t-1}^g + a_2 E_t(Y_{t+1}^g) + a_3[R_t - E_t(p_{t+1})] + a_4(rer)_t + s_6 \tag{2.1}'$$

$$(\text{PSBR})_t = (\text{PSBR})_0 - c_1 Y_{t-1}^g - c_2(p_{t-1} - p^T) + s_7 \tag{2.3}'$$

where the variables are as above, with the exception of PSBR, which stands for Public Sector Borrowing Requirement, and $(\text{PSBR})_0$, which is a constant that purports to capture the structural 'dimension' of PSBR and is actually invariant to short-run disturbances. In fact, formula (2.3)′ can be thought of as decomposing PSBR into a structural part and a cyclical part. (PSBR_0) is the structural part, and it represents the result of discretionary fiscal actions. The cyclical part is the rest of the right-hand side in equation (2.3)′ other than PSBR_0, with c_1 proxying the effect of automatic stabilizers.

An additional assumption is necessary to close the model, as in equation (2.7):

$$[R_t - E_t(p_{t+1})] = RR^* \tag{2.7}$$

i.e. the actual real rate of interest is continuously equal to the equilibrium real rate of interest.

The new model comprises equations (2.1)′, (2.2), (2.3)′, (2.4), (2.5), (2.6) and (2.7). Fiscal policy in this revised model overcomes the problem relating RR^* and the monetary policy rules, as in equations (2.1) to (2.6) of the model discussed earlier. Some of the differences between the two models can actually be significant. One in particular stands out. This relates to the RR^*, which is no longer important in the fiscal rule reformulation. The argument that relates to the uncertainty that surrounds RR^* in terms of its imprecise nature when it comes to empirically verifying it (see Weber, 2006; and the discussion earlier in this chapter), is no longer relevant. We should also note at the same time, though, that Y^g is still the same in both cases, with all the difficulties in attempting to estimate it. A further important difference is that to the extent that expenditure is insensitive to changes in the real rate of interest, then the coefficient a_3 is not statistically different from zero, a matter of grave importance to the monetary policy rule case. Such a case, though, is of no consequence in terms of the effectiveness of fiscal policy rules. A remaining problem is, of course, the decision upon the 'right' inflation target in the long run.

Still the question remains as to whether fiscal policy rules are effective. No straightforward answer is possible. To begin with, it ought to be acknowledged that for policy rules to be effective, they should be enforced. Furthermore, since fiscal outcomes are the result of both policy and endogenous economic outcomes, it becomes difficult to judge whether they comply with a rule or they are the result of other economic circumstances. The two should then be separated in an attempt to ascertain the extent to which fiscal policy rules can affect budgetary policy. This is by no means an exercise that can be undertaken with clear-cut results.

What role for fiscal policy?

The overall conclusion of this brief excursion into the recent developments on the effectiveness of fiscal policy is that incorporating a number of additional assumptions to NCM, implies favourable results for fiscal policy. The most important of which can be succinctly and briefly summarized (see, for example, Botman and Kumar, 2006). Overlapping generation models in the tradition of Blanchard (1985) and Weil (1989), which enable the relaxation of the Ricardian equivalence assumption, is probably the most important one. It implies short-planning horizons by households so that intertemporal smoothing of consumption is not possible. This implies, of course, that even temporary changes in fiscal policy affect household decisions to consume and work. Another assumption is that of liquidity-constrained households, consistent with the evidence that even in developed countries up to a third of households do not have sufficient access to financial markets (Botman and Kumar, 2006). Under such circumstances, changes in fiscal policy that affect household disposable income would have significant real effects. Still another feature is the endogenization of labour supply and capital accumulation. Since they are affected by after-tax real wage and after-tax rate of interest, respectively, changes in fiscal stance, as they affect after-tax real wage and the rate of interest, can have real effects.

It clearly follows that fiscal multipliers and other relevant exercises undertaken, tend to provide strong support to fiscal policy as an instrument of stabilization policy. This conclusion is strengthened by more recent findings, which are based on the value of the fiscal multipliers under conditions of coordination between fiscal and monetary policy.

Eggertsson (2006) utilizing a calibrated model, not dissimilar in substance to the one portrayed in the section titled 'An open economy NCM', concludes that under fiscal and monetary policy coordination fiscal multipliers are higher than when no policy coordination prevails. Indeed, they are bigger than those found in the traditional Keynesian literature.[10] This large difference in fiscal multipliers is explained by the expectations channel, which is very much emphasized in the Eggertsson (2006) study. This channel works via inflation expectations. Fiscal expansion increases expectations about future inflation, real rate of interest is reduced (provided the central bank collaborates with the fiscal authority) and spending is stimulated. Expectations of future income also improve, thereby stimulating spending further. This result is particularly important in view of much current theory and practice that see fiscal policy better divorced from monetary policy, as shown in the 'An open economy NCM' section. This contribution would suggest that macroeconomic stability is the joint responsibility of the monetary and fiscal authorities. Potentially destabilizing behaviour by one authority can be offset by an appropriate stance of the other authority. Perhaps more importantly the monetary authority can trade off some inflation for lower unemployment, even in the long run.

Coordination of fiscal and monetary policy does not imply that the respective authorities need to lose their 'independence'. For example, this cooperation need not mean that central bank independence is reduced. So long as the fiscal and monetary authority have *a common objective*, for example maximization of social welfare, this need not imply that the two authorities should lose their 'independence' (Eggertsson, 2006). In the words of the current Fed Chairman 'any more than cooperation between two independent nations in pursuit of a common objective is inconsistent with the principle of national sovereignty' (Bernanke, 2003). This is not dissimilar to Wren-Lewis's (2000) proposal for delegating fiscal actions to an independent body, outside the government. This could take the form of a 'fiscal regulator' with two objectives: to advise on short-run discretionary action and to supervise the long-run sustainability of government finances. It is also argued that the Bank of England Monetary Policy Committee (MPC) can play such a role, alongside monetary policy. This is paramount in this view, given the requirement of proper coordination of fiscal and monetary policies (Wren-Lewis, 2000, p. 104).[11] In the same spirit of analysis, Linnemann and Schabert (2003), utilizing a model of wage and price stickiness, demonstrate that fiscal policy can affect output if the monetary authority does not react aggressively to output changes. Furthermore, in models where capital accumulation is also accounted for, as in Arestis *et al.* (2007) for example, aggregate demand, which would now include investment expenditure more prominently, would be more susceptible than otherwise to changes in the rate of interest. This consideration gives more credence to the proposition that coordination of fiscal and monetary policy becomes paramount.

These policy prescriptions are rather different from Taylor's (2000) suggestion of fiscal policy and monetary policy coordination, with the two policies being interdependent but *with different objectives*. A monetary policy concerned with output stabilization around the cycle in the short-run and with controlling inflation in the long run, and a fiscal policy that focuses on a passive act in the short run through automatic stabilizers, but on a series of medium- to long run-run objectives to be achieved by discretionary action. The UK appears to be a good example of this policy prescription. An activist monetary policy as just described, along with a passive short-run fiscal policy (which supports monetary policy via the operation of the automatic stabilizers), but with an active long-run fiscal policy to deal with objectives that include low debt, the provision of public services and investment, social equality, and economic efficiency. The success of this coordination is predicated on a leadership role for fiscal policy (it takes precedence in cases of conflict), but without either policy losing its ability to act independently (HM Treasury, 2003; Hughes Hallett, 2004).

The conclusion from this discussion is two-fold. The first is that fiscal policy does have a significant role to play as an instrument of economic policy. Second, coordination of fiscal and monetary policies is probably the best way forward in terms of macroeconomic stabilization.

Summary and conclusions

In this chapter, we have examined the role of fiscal policy in the NCM. We have shown that this policy has been downgraded for a number of reasons, which have been explained. Similarly, we have produced a number of arguments that suggest that the reasoning behind these arguments can be shown to rely on weak foundations. The empirical evidence on the effectiveness of fiscal policy is not always supportive of the NCM view on it. This is particularly the case in view of recent theoretical developments and new evidence produced. Modifying the NCM model from monetary policy rules to fiscal policy rules is shown to possess certain advantages. We are thus led to the conclusion that although problems would always prevail on the policy arena, fiscal policy does not deserve to be so downgraded as in the new macroeconomics consensus. In any case, it is true to say that there is broad agreement, at least, about the main factors that can influence the size and sign of fiscal multipliers. The complexity of the theoretical arguments and the difficulty of arriving at clear-cut empirical results notwithstanding, the analysis in this chapter suggests that fiscal policy can be an effective instrument for regulating the level of aggregate demand. This is particularly so when fiscal policy is properly coordinated with monetary policy. It would appear to be the case that coordination of fiscal and monetary policies appears to gain a great deal of support.

Still, proponents argue, there are perceived risks of deficits that block the use of fiscal policy. They revolve around three arguments: solvency and sustainability; generational issues; financial burdens and danger of high interest rates due to deficits. We briefly comment on these issues as an overall conclusion.

Solvency and sustainability: proponents continually warn that deficits are unsustainable and that national solvency is at risk. For example, they argue that when the debt interest rate is higher than the rate of growth it leads to insolvency. Also, they warn that markets will 'punish' the government well in advance should they take the first step in this direction. This is unsupported rhetoric. The risk of deficits may be inflation.

Generational issues: 'We are leaving this debt to our children' is heard repeatedly. This would imply that 20 years from now if our children build 20 million cars they will need to send them back to 2007 to pay off the debt, for example. At the macro level each year's GDP gets distributed to whoever is alive, and the distribution process is under the full control of the government at any time.

Financial burdens and danger of high interest rates due to deficits: it is heard repeatedly that if the debt gets large enough all the government's income will go towards interest and there will not be anything left for other spending. This is inapplicable. Government spending is not operationally revenue constrained. Government can spend whatever it wants regardless of whether it is in surplus or deficit. Any constraints are self-imposed. And, of course, the government sets the interest rate it pays on its debt, not the market. Note that Japan paid near zero rate of interest for a decade with a debt of 150% of GDP, annual deficits of 7% of GDP, and a very low credit rating; the ability to make payment was never even the slightest issue.

There is, thus, very little theoretical and empirical grounds to suggest that fiscal policy should not be used as an instrument of stabilization policy. Indeed, proper coordination with monetary policy might be the way forward.

Notes

1. I am grateful to Warren Mosler, and to the two editors of this volume, for helpful comments.
2. Automatic stabilizers are 'those elements of the tax and spending regime which 'automatically' tend to stabilize the economy over the cycle. For example, during an upswing, incomes will rise and tax receipts will increase tending to dampen the cycle. Similarly, in a downturn, unemployment benefit payments will rise tending to moderate the slowdown' (HM Treasury, 2003, p. 4).
3. It should be noted that the main theoretical property of RET is the irrelevance of the government's financing decisions *vis-à-vis* taxes and debt. For example, a fiscal expansion prompts expectations of future fiscal contractions regardless of the way financing is undertaken. Private savings increase to compensate for the reduction in government saving, in the expectation of future tax increases, with the multiplier effect of the fiscal expansion brought to zero in the limit (Barro, 1974).
4. Coenen and Straub (2005) offer a comprehensive summary of the literature on the two contrasting issues discussed in the text.
5. The study by Smets and Wouters (2003) is used as a benchmark specification in the Coenen and Straub (2005) study. The latter is an augmented specification with non-Ricardian households in relation to Smets and Wouters (2003).
6. Bayesian inference methods rely on the use of prior information obtained from earlier studies in the estimation of a stochastic dynamic general equilibrium model. Such methods are particularly useful when the sample period of the data is short, and also when it is necessary to solve highly non-linear estimation relationships.
7. Alesina and Tabellini (2005) note that pro-cyclicality can only materialize in democratic regimes. In a dictatorship where corruption may be thriving, voters cannot influence fiscal decisions and thus pro-cyclicality would not be observed.
8. It should actually be 'additional' fiscal policy rules. Additional, that is, to the automatic stabilizers that are embodied in equations (2.1) to (2.6) and discussed above.
9. Time inconsistency problems prevail when governments announce *ex ante* fiscal adjustments, but *ex post* there may always be economic or political reasons for governments to renege on the *ex ante* promises (Kydland and Prescott, 1977). A deficit bias emanates from the democratic political process (Mueller, 2003). For example, rational but imperfectly informed voters are able to influence politicians and indeed persuade them to pursue expansionary policies before elections.
10. The fiscal multipliers reported in Eggertsson (2006) under fiscal and monetary policy coordination are 3.4, in the case of the real spending multiplier,

and 3.8, in the case of the deficit spending multiplier. When there is no policy coordination, i.e. when the central bank is 'goal independent', the real spending multiplier is unchanged, while the deficit spending multiplier is zero.

11. A number of authors have proposed delegating decisions on fiscal policy to 'an independent fiscal policy committee' to improve its effectiveness and the financial discipline of the government. See HM Treasury (2003, p. 74) for a brief summary of a number of these propositions.

References

Agénor, P. (2002) 'Monetary policy under flexible exchange rates: An introduction to inflation targeting', in N. Loayza and N. Soto (eds), *Inflation Targeting: Design, Performance, Challenges*, Santiego, Chile: Central Bank of Chile.

Agénor, P-R., McDermott, C.J. and Prasad, E.S. (1999) 'Macroeconomic fluctuations in developing countries: Some stylised facts', *IMF Working Paper 99/35*, Washington, DC: International Monetary Fund.

Alesina, A. and Tabellini, G. (2005) 'Why is fiscal policy often procyclical?', *Discussion paper No. 2090*, Cambridge, MA: Harvard University.

Arestis, P. (2007) 'What is the new consensus in macroeconomics?', in P. Arestis (ed.), *Is There a New Consensus in Macroeconomics?*, Basingstoke: Palgrave Macmillan.

Arestis, P. and Sawyer, M. (2003) 'Reinstating fiscal policy', *Journal of Post Keynesian Economics*, 26(1), 4–25.

Arestis, P. and Sawyer, M. (2006) 'Fiscal Policy matters', *Public Finance*, 54(3–4): 133–53.

Arestis, P., Baddeley, M. and Sawyer, M. (2007) 'The relationship between capital stock, unemployment and wages in nine EMU countries', *Bulletin of Economic Research*, 59(2), 125–48.

Barro, R.J. (1974) 'Are government bonds net wealth?', *Journal of Political Economy*, 82, 1095–117.

Bernanke, B.S. (2003) 'Some thoughts on monetary policy in Japan', *Speech at the Japan Society of Monetary Economics*, May.

Bilbiie, F.O., Meier, A. and Müller, G.J. (2006) 'What accounts for the changes in U.S. fiscal policy transmission?', *ECB Working Paper Series No. 582*, January, Frankfurt: European Central Bank.

Blanchard, O. and Perotti, R. (2002) 'An empirical characterization of the dynamic effects of changes in government spending and taxes on output', *Quarterly Journal of Economics*, 117(2), 1329–68.

Blanchard, O.J. (1985) 'Debt, deficits and finite horizons', *Journal of Political Economy*, 93(2), 223–47.

Botman, D. and Kumar, M.S. (2006) 'Fundamental determinants of the effects of fiscal policy', *IMF Working Paper 06/72*, Washington, DC: International Monetary Fund.

Briotti, M.G. (2005) 'Economic reactions to public finance consolidation: A survey of the literature', *Occasional Paper Series No. 38*, Frankfurt: European Central Bank.

Campbell, J.Y. and Mankiw, N.G. (1989) 'Consumption, income and interest rates: Reinterpreting the time series evidence', in O.J. Blanchard and S. Fischer (eds), *NBER Macroeconomics Annual 1989*, Boston: MIT Press, pp. 185–216.

Chirinko, R.S., Fazzari, S.M. and Meyer, A.P. (1999) 'How responsive is business capital formation to its user cost? An exploration with micro data', *Journal of Public Economics*, 74(1), 53–80.

Coenen, G. and Straub, R. (2005) 'Does government spending crowd in private consumption? Theory and empirical evidence for the euro area', *IMF Working Paper 05/159*, Washington, DC: International Monetary Fund. Also *ECB Working Paper Series No. 513*, August, Frankfurt: European Central Bank.

Creel, J., Monperrus-Veroni, P. and Saraceno, F. (2006) 'Estimating the impact of public investment for the United Kingdom: Has the golden rule of public finance made a difference?', *Mimeo*, Paris: OFCE Research Department.

Eggertsson, G.B. (2006) 'Fiscal multipliers and policy coordination', *Federal Reserve Bank of New York Staff Reports, No. 241*, New York: Federal Reserve Bank of New York.

Eisner, R. (1989) 'Budget deficits: Rhetoric and reality', *Journal of Economic Perspectives*, 3(2), 73–93.

Eisner, R. and Pieper, P.J. (1984) 'A new view of the Federal debt and budget deficits', *American Economic Review*, 74(1), 11–29.

Galí, J., López-Salido, J.D. and Vallés, J. (2004) 'Understanding the effects of government spending on consumption', *ECB Working Paper Series No. 339*, Frankfurt: European Central Bank.

Hemming, R., Kell, M. and Mahfouz, S. (2002) 'The effectiveness of fiscal policy in stimulating economic activity: A review of the literature', *IMF Working Paper 02/208*, Washington, DC: International Monetary Fund.

Hemming, R., Mahfouz, S. and Schimmelpfennig, A. (2002) 'Fiscal Policy and economic activity in advanced economies', *IMF Working Paper 02/87*, Washington, DC: International Monetary Fund.

Hjelm, G. (2002) 'Is private consumption higher (lower) during periods of fiscal contractions (expansions)?',*Journal of Macroeconomics*, 24(1), 17–39.

HM Treasury (2003) *Fiscal stabilisation and EMU*, HM Stationary Office, Cmnd 799373, Norwich, online at: www.hm-treasury.gov.uk

Hughes Hallett, A. (2004) Post-Thatcher fiscal strategies in the UK: An interpretation', *CESifo Working Paper No. 1372*, Category 5: Fiscal Policy, Macroeconomics and Growth, December.

Kaminski, G., Reinhart, C. and Vegh, C. (2004) 'When it rains it pours: Procyclical capital flows and macroeconomic policies', in M. Gertler and K. Rogoff (eds), *NBER Macroeconomic Annual 2004*, Cambridge, MA: MIT Press.

Kydland, E.F. and Prescott, E.C. (1977) 'Rules rather than discretion: The inconsistency of optimal plans', *Journal of Political Economy*, 85(4), 473–91.

Lane, T.D., Ghosh, A., Hamann, J., Phillips, S., Schulze-Ghattas, M. and Tsikata, T. (1999) 'IMF-supported programs in Indonesia, Korea, and Thailand: A preliminary assessment', *IMF Occasional Paper, No. 178*, Washington, DC: International Monetary Fund.

Linnemann, L. and Schabert, A. (2003) 'Fiscal Policy in the New Neoclassical Synthesis', *Journal of Money, Credit and Banking*, 35(6) Part 1, 911–29.

Mankiw, G.N. (2000) 'The savers-spenders theory of fiscal policy', *American Economic Review*, 90(1), 120–5.

Mihov, I. (2003) 'Discussion of "Understanding the effects of government spend-ing on consumption" by Jordi Galí, J. David López-Salido and Javier Vallés', *Mimeo*, Paris: INSEAD.

Mueller, D. (2003) *Public Choice III*, Cambridge: Cambridge University Press.

Perotti, R. (2005) 'Estimating the effects of fiscal policy in OECD countries', *CEPR Discussion Paper 4842*, London: Centre for Economic Policy Research.

Persson, T. and Tabellini, G. (2000) *Political Economics: Explaining Economic Policy*, Cambridge, MA: MIT Press.

Setterfield, M. (2006) 'Is there a stabilizing role for fiscal policy in the new consensus?', *Mimeo*, Department of Economics, Trinity College.

Smets, F. and Wouters, R. (2003) 'An estimated stochastic dynamic general equi-librium model of the euro area', *Journal of the European Economic Association*, 1(4), 1123–75.

Taylor, J.B. (2000) 'Discretionary fiscal policies', *Journal of Economic Perspectives*, 14(1), 1–23.

Van Aarle, B. and Garretsen, H. (2003) 'Keynesian, non-Keynesian or no effects of fiscal policy changes? The EMU case', *Journal of Macroeconomics*, 25(2), 213–40.

Weber, A. (2006) 'Interest rates in theory and practice – how useful is the concept of the natural real rate of interest for monetary policy?', *Inaugural G.L.S. Shackle Biennial Memorial Lecture*, University of Cambridge, 9 March.

Weil, P. (1989) 'Overlapping families of infinitely-lived agents', *Journal of Public Economics*, 38(2), 183–98.

Wren-Lewis, S. (2000) 'The limits to discretionary fiscal stabilisation policy', *Oxford Review of Economic Policy*, 16, 92–105.

3
Fiscal Policy in Today's Endogenous Money World

Giuseppe Fontana

Introduction

There is now a well established proposition in our profession, namely that there is a New Consensus in macroeconomics, which can be easily deployed to analyse a broad range of policy issues. In fact, the New Consensus model is so popular and easily applicable to a variety of policy exercise, that it is slowly but increasingly used to replace the iconic *IS-LM* model in undergraduate macroeconomic textbooks (e.g. Carlin and Soskice, 2006, ch. 3). Most, if not all, of the success is related to a combination of theoretical and practical arguments.

Starting with the theoretical arguments, the New Consensus model marks a dramatic shift from the quantity-theoretic framework defended by monetarists and neo-classical synthesis Keynesians alike, toward a non-quantity theoretic framework in the spirit of the monetary contributions of Wicksell and Keynes (Fontana, 2007, table 1). This non-quantity theoretic framework has shown remarkable flexibility, being able to encompass modern theoretical advances, including the natural rate hypothesis, and the expectations-augmented or inertial Phillips curve. It has also absorbed the rational expectation hypothesis, and built on the insights and methodology of the real business cycle theory.

The practical arguments in favour of the New Consensus view are no less powerful and innovative. Most central banks around the world including the Bank of England and the Federal Reserve have all rejected the monetarist credo and its policy prescriptions. Central banks do not control monetary aggregates, but the short-run nominal interest rate. The stock of money is thus a residual, an endogenous rather than an exogenous element of the economic process. The old causal relationship between money and prices is untenable. Similarly, any recommended cure for inflation based on a monetary targeting rule is considered impracticable. The void left by the monetarist credo and its policy implications has been replaced by new analyses and policies, which are consistent with the New Consensus view. Central banks now use the short-run nominal interest rate to achieve a particular combination of current and potential levels of output, the so-called output gap, which delivers the desired rate of inflation.

An interesting but often ignored implication of modern developments in macroeconomics is that the role of central banks and monetary policy in the New Consensus view is now so prominent that discretionary fiscal policy is rarely mentioned in modern economics or policy making alike. The purpose of this chapter is to challenge this view in several ways. First, the chapter will argue that there is nothing inherently monetary about the nature of stabilization policy in the New Consensus view. Second, it will lend support to the view that ideology, policy mistakes and particular historical circumstances have played a role at least as important as economic theory in the rejection of post-war Keynesianism, and the consequent downgrading of fiscal policy. Finally, it will suggest that the existence of partial or complete crowding-out in the modern New Consensus/endogenous money framework is decided by the central bank rather, than by the 'market'. Also, in this framework the different forms of financing real government spending are endogenously decided by private agents rather than exogenously set by policy makers.

The chapter is organized in three main sections. The next section presents a simplified algebraic representation of the New Consensus view, and it discusses its policy implications. The following section reviews recent works on the possible historical causes of the current downgrading of fiscal policy to the advantage of monetary policy. The final section considers the theoretical explanations that are traditionally used to explain the ineffectiveness of fiscal policy, with a particular focus on the crowding-out arguments, within both an exogenous money framework and an endogenous money framework.

The New Consensus view and its policy implications

The New Consensus view is based on a three-equations model: a Phillips curve, an *IS*-type curve, and a monetary policy equation. The model has several standard New Keynesian features. All three equations can be derived from the explicit optimizing behaviour of individual agents in the presence of market failures, including imperfect competition, incomplete markets, and asymmetric information. These market failures generate transitory price and wage stickiness, which in turn give support to the view that in the short run the aggregate supply responds to changes in the aggregate demand. Aggregate demand has thus a transitory, yet non-trivial role in determining the equilibrium level of output and employment in the economy. In other words, where individual agents behave rationally, the outcome of their actions has adverse macroeconomic effects. On this basis, activist government actions are then justified to eliminate or limit some of these effects.

In terms of the mechanics of the model, price and wage stickiness plays a key role in relating the monetary policy rule to the *IS*-type curve. The central bank via changes in the short-run nominal interest rate is actually able to control the short-run real interest rate. In this way, the central bank is able to affect the consumption and investment components of aggregate demand. This is an important theoretical result, because it goes well with another important tenet of the New Consensus view, namely that low and stable inflation is conducive to growth, stability and the efficient functioning of the market. When the economy is hit by shocks, taking it away from its natural path, it is the central bank which is responsible for achieving the desired rate of inflation in the medium term, and subject to that, also for bringing output and employment to their equilibrium levels in the shorter term (Allsopp and Vines, 2005).[1] However, in pursuit of its objectives the central bank faces a (short-run) trade-off between inflation and output. This trade-off is captured by the Phillips curve, which can be thought as the aggregate supply component of the New Consensus model.[2]

Drawing on Carlin and Soskice (2005), Clarida *et al.* (1999), Meyer (2001) and Walsh (2002) a simplified version of the New Consensus model can thus be represented by a set of three equations describing the dynamics of changes in the inflation rate (Equation 3.1), the output gap (Equation 3.2), and the interest rate policy rule (Equation 3.3):[3]

$$\dot{\pi} = g\left(y - \bar{y}\right) \tag{3.1}$$

$$y - \bar{y} = f\left(r; X\right) \tag{3.2}$$

$$r - r^* = h\left(\pi - \pi^T\right) \tag{3.3}$$

Equation (3.1) is a Phillips equation explaining changes in the inflation rate in terms of the output gap, namely the difference between current (y) and potential levels of output $(\bar{y})$. The *IS* curve is represented by Equation (3.2). The output gap is influenced by changes in the real interest rate (r), and by a vector of exogenous variables (X) like government expenditure, the tax structure, and net exports that also influence the *IS*-type curve. Finally, Equation (3.3) is a simple monetary policy rule. The difference between the actual real interest rate (r), and its long-run equilibrium level (r^*) is a function of the difference between current (π) and target (π^T) rates of inflation.

The set of Equations (3.1–3.3) summarizes the core propositions of the 'New Consensus' view, and its policy implications: given short-run price and wage rigidities, by changing the short-run nominal interest rate, central banks are able to influence the short-run real interest rate (r). Equation (3.2) then shows that central banks change the output gap, which via Equation (3.1) affects the rate of change in the inflation rate. When the rate of inflation is at its target level (Equation 3.3), the actual real interest rate (r) is equal to its long-run equilibrium level (r^*), and the output gap is nil.

However, there is nothing intrinsically monetary about the nature of stabilization policy in the New Consensus view. If anything, from a theoretical point of view fiscal policy should actually have the most prominent role in the New Consensus view. Basically, the role of the policy instrument in the New Consensus model can be theoretically played by any variable affecting demand and thereby the output gap (Equation 3.2), which in this way is used to control changes in the inflation rate (Equation 3.1), and hence to achieve the desired or targeted inflation target (Equation 3.3). For instance, Equation (3.2) could be replaced with Equation (3.4) below, which highlights the role of fiscal policy variables rather than the standard monetary policy instrument. In its new version, the *IS* curve explains that the output gap is influenced by changes in real government expenditure (G), taxes (T), and by a vector of exogenous variables (X), which in this case include the real interest rate (r) as well as net exports. This means that government expenditure, tax structure and net exports are not entirely exogenous. Equation (3.4) makes plainly evident that governments are not fully responsible for fiscal deficits, since at least in part they respond to the inflationary or deflationary effects of changes in the output gap:

$$y - \bar{y} = f(G, T, X) \tag{3.4}$$

Theoretically the replacement of Equation (3.2) with Equation (3.4) in the New Consensus model should reinforce the policy transmission mechanism described above. It is worth remembering that in the set of Equations (3.1–3.3), the central bank is able to affect the output gap, and hence hit the inflation target only in the restrictive case of some price and wage stickiness; the reason being that the central bank controls the nominal short-run interest rate (i) rather than the real short-run interest rate (r). The difference between the two rates is measured by the change in the price level. Therefore, it can be safely assumed that the central bank can control the real short-run interest rate (r) only when prices and wages are sticky. This is the essence of the so-called Taylor principle, namely the proposition that central banks can stabilize the economy by raising the nominal short-run interest rate (i) instrument more than one-for-one in response to higher inflation (Davig and Leeper, 2005).

The Taylor principle implicitly assumes either that prices and wages are fixed in the short-run, or that whatever little change in their value, this is known to the central bank, which can then use this information in order to attain, via changes in the controlled nominal interest rate (i), the desired level of the real short-run interest rate (r). These assumptions severely limit the applicability of the New Consensus model, and the effectiveness of its monetary policy prescriptions. However, in the long run prices and wages are flexible by assumption, which automatically rules out any possibility for the central bank to affect the real interest rate, and hence to influence real variables in the long run.[4]

By contrast, the fiscal authority does not encounter any of these problems or limitations: there are no implicit or explicit assumptions on the values that prices and wages can take either in the short or long run. Furthermore, it is not necessary to make unrealistic assumptions about the level of knowledge required by the fiscal authority in order to achieve its New Consensus policy prescriptions. The fiscal authority can directly affect aggregate demand, and hence the output gap, by moving real government expenditure (G) and/or taxes (T) (Equation 3.4). Like in the traditional interpretation of the New Consensus model, then the fiscal authority can manipulate the output gap in order to bring the inflation rate to its target level, and the actual real interest rate (r) to its long-run equilibrium level (r^*).[5]

Why fiscal policy fell out of use: a speculative history

The previous section has argued that one of the most important practical implications of the New Consensus view in modern macroeconomics is the prominent role assigned to central banks in achieving an inflation target either explicitly, as in the case of the UK and Sweden, or implicitly, as in the case of the US. In fact, the role of monetary policy in the New Consensus view is so prominent that today the macroeconomic role of discretionary fiscal policy is rarely mentioned in economics or policy making alike.[6] In the few cases when fiscal policy is discussed, the aim is to limit its role to exceptional circumstances, when monetary policy is either unusable or lacking effectiveness, as in the case of the lower bound problem on the short-run interest rate (Krugman, 2005), or country-specific shocks in monetary unions (Kirsanova *et al.*, 2007). But why has the role for fiscal policy been downgraded? Is this a novel feature of modern macroeconomics or has the New Consensus view borrowed it from past contributions?

The few recent papers on the subject almost universally start with a statement about the hegemonic role of fiscal policy over monetary policy in the 1940s and 1950s, reaching its apogee in the 1960s (see, for instance, the papers in Symposium, 2005). It is also hinted that the success of monetarism in the 1970s and 1980s has played an important role in the modern downgrading of fiscal policy, but little is told of this historical change. A possible reason for the unspoken downgrading of fiscal policy is that this historical shift is rather complex, possibly an interplay of theoretical and practical factors. It is also likely that these factors have played distinct roles at different times, and in different countries. For instance, as the standard Mundell-Fleming model shows, a move from a fixed to a floating exchange rate system affects the effectiveness of fiscal policy to the advantage of monetary policy. Following the US decision to suspend the convertibility of dollars to gold in 1971, the Bretton Woods system of fixed exchange rate *de facto* collapsed. However, countries adopted a flexible exchange rate at different times, and in different ways. Furthermore, the policy implications of a move from a fixed to a floating exchange rate system depends on the size and position of the country in the world economy, and on its membership of a monetary union like the Euro area.

Notwithstanding the likely complexity of the historical process that has led to a downgrading of fiscal policy, to the advantage of monetary policy, it may be worth speculating on some of the possible causes of it, by looking at some recent contributions on the subject. In a recent paper aptly titled 'The case against the case against discretionary fiscal policy' Alan Blinder has reminded us that in the three decades following the publication in 1936 of the *General Theory of Employment, Interest, and Money* (Keynes, 1973[1936]), discretionary fiscal stabilization policy gradually but steadily conquered hearts and minds of academics and practitioners alike. By the 1960s it was a common proposition that governments should cut taxes, increase cash transfer payments as well as goods and services purchases in order to combat a recession. Blinder also refers to some anecdotal evidence about the marginal role in policy making assigned to the chairman of the Federal Reserve Board. It is said that President Kennedy (1961–63) only remembered the name of the chairman of the Federal Reserve Board, namely William McChesney Martin, because his surname started with the same first letter of monetary policy. Still more indicative of the time is the fact that Walter Heller, the then chairman of the Council of Economic Advisors, in the index of his well-know book *New Dimensions of Political Economy* (Heller, 1966) does not make any reference to William McChesney Martin. However, Blinder (2004, p. 1) argues that times have dramatically changed: 'Multiply by −1, and you have a capsule summary of the conventional wisdom today ... Discussion of stabilization policy by economists – whether it is abstract or concrete, theoretical or practical – is about monetary policy, not fiscal policy.'

The past few decades have in fact witnessed a decline of interest in discretionary fiscal stabilization policy at the advantage of monetary policy. Blinder complains that it is not only academics, but also policy makers who discuss almost exclusively monetary policy strategies. On the rare occasions when fiscal policy is discussed, it is mostly to argue against its use for stabilization objectives or inflation control. The present writer has tried to replicate the 'Kennedy-experiment' with his macroeconomics students during a seminar on monetary and fiscal policy strategy in the US: all students knew the name and the policy view of the current chairman of the Federal Reserve Board, namely Ben S. Bernanke, but no one was familiar with the name, let alone the policy view of the current chairman of the Council of Economic Advisors, namely Edward P. Lazear.

According to Blinder, there are two main reasons explaining the current decline of interest in discretionary fiscal policy. First, there are potentially long inside lags for fiscal policy compared to monetary policy. In other words, there are long delays between a disturbance in the economy and the time policy makers recognize that a policy action is required and then implemented. This is what Blinder calls practical or political arguments against discretionary fiscal policy.[7]

Second, there is the so-called 'Ricardian equivalence' view suggesting that it does not matter whether a government finances spending with debt or tax increase, the total level of demand in the economy is the same. This means that any attempt by the government to influence aggregate demand, and hence the level of income and employment in a country by using fiscal policy, will prove fruitless. Putting it boldly, if consumers are 'Ricardian' they will save more now to compensate for current higher taxes (in the case of tax-financed government expenditure), or future higher taxes (in the case of bond-financed government expenditure), as the government has to pay back its debts. The increased government spending is therefore exactly offset by decreased consumption on the part of private agents, with the result that aggregate demand does not change. This is what Blinder calls theoretical or economic arguments against discretionary fiscal policy.

Blinder maintains that the interplay of these practical and theoretical arguments together with adverse historical circumstances explain the dramatic debacle in the late 1960s of the post-*General Theory* support for discretionary fiscal stabilization policies. He uses the case of the US with great effect. The Vietnam War caused a massive increase in public spending at a time of a near-full employment situation. Against the counsel of his Keynesian advisers, the US President, Lyndon Johnson (1963–69), neither reduced public spending nor raised taxes with the result that inflation kept rising. When in 1968 taxes were finally raised, the Vietnam-induced inflation was unaffected. This historical accident supported well the practical and theoretical arguments against the use of discretionary fiscal policy. First, it showed that the inside lags for fiscal policy could be very long. Okun (1970, ch. 3) argues that the advisers to President Johnson urged an increase in taxes as early as 1965. The President resisted the advice till mid 1967, and it then took another 18 months for the Congress to approve the temporary income tax increase. Second, consistently with the 'Ricardian equivalence' view, the 1968 income tax increase proved to be ineffective. The change in fiscal policy failed to affect consumer spending, and hence the rate of inflation.

It should be added that whereas the long inside lag of the 1968 fiscal restraint is unanimously accepted, Blinder is sceptical of the 'Ricardian equivalence' interpretation of the event. He laments that the 'Ricardian equivalence' view is based on unrealistic theoretical assumptions, including long time horizons, perfect foresight, perfect capital markets, and the absence of liquidity constraints. It is also poorly supported by empirical evidence (see, also, Hemming *et al.*, 2002). Drawing on his own study of the 1968 episode (Blinder, 1981), Blinder blames the temporary nature of the income tax rise as the cause of the poor impact on aggregate demand. In any case, a similar experience followed with the deep recession of 1974–75, when first President Richard Nixon (1964–74), and then President Ford (1974–77), failed to use countercyclical fiscal measures until it was too late, and with little impact. Blinder concludes that these practical and theoretical factors apparently supported by historical circumstances destroyed faith in fiscal policy, and more generally discretionary stabilization policy:

> Long inside lags, weak tax effects due to the PIH [the permanent income hypothesis (PIH) implies that temporary tax changes should

have small effects on consumer spending], and the vertical long-run Phillips curve have precious little to do with the monetarist claim of fiscal impotence owing to a vertical LM curve. But all these problems with fiscal policy seemed to get mixed up together in the anti-Keynesian backlash, and fiscal stabilization fell deeply out of favour. (Blinder, 2004, p. 12)

From this perspective, the modern New Consensus view represents the final outcome of a historical process that started in the late 1960s and steadily downplayed the role of discretionary fiscal policy, to the advantage of discretionary monetary policy. Interestingly, in his concluding remarks just quoted, Blinder introduces two new causes for the downgrading of fiscal policy, namely the emergence of monetarism and the existence of a vertical Phillips curve. Monetarism and the Phillips curve are actually the main topics of another recent contribution on the subject.

James Forder (2007a, 2007b) argues that the historical downgrading of fiscal policy in the past few decades is due in large part to the success of the 'expectations critique' of the Phillips curve. According to this critique, expected inflation affects the wage bargaining process such that any reduction in unemployment would be short-lived. The expectation critique is usually attributed to Milton Friedman (1968) and Edmund Phelps (1967). It is, therefore, dated towards the end of the 1960s, which marks roughly the beginning of the end of the use of discretionary fiscal policy for stabilization purposes. More importantly, Forder maintains that the expectation critique forms the backbone of a convenient myth in economics about the supposed weaknesses of Keynesian economics, and its support for discretionary fiscal policy:

Mythology has it that, until the view was rebutted by Friedman (1968), or Phelps (1967), or perhaps Friedman (1966), the work of Phillips (1958) had the economics profession, and the Keynesians in particular, convinced of the exploitability of an inflation-unemployment trade off. That rebuttal, it is held, came in the form of what is now sometimes called 'the expectations critique' ... One can only speculate. But there is a certain utility in dating the discovery of the expectations critique late in the Keynesian era. For one thing, it helps to provide the profession with a collective excuse for the inflation of the 1970s. Whilst there are other aspects to this, it should be apparent that with the inflationary failures of that period so evident, it is convenient to be able to lay the blame as fully as possible on a single mistake. There is no fundamental flaw in the system, and perhaps not in the operators; there was one error and that has now been corrected. By this line of thinking, the myth of Friedman's innovation is made to provide absolution through logical insight.

It is also the case that according to the conventional presentations, attempts to exploit the Phillips curve were at the center of Keynesian policy. Although a history may be fictitious, it still benefits from being internally consistent, and that requires that the 'failure of Keynesianism' be explicable in terms of the discovery of the flaw in reasoning about the Phillips curve. One could not tell even a superficially convincing story to the effect that practical Keynesianism revolved around a stable Phillips curve if one acknowledged the common sense status of the expectations critique all through the period...

So the deprecation of Keynesianism, the wisdom of the post-Friedmanite orthodoxy, and the scientific status of economics are all buttressed by this particular piece of amnesia. One should perhaps not be too surprised that such a convenient myth persists. (Forder, 2007a, pp. 1, 12–13)

There are two major points in these long quotations, which are relevant for the purpose of this chapter. First, Forder (2007a) argues that the expectation critique of the Phillips curve originates much earlier than the end of the 1960s. He maintains that even before the publication of 'The relation between unemployment and rate of change of money wage rates in the United Kingdom' by Phillips (1958), it was a well-accepted proposition in economics that expected inflation will affect the wage bargaining process such that any reduction in unemployment would not last forever (see, for instance, Champernowne, 1936). It is therefore, misleading to present, like Friedman (1968) did, the expectation critique of the Phillips curve as the reason for the rejection of Keynesianism and discretionary fiscal policy by academics and policy makers alike.

Second, Forder (2007b) challenges the role usually assigned to the Phillips curve in the development of post-war macroeconomics. In his Nobel lecture, Friedman (1977) argues that Keynesian scholars adopted with alacrity Phillips' analysis and used it, or better misused it, for policy purposes by arguing in favour of inflationary policies with the aim of lowering unemployment. In this way, Friedman set the Phillips curve at the heart of all post-war attempts by Keynesian economists to lower unemployment. The rise of inflation and unemployment in the 1970s could then easily be used as historical evidence against Keynesian theories and policies. By contrast to this view, Forder actually shows that Keynesian scholars were sceptical of the Phillips curve, and there is very little evidence to suggest that they used the trade-off between inflation and unemployment in order to lower unemployment:

> It should be noted, however, that although it is only a myth, Friedman's depiction of a naïve and indeed rather stupid professional consensus of the 1960s may not be entirely harmless. Two consequences in particular should be considered. The first is that Friedman subjected the Keynesians not merely to criticism, but to derision. He suggested that the greatest economists of the time had, to what can only be the deepest professional discredit, committed the most foolish of intellectual blunders. Once that is accepted, it hardly needs to be added that, shameful as it was ever to have made those inflationary mistakes, it would be more shameful still ever to make them again. Thus this romance of a Dark Age of Economics does much, I suggest, to shore-up support for approaches to policymaking based on central bank independence, inflation targeting, and fiscal conservatism . . .
>
> Secondly, whilst he is remembered for dismissing the possibility of a long-run trade-off, Friedman's greater achievement was to put the short-run trade-off at the centre of almost everyone's macroeconomic analysis. The historically attested theoretical alternative to the vertical Phillips curve is not a trade-off in the long-run, but a denial of it in the short-run. To the Keynesians, the problem of unemployment was, over a very wide range, simply a different problem from the problem of inflation. It is as much the triumph of Friedman's history as of his theory that it has become almost impossible to articulate the view that macroeconomic policy should be concerned with unemployment without seeming merely to plan a day-trip up the Phillips curve. But this is in fact not the only view one might take. (Forder, 2007b, pp. 16–17)

For the purpose of this chapter, it is thus interesting to record that the traditional explanation for the current disaffection with discretionary fiscal stabilization policy is, to say the least, not unanimously supported by historical evidence. The traditional story goes that *IS-LM* Keynesianism and its policy implications failed to provide any understanding of the events of the 1970s, let alone to solve them, and hence it was replaced by a new theoretical framework, namely New Classical Macroeconomics (Lucas and Sargent, 1978). Whatever the merit of the contributions by New Classical macroeconomists, the work of Blinder and Forder discussed above seems to suggest an alternative story, where ideology, policy mistakes and particular historical circumstances played a role at least as important as economic theory in the rejection of *IS-LM* Keynesianism, and the consequent downgrading of fiscal policy.[8]

Why fiscal policy is ineffective: an endogenous money perspective of the crowding-out debate

The previous sections have discussed the main features of the New Consensus view in macroeconomics and its policy implication that monetary policy must play the dominant role in order to deliver price stability in the medium-to-long run. They have also argued that theoretically there is nothing inherently monetary about the nature of stabilization policy in the New Consensus view. Any policy instrument affecting the *IS*-type equation, and hence the output gap (Equation 3.2), could deliver price stability.[9] In other words, theoretically fiscal policy could well play the current role assigned to monetary policy.

Over the past few decades several arguments have been developed to the effect that fiscal policy instruments are ineffective. Hemming *et al.* (2002), and Arestis and Sawyer (2003) provide an excellent review of the theoretical and empirical literature on the effectiveness of fiscal policy in stimulating output and employment. Following their works, the arguments supporting the view that fiscal policy is ineffective could be grouped under three headings. First, there is the crowding-out debate, which discusses the effects in the economy of changes in interest rates and the exchange rate due to a fiscal expansion. Second, there is the natural rate of unemployment or NAIRU literature, which discusses the role of changes in the aggregate demand in the context of a supply-determined level of output and employment (Sawyer, 2002). Finally, there is the so-called 'Ricardian equivalence' view (Barro, 1974), which analyses the conditions under which a reduction in public savings is compensated by an increase in private savings.

Fontana and Palacio-Vera (2007) and previous sections had already dealt with the second and the third arguments supporting the view that fiscal policy is ineffective (see, for an elaborated critical view of the 'Ricardian equivalence', Arestis and Sawyer, 2006). Therefore, the main focus of this section is on the crowding-out debate in the case of the traditional *IS-LM* exogenous money framework, and of the modern New Consensus endogenous money framework. For the sake of simplicity, the crowding-out debate is discussed in the case of a closed economy.

The crowding-out debate concerns the efficacy of fiscal policy in stimulating the level of output and employment in the economy. The debate is usually set in a standard *IS-LM* and *AD-AS* framework, with finite elasticity in the *IS* and *LM* curves with or without the existence of wealth effects. For simplicity, let us assume that the private sector does not have liabilities, and that wealth consists only of money (*M*) and perpetual bond holdings (*B*). Private wealth (*a*) is then defined as following:

$$a_t = \frac{1}{P_t} \left(M_t + \frac{B_t}{i_t} \right) \tag{3.5}$$

where *P* and *i* are the price level and the nominal interest in period *t*, respectively. Similarly, for simplicity let us ignore interest-induced wealth effects, and the full-employment case (i.e. a vertical *AS* curve). In the case of a money-financed increase in real government spending, the results are unequivocal: the *IS* curve shifts rightwards, as does the *LM* curve, and as a result of these shifts the level of output and employment rises. In Figure 3.1, the new equilibrium in the economy is at point (*B*).

These results are not overturned by considering wealth effects. For any given level of money, the increase in income triggers wealth effects in the demand for money function, the reason being that as wealth rises, a person wishes to hold more money. The interest raises, and the *LM* curve shifts slightly leftwards (i.e. LM_2), whereas at the same time the *IS* curve shifts further rightwards (i.e. IS_2). The final equilibrium in the economy is thus at point (*C*), where (*C*) could be on the right or slightly on the left of point (*B*). In short, there is only partial crowding out (i.e. Y_2 is always on the right of Y_0).

A different case is that of a bond-financed increase in real government spending (Blinder and Solow, 1974). It is now important to distinguish first-round effects from second-rounds effects. In the former case, wealth effects are absent. The *IS* curve shifts rightwards (i.e. IS_1), but the *LM* curve does not move. In other words, as a result of the increase in real government spending, the level of output and employment rises, though to a lesser extent than the money-financed case, because by assumption the money supply does not change. In Figure 3.2, the new equilibrium in the economy is at point (*B*). Second-rounds effects include wealth effects, which now shifts the *IS* curve further rightwards (i.e. IS_2), whereas the *LM* curve moves leftwards (i.e. LM_2).

As in the case of a money-financed increase in real government spending, the *LM* curve shifts leftwards because of negative wealth effects on the demand for money. However, in this case the wealth-induced *LM* curve shift may even offset the expansionary effect of the wealth-induced *IS* curve shift altogether, the reason being that *ceteris paribus* with a fixed money supply the interest rate must rise higher than the previous case to

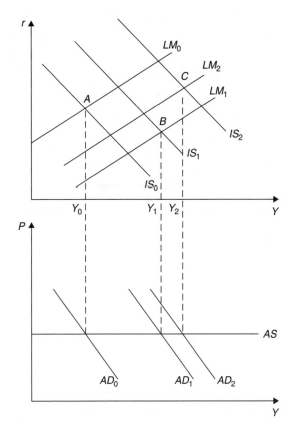

Figure 3.1 A money-financed increase in real government spending with wealth effects

compensate for the wealth-induced increase in the demand for money. In Figure 3.2, the final equilibrium in the economy is at point (C), with an output level equal to (Y_0). In other words, in this case the wealth effects bring the economy back to the original position. The aggregate demand curve moves rightwards and then leftwards (i.e. from AD_0 to AD_1 and then back to AD_0). In short, there is a complete crowding-out.

In summary, in a standard *IS-LM* closed economy framework with finite elasticity in the *IS* and *LM* curves, and in presence of wealth effects, the economy experiences partial crowding-out in the case of a money-financed increase in real government spending, and possibly a complete crowding out, like in Figure 3.2, in the case of a bond-financed increase in real government spending.[10]

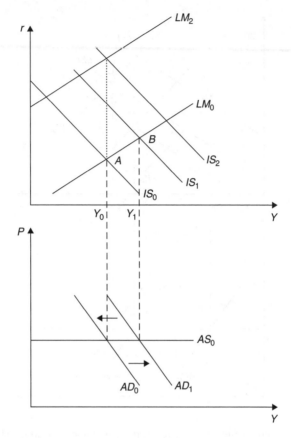

Figure 3.2   A bond-financed increase in real government spending with wealth effects

Let us now repeat the same type of exercise, namely the analysis of a money-financed and a bond-financed increase in real government spending, when money is endogenous rather than exogenous like in the *IS-LM* model (Fontana, 2008, chs 6 and 7). For the purpose of the analysis here, an endogenous money model is simply the *IS-LM* model with the central bank setting the short-run interest rate on monetary reserves rather than the quantity of money, either directly or indirectly via the standard reserves multiplier story (Fontana, 2004, 2006). This seemingly innocuous change in central banking behaviour has dramatic implications for the analysis of the crowding-out phenomenon. Immediately there is a problem of definitions, because in the endogenous

Table 3.1   A bond-financed increase in real government spending without banknotes

Commercial Banks	
Assets	**Liabilities**
Treasury bills: +100	Treasury deposits: +100
Treasury bills: +100	Households' deposits: +100

money case it is arbitrary to differentiate money-financing and bond-financing real government spending. As argued below, the decision of money-financing or bond-financing real government spending rests with the private sector rather than the public sector. The different forms of financing real government spending are endogenously decided by private agents rather than exogenously set by policy makers. In other words, the form of financing government spending is a residual outcome of the portfolio preference of households between different liquid assets. Tables 3.1 and 3.2 show the effects of an increase in government spending, through an analysis of the balance sheets of commercial banks and the central bank.[11]

Let us suppose that the government wants to increase spending by £100 million in order to employ more nurses in public hospitals. Table 3.1, row 1 illustrates that the government will then sell £100 millions short-run bonds (i.e. Treasury bills) to commercial banks in return for the opening of deposits of equal value. Table 3.1, row 2 shows the second-round effects of the government spending. As the Treasury fulfils its spending plans, the deposits are transferred from the government to households. If the economic process stopped here, it could be concluded that the £100 million increase in government spending is bond-financed. However, once households receive their payments, they may wish to hold part or all of it in banknotes. Let us suppose that households wish to hold all deposits in banknotes. Table 3.2, row 1 shows the effects of this decision on the balance sheets of commercial banks and the central bank, respectively.

Banks sell Treasury bills to the central bank in return for the opening of deposits of equal value. This means that banks have now replaced Treasury bills with reserves at the central bank. Table 3.2, row 2 records the second-round effects of the process. Since households wish to hold all deposits in banknotes, they withdraw money from banks. Commercial banks accommodate the request by using their reserves of banknotes

Table 3.2 A bond-financed increase in real government spending
with banknotes

Commercial Banks		Central Bank	
Assets	Liabilities	Assets	Liabilities
Reserves: +100	Households' deposits: +100	Treasury bills: +100	Banks' deposits: +100
Reserves: 0	Households' deposits: 0	Treasury bills: +100	Banknotes: +100

Table 3.3 A money-financed increase in real government spending

Commercial Banks		Central Bank	
Assets	Liabilities	Assets	Liabilities
		Treasury bills: +100	Treasury deposits: +100
Reserves: +100	Households' deposits: +100	Treasury bills: +100	Banks' deposits: +100

at the central bank. In this case, the £100 million increase in government spending is money-financed. In reality, it is likely that households
wish to hold only part of their deposits in banknotes. This means that
the proportion of government spending that is bond-financed or money
financed is the outcome of households' choice between deposits and
banknotes, and it can be represented by a combination of Table 3.1 and
Table 3.2.

Before moving to an analysis of a money-financed increase in real
government spending, it is worth highlighting some of the implications of replacing the exogenous money hypothesis of the *IS-LM* model
with the endogenous money hypothesis. They are related to the role of
the central bank as the residual supplier of liquidity to the economy.
The acceptability of bank deposits as means of payments rests on the
confidence of households that deposits can always be used for buying
goods and services. This means that deposits must always be exchange-
able for legal tender, i.e. banknotes, on demand. Therefore, whenever
households desire to have some deposits transformed into banknotes,
the commercial bank cannot but borrow reserves from the central bank.

Table 3.3 show the effects of a money-financed increase in government
spending, through an analysis of the balance sheets of commercial banks

and the central bank. Like before, let us suppose that the government wants to increase spending by £100 millions in order to employ more nurses in public hospitals. Table 3.3, row 1 illustrates that government will then sell £100 millions short-run bonds (i.e. Treasury bills) to the central bank in return for the opening of deposits of equal value. Table 3.3, row 2 shows the second-round effects of the government spending. As the Treasury fulfils its spending plans, the deposits are transferred from the government to households, which place them at the commercial banks. This means that £100 million reserves are recorded on the assets side of the commercial banks, where £100 million household deposits are recorded on the liabilities side of commercial banks.

Table 3.3, row 2 corresponds to Table 3.2, row 1. Therefore, the analysis of previous paragraphs also applies to this case. In particular, like in the case of a bond-financed increase in government spending, the proportion of government spending that is bond-financed or money-financed does not depend on the favoured finance choice of the government, but rather on the choice of households between holding liquidity in the form of deposits or banknotes.

There is a second important difference for the analysis of an increase in real government spending, when money is endogenous, rather than exogenous like in the *IS-LM* model. When money is endogenous, the existence of a partial or complete crowding-out is decided by the central bank.[12] It is worth recalling that in the standard *IS-LM* framework with finite elasticity in the *IS* and *LM* curves and in presence of wealth effects, the economy experiences crowding-out because of the assumption of a fixed money supply. For instance, in the case of a bond-financed increase in real government spending, the wealthier households are, the more money they wish to hold. With a fixed supply of money, this means that the interest rate must increase to release some money from idle balances to active balances. The higher interest rate crowds-out private-sector investments, and it offsets completely the positive income effects of the increase in government expenditure. Similarly, in the case of a money-financed increase in real government spending, the interest rate will rise to accommodate the wealth-induced increase in the demand for money. However, in this case the higher interest rate does not fully crowd-out private-sector investments, because part of the increase in the money demand is accommodated by the increase in the money supply in order to finance government spending.

It should then be clear the reason for the absence of a partial or complete crowding-out in the case of an increase in real government spending, when money is endogenous. Partial or complete crowding-out is the final outcome of increases in the interest rate due to an excess of the demand for money over a fixed supply of money. But, when money is endogenous, by definition the money supply responds to the demand for money, though the central bank may raise the price for supplying monetary reserves (i.e. the short-run interest rate). This means that when money is endogenous, there is no such a thing as a market-driven interest rate response to the wealth-induced excess of money demand. Therefore, no crowding-out needs to take place. It is, rather, an autonomous and deliberate decision of the central bank to intervene in the money market by increasing the interest rate that creates the conditions for the crowding-out of private investments. The adjustment process in the monetary market becomes a matter of administrative decision rather than a market mechanism.

Conclusions

This chapter has presented the New Consensus view and its major policy implications, namely the prominent role assigned to central banks in achieving desired inflation target strategies. The role of central banks and monetary policy in the New Consensus view is so prominent that the macroeconomic role of discretionary fiscal policy is rarely mentioned in modern economics or policy making alike. In the few cases when fiscal policy is discussed, the aim is to limit its role to exceptional circumstances, when monetary policy is either unusable or little effective, like in the case of the lower bound problem on the short-run interest rate, or country-specific shocks in monetary unions. But why has the role for fiscal policy been downgraded? Is this a novel feature of modern macroeconomics or has the New Consensus view borrowed it from past contributions?

This chapter has tried to answer these questions. First, the chapter has reviewed recent works on the possible historical causes of the modern downgrading of fiscal policy. The traditional story is that post-war Keynesianism failed to provide any understanding of the stagflation of the 1970s, let alone to solve it, and hence it was replaced by a new theoretical framework, namely New Classical Macroeconomics. However, recent work on the subject seems to suggest an alternative story, where ideology, policy mistakes and particular historical circumstances played a role at least as important as economic theory in the rejection of post-war Keynesianism, and the consequent downgrading of fiscal policy.

Second, the chapter has considered the theoretical explanations that are traditionally used to explain the ineffectiveness of fiscal policy, with a particular focus on the crowding-out arguments, within both the standard *IS-LM* (exogenous money) framework and the modern New Consensus (endogenous money) framework. The analysis has led to two main conclusions. The different forms of financing real government spending are endogenously decided by private agents rather than exogenously set by policy makers. More importantly, the existence of partial or complete crowding-out is decided by the central bank rather than by the 'market'.

Acknowledgements

The paper on which this chapter is based was mostly written when the author was Visiting Research Professor at the Observatoire Français des Conjonctures Economiques (OFCE), Sciences Po, Paris, France. I would like to express appreciation to members of this institution for providing a stimulating and pleasant working environment, especially Jacques Le Cacheux, Gérard Cornilleau, Jérôme Creel and Laurence Duboys Fresney. I am also grateful to Philip Arestis, Jérôme Creel, Francesco Saraceno, Malcolm Sawyer, and participants at the 4th International conference 'Developments in Economic Theory and Policy' (Bilbao, 5–6 July 2007), and at the OFCE Research Seminar (OFCE, Paris, 7 January 2008) for comments and discussion on a previous draft of this chapter. The usual disclaimer applies.

Notes

1. The reader should note this New Consensus policy prescription implicitly assumes that this output stabilization objective does not leave any long lasting effect on the economy. In other words, the New Consensus view subscribes to the axiom of neutrality of money and monetary policy in the long run. See Fontana (2007), and Fontana and Palacio-Vera (2004, 2007) for a critical assessment of this axiom.
2. Interestingly, the Phillips curve has gone through some unnoticed change in the past couple of decades: in the New Consensus view causation runs from the output gap to inflation (see Equation 3.1), whereas in the supply component of the traditional New Classical macroeconomic model, causation runs from inflation (surprises) to output (see, on the policy implications of this change, Sawyer, 2008).
3. More realistic representation of the 'New Consensus model' will include distributed lag relations, expected values of the exogenous variables, as well as complex monetary policy rules *à la* Taylor (see, for instance, papers in Arestis, 2007). However, in order to keep the analysis as simple as possible, these complications are set aside.
4. This is another way of saying that the New Consensus model assumes the existence in the long run of a market-determined equilibrium real interest

rate, to which the Central Bank has to conform. In Wicksellian terms, the Central Bank has to conform to the 'natural rate' of interest in pursuit of a constant rate of inflation (Fontana, 2007).

5. A different issue is the repayment of the national debt and the debt service payments, a problem faced by the fiscal authority, but not by the monetary authority. This issue is not discussed here, though it is worth recalling that it cannot be excluded that public expenditure is self-financing in the long run (e.g., Christ, 1968).

6. A noteworthy exception is Taylor (1993, 2000).

7. These potentially long inside lags for fiscal policy are also used by more sympathetic supporters of fiscal policy to justify support for changes in taxes and government transfers at the expenses of countercyclical variations in government purchases (e.g. Seidman, 2003; Solow, 2005).

8. This alternative story also draws attention to the misleading calculations in the 1970s of the impact of fiscal policy. Budget deficits were usually calculated in nominal but not real terms, with the result that higher inflation led to higher nominal interest rates and apparently increasing budget deficits (e.g. Eisner and Pieper, 1984)

9. Of course, strictly speaking a zero output gap can deliver constant inflation, not price stability. Also, the delivery of the target rate of inflation depends on expectations. One simple argument to finesse these issues is that the use of an inflation targeting regime is uniquely able to foster the 'right' expectations (see, for instance, Goodfriend, 2007).

10. The form of financing of the increase in real government spending explains the size of interest rate rise, hence the nature and origin of any crowding-out. How this rise feeds through to other interest rates in the economy, the interest rate responsiveness of investment or consumer expenditure, and the phase of the business cycle are the remaining factors accounting for the full extent of the crowding-out. These factors explain the slope of IS and LM curves and, for the sake of simplicity, are ignored in the analysis of Figures 3.1 and 3.2.

11. See, for a further discussion of balance sheet analysis, Lavoie, 2003.

12. An early suggestion in this direction is to be found in Champernowne (1936, pp. 204–6), who argued that monetary authorities are responsible for moving actual unemployment toward basic unemployment, where the latter is 'the amount of unemployment that there would be in that situation if each man demanded neither more nor less than his basic real wage' Champernowne (1936, p. 203).

References

Allsopp, C. and Vines, D. (2005) 'The macroeconomic role of fiscal policy', *Oxford Review of Economic Policy*, 21(4), 485–508.

Arestis, P. (2007, ed.) *Is there a New Consensus in Macroeconomics?*, Basingstoke: Palgrave Macmillan.

Arestis, P. and Sawyer, M. (2003) 'Reinventing fiscal policy', *Journal of Post Keynesian Economics*, 26(1), 3–25.

Arestis, P. and Sawyer, M. (2006) 'Fiscal policy matters', *Public Finance/Finance Publiques*, 54(3–4), 133–53.

Barro, R.J. (1974) 'Are government bonds net wealth?', *Journal of Political Economy*, 82(6), 1095–117.

Blinder, A. (1981) 'Temporary income taxes and consumer spending', *Journal of Political Economy*, 89(1), 26–53.

Blinder, A. (2004) 'The case against the case against discretionary fiscal policy', *CEPS Working Paper*, No. 100, June. An abridged version of the paper is 'The case against the case against discretionary fiscal policy', in R.W. Kopcke, G.M.B. Tootell, and R.K. Triest (eds) (2006) *The Macroeconomics of Fiscal Policy*, London: MIT Press.

Blinder, A. and Solow, R. (1974) 'Analytical foundations of fiscal policy', in A. Blinder *et al.* (eds), *The Economics of Public Finance: Essays*, Washington: The Brookings Institution.

Carlin, W. and Soskice, D. (2005) 'The 3-equation new Keynesian model: A graphical exposition', *Contributions to Macroeconomics*, 5(1), 1–36.

Carlin, W. and Soskice, D (2006) *Macroeconomics: Imperfections, Institutions and Policies*, Oxford: Oxford University Press.

Champernowne, D.G. (1936) 'Unemployment, basic and monetary: The classical analysis and the Keynesian', *Review of Economic Studies*, 3(3), 201–16.

Christ, C. (1968) 'A simple macroeconomic model with a government budget restraint', *Journal of Political Economy*, 76(1), 53–67.

Clarida, R., Galí, J. and Gertler, M. (1999) 'The science of monetary policy', *Journal of Economic Literature*, 37(4), 1661–707.

Davig, T. and Leeper, E.M. (2005) 'Generalizing the Taylor principle', *NBER Working Paper, No. 11874*, December.

Eisner, R. and Pieper, P.J. (1984) 'A new view of the federal debt and budget deficits', *American Economic Review*, 74(1), 11–29.

Fontana, G. (2004) 'Rethinking endogenous money: A constructive interpretation of the debate between accommodationists and structuralists', *Metroeconomica*, 55(4), 367–85.

Fontana, G. (2006) 'Telling better stories in macroeconomic textbooks: Monetary policy, endogenous money and aggregate demand', in M. Setterfield (ed.), *Complexity, Endogenous Money and Exogenous Interest Rate, Essays in Honour of Basil Moore*, Cheltenham (UK): Edward Elgar.

Fontana, G. (2007) 'Why money matters: Wicksell, Keynes, and the New Consensus view on monetary policy', *Journal of Post Keynesian Economics*, 30(1), 43–60.

Fontana, G. (2008) *Money, Time and Uncertainty*, London: Routledge.

Fontana, G. and Palacio-Vera, A. (2004) 'Monetary policy uncovered: Theory and practice', *International Review of Applied Economics*, 18(1), 25–42.

Fontana, G. and Palacio-Vera, A. (2007) 'Are long-run price stability and short-run output stabilization all that monetary policy can aim for?', *Metroeconomica*, 58(2), 269–98.

Forder, J. (2007a) *The Historical Place of the Friedman-Phelps' Expectation Critique*, Mimeo, Presented at OFCE seminar, Paris, December.

Forder, J. (2007b) *Friedman's Nobel Lecture Reconsidered*, Mimeo, Presented at Ecopol seminar, Sciences Po, Paris, December.

Friedman, M. (1966) 'What price guideposts?', in G.P. Schultz and R.Z. Aliber (eds), *Guidelines, Informal Controls, and the Market Place*, Chicago: Chicago University Press.

Friedman, M. (1968) 'The role of monetary policy', *American Economic Review*, 58(1), 1–17.

Friedman, M. (1977) 'Nobel lecture: Inflation and unemployment', *Journal of Political Economy*, 85(3), 451–72.

Goodfriend, M. (2007) 'How the world achieved consensus on monetary policy', *NBER Working Paper Series*, No. 13580, November.

Heller, W.W. (1966) *New Dimensions of Political Economy*, Cambridge, MA: Harvard University Press.

Hemming, R., Kell, M. and Mahfouz, S. (2002) 'The effectiveness of fiscal policy in stimulating economic activity: A review of the literature', *IMF Working Paper, No.* 02/208, Washington, DC: International Monetary Fund.

Keynes, J.M. (1973, orig. 1936) *The General Theory of Employment, Interest, and Money, The Collected Writings of J.M. Keynes*, Vol. VII, London: Macmillan.

Kirsanova, T., Satchi, M., Vines, D. and Wren-Lewis, S. (2007) 'Optimal fiscal policy rules in a monetary union', *Journal of Money, Credit and Banking*, 39(7), 1759–84.

Krugman, P. (2005) 'Is fiscal policy poised for a comeback?', *Oxford Review of Economic Policy*, 21(4), 515–23.

Lucas, R.E. Jr. and Sargent, T.J. (1978) 'After Keynesian macroeconomics', in R.E. Lucas Jr. and T.J. Sargent (eds), *After the Phillips Curve: Persistence of High Inflation and High Unemployment*, Boston, MA: Federal Reserve Bank of Boston.

Meyer, L.H. (2001) 'Does money matter?', *Federal Reserve Bank of St. Louis Review*, 83(5), 1–15.

Okun, A.M. (1970) *The Political Economy of Prosperity*, Washington: The Brookings Institution.

Phelps, E.S. (1967) 'Phillips curves, expectations of inflation and optimal unemployment over time', *Economica* (NS), 34(135), 254–81.

Phillips, A.W.H. (1958) 'The relation between unemployment and rate of change of money wage rates in the United Kingdom: 1861–1957', *Economica* (NS), 25(100), 283–99.

Sawyer, M.C. (2002) 'The NAIRU, aggregate demand and investment', *Metroeconomica*, 2002, 53(1), 66–94.

Sawyer, M.C. (2008) 'Phillips' curve', in W.A. Darity, Jr. (ed.), *International Encyclopaedia of the Social Sciences*, Vol. 6 (2nd edn) Detroit: Palgrave Macmillan.

Seidman, L. (2003) *Automatic Fiscal Policies to Combat Recessions*, London: M.E. Sharpe.

Setterfield, M. (2007) 'Is there a stabilising role for fiscal policy in the New Consensus?', *Review of Political Economy*, 19(3), 405–18.

Solow, R.M. (2005) 'Rethinking fiscal policy', *Oxford Review of Economic Policy*, 21(4), 509–14.

Symposium on Fiscal Policy (2005) *Oxford Review of Economic Policy*, 21(4) 485–635.

Taylor, J.B. (1993) 'Discretion versus policy rules in practice', *Carnegie-Rochester Conference Series in Public Policy*, 38, 195–214.

Taylor, J.B. (2000) 'Reassessing discretionary fiscal policy', *Journal of Economic Perspectives*, 14(3), 21–36.

Walsh, C.E. (2002) 'Teaching inflation targeting: An analysis for intermediate macro', *Journal of Economic Education*, 33(4), 333–46.

4
Minsky's Financial Instability Hypothesis: The Crucial Role of Fiscal Policy

Philip Arestis and Elisabetta De Antoni

Introduction

Over the past two decades or so, monetary policy has gained considerably in importance as an instrument of macroeconomic policy. Fiscal Policy, on the contrary, has been so much downgraded that it is rarely mentioned in policy discussions, apart from arguing to place limits on budget deficit and fiscal variables. Arestis and Sawyer (2003) argue that 'fiscal policy remains a powerful instrument of regulating the level of aggregate demand' (p. 23). This chapter aims to consider that particular conclusion within the context of the work of Hyman P. Minsky.

By focusing on the financial instability of advanced capitalist economies, Hyman Minsky greatly extends the effectiveness and role of fiscal policy. In his view, the effects of fiscal policy do not only work through the goods market, but also impinge upon the financial system. Government intervention is not only necessary to reach and maintain full employment; it is also indispensable to contain capitalist instability, thereby avoiding financial crises followed by debt deflations and deep depressions.

This work aims to present Hyman Minsky's financial instability hypothesis and the crucial role it assigns to the government. In the next section we consider the heterodox presuppositions of Hyman Minsky's analysis. Following this we examine his 'financial instability hypothesis'. In the following three sections, we analyse the role that Hyman Minsky assigns to fiscal policy considering first a closed and then an open economy. The penultimate section extends the analysis to the prospects of capitalism, with the summaries and conclusions presented in the final section.

The heterodox nature of Hyman Minsky's economics

Over the past 70 years, the dominant macroeconomic theory has assumed ever new and more sophisticated facets. There seems to be, however, a continual thread in its evolution: the constant reference to General Equilibrium Theory (GET). It is thus this aspect that seems to qualify macroeconomic orthodoxy. Among other things, standard GET is based on two fundamental pillars: i) the assumption of unbounded individual rationality, according to which at any given price vector perfectly competitive agents choose the quantities supplied and demanded that maximize their target function; and ii) the assumption of unbounded collective rationality, according to which there is instantaneous and generalized market clearing. The omniscient auctioneer (the personification of the equally occult 'invisible hand' of the market) instantaneously finds and announces the equilibrium price vector. S/he then signals the start of trading, coordinating ex ante the whole system.

Seventy years ago, *The General Theory* rejected the individual and collective perfect rationality assumptions. First, in Keynes's world agents have a bounded rationality – the future, in particular, is totally unknown. Second, the general equilibrium price vector may not exist. The existence of a positive interest rate level able to align full-employment savings and investments is, for instance, not granted. Moreover, even if the equilibrium price vector did exist, there is no auctioneer that leads prices to their equilibrium level.[1] The perfect rationality pillars, and with them GET, are totally unrealistic and thus have to be rejected. In short, this seems to be the essence of the Keynesian 'revolution'.

Revolutions, as we know, are usually followed by counter-revolutions. In the case under examination, the counter-revolution (the Neoclassical Synthesis) takes place immediately after the publication of *The General Theory*. In its course, which starts with Hicks (1937) and culminates with Patinkin (1956), the Synthesis ends up with recovering the GET as a benchmark. In other words, GET is again proposed as a reliable approximation of the reality. It is simply necessary to take into account that in the short-run some gears of the adjustment mechanism can jam, giving rise to deviations from general equilibrium. Specifically, the Synthesis believes that in the short-run nominal wages are rigid. In the presence of a recessionary shock, aggregate demand thus temporarily gains the facility to contain economic activity below its full employment level.

Monetarism also adopted the general equilibrium as a benchmark. In its evolution, however, short-run deviations from general equilibrium become supply (rather than demand) phenomena (Friedman, 1968). Moreover, the maladjustment causing these deviations concerns inflationary expectations in Friedman's Monetarism Mark 1 and intertemporal relative prices in Lucas's Monetarism Mark 2.[2] In the latter case, rational expectations take the place of the auctioneer. Agents are now able to find by themselves the equilibrium price vector. Except for unforeseeable random surprises, the system is in its general equilibrium. With the Real Business Cycle Theory, maladjustments disappear and shocks determine general equilibrium fluctuations.[3] With this, the rehabilitation of GET was complete.[4]

Hyman Minsky's contributions appeared over the period 1954 to 1996 and thus coincided with the aforementioned resurface of the GET. Drawing on *The General Theory*, of which he is one of the most famous and original interpreters, Minsky (1975) rejects as unrealistic the unbounded rationality pillars and thus the GET. In Hyman Minsky's view, the limits of collective and individual rationality feed each other, generating deviation-amplifying mechanisms that make the economy unstable.

Starting with the collective rationality, Minsky (1975, 1982a, 1986) radicalizes Keynes's arguments. He does not limit himself to rejecting the auctioneer, but banishes the concept of equilibrium itself. Hyman Minsky's economics is not unstable because it lacks the tendency to general (or any other) equilibrium. It is unstable because its structure and the qualitative characteristics of its dynamic behaviour autonomously evolve with the simple passing of time (Vercelli, 2001).

We turn our attention next to individual rationality. In Minsky's (1975, 1982a, 1986, 1996) evolving world, learning processes are comparatively slow. Agents do not succeed in knowing the model and (above all) are conscious of this. To quote Minsky (1996): 'The uncertainty that permeates the economics of Keynes and the economics of bounded rationality is due to the unsureness about the validity of the model that enters in the decision process' (p. 2). What matters is not only the expectation about the future, but also the confidence placed in it. Given the ignorance of the future, expectation and confidence are based on recent past and consequently end up with performing a deviation-amplifying role. To quote Minsky (1986), 'A history of success will tend to diminish the margins of safety that business and bankers require and will thus tend to be associated with increased investment; a history of failure will do the opposite' (p. 187). The limits of individual rationality thus hinder the yet bounded collective rationality.

Drawing on *The General Theory*, Minsky (1975, 1986) places the uncertainty about the future at the centre of his analysis. This leads him to recognize the crucial role of finance. Uncertainty mainly hits perspective yields on financial and real assets. The external financing of investment, thus, becomes a crucial issue.[5] An important characteristic of advanced economies is that large and expensive long-term investment takes place that needs to be debt financed. The underlying assumption is that this type of investment generates sufficient profits to service the necessary debt commitments. This assumption, however, is not necessarily confirmed by empirical evidence.[6] In this sense one might observe that the coherence of a market economy not only does it require the clearing of all individual markets. It also requires that investment actually generates profits greater than debt commitments, which is not necessarily met in the real world (Minsky, 1986, p. 141).

Starting from these presuppositions, Minsky (1975, 1978, 1982a, 1986) launches his attack on the dominant theory. Even if general equilibrium did represent a reliable approximation to reality, the price mechanism would not necessarily be able to coordinate the system. Let us consider a situation of unemployment. Insofar as wage and price deflation is associated by a fall in profits, it decreases firms' ability to fulfil inherited debt commitments. In this way it jeopardizes the robustness of the financial system, with depressing effects on long-term expectations and investments. In conformity with the experience of 1929–33 and to the 'true' thought of Keynes, the fall in prices can thus depress aggregate demand, accentuating unemployment instead of reabsorbing it.

In addition to the realism and stability of the general equilibrium, however, Hyman Minsky also questions the less ambitious concept of short-run unemployment equilibrium. Subjective evaluations ruling financial markets and expected returns on real assets are changeable and consequently investment is volatile. The equilibrium continuously changes with the passing of time and the system never succeeds in reaching it. Instead of speaking of equilibrium or disequilibrium, Minsky (1986, p. 176), just like Joan Robinson (1971), argues in terms of states of tranquillity, which hide in themselves disequilibrating forces destined to gain strength with the simple passing of time. Every state nurtures the forces destined to change it.

In Hyman Minsky's view, the dominant theory has been able to adopt an equilibrium framework since it has cut out crucial aspects of the reality as uncertainty, the external financing of capital accumulation, the relevance of monetary and financial factors, the structural instability of capitalism and the crucial role of institutions. The originality and the importance of Hyman Minsky's contributions lies precisely in recovering these issues and placing them at the centre of his financial instability hypothesis. This made his theory extremely modern and allowed it to influence a whole generation of Keynesian economists.

Hyman Minsky's financial instability hypothesis

Hyman Minsky presented his financial instability hypothesis as an authentic interpretation, or as a legitimate extension, of Keynes' thought.[7] As a matter of fact, the basic vision of the two authors is the same. Let us dwell, for instance, on the rejection of the assumption of unbounded individual and collective rationality, on the relevance attributed to uncertainty and accumulation, to monetary and financial factors, to institutions and so on. The two authors, however, might be considered as two faces of the same coin that look in opposite directions. Keynes focuses on a depressed economy, tending to chronic underinvestment and thus to high and long lasting unemployment. Hyman Minsky, on the other hand, looks to a vibrant economy naturally inclined to overinvestment and over-indebtedness.[8]

Specifically, Minsky's (1978) starting point is that 'Stability – or tranquillity – is destabilising' (p. 37) and that 'the fundamental instability is upward' (Minsky, 1975, p. 165). A period of tranquillity (in which the financial system is robust and there are no relevant shocks, so that profits are systematically greater than debt commitments) increases the confidence in the future, giving rise to a wealth re-allocation from money to other assets. The result is an increase in investment financed with indebtedness. Thus, stability turns into an expansion.

Expansion triggers a deviation-amplifying mechanism primarily based on the link investments-profits-investments. An initial rise in investment provokes an income expansion, which partly turns into a rise in profits. Besides validating past investment decisions, this rise improves profit expectations and confidence. In this way, the higher profits give rise to a further increase in the volume of investment financed by indebtedness. The deviation-amplifying mechanism based on the link investments-profits-investments is strengthened by the money and financial markets. With the growing optimism, the speculative demand for money shrinks in favour of other assets inducing expansionary effects on credit and investments (and thus on income and profits). The money supply increases associated with income expansion also lead to the same results. Through its wealth effects, the rise in asset prices stimulates credit and capital accumulation as well. Lastly, as we have seen, expectations and confidence also perform a deviation-amplifying role. Thanks to the aforementioned processes, expansion turns into a debt-financed investment boom.

At this point, Minsky (1975, 1978, 1982a, 1982b, 1986) focuses on two drawbacks of such a boom. The first one refers to the general euphoria, whereby firms' debt commitments increase more rapidly than profits, ending by rising above them. Given the expectation of a future bonanza, firms start financing the principal by indebtedness (speculative financing) and also interest payments (ultra-speculative or Ponzi financing). The fulfilment of debt commitments is based no longer on profits but, respectively, on the rolling over or the automatic increase in indebtedness. From being initially robust, the financial system becomes fragile.[9] Turning to the second drawback, the persistence of the boom inevitably ends up creating either bottlenecks in the financial system or inflationary pressures in the goods market that push the central bank in a deflationary direction. In both cases, the result is an increase in the rate of interest.[10]

The rise in the interest rate ends the boom, turning the investments-profits-investments chain into a downward spiral. The unexpected increase in the cost of funds is thus associated with the unexpected fall in (the yet insufficient) profits. Given the situation of financial fragility, the fulfilment of inherited debt commitments would require an increase in (the already high) indebtedness. This solution, however, is neither desirable nor possible since the confidence underlying indebtedness fades away. We thus come to the financial crisis, defined (Minsky, 1982b) as a situation in which firms' debt commitments cannot be fulfilled any more in the normal way, i.e. by profits (hedge finance) or indebtedness (speculative and Ponzi finance).

Under the new circumstances, the only way to fulfil the debt commitments is the sale of assets, which after the boom are mainly illiquid assets. The fall in the asset prices reduces the net wealth of firms and financial intermediaries. This reinforces the need to squeeze indebtedness by selling assets. Asset prices fall precipitously. The fall of capital asset prices strengthens the fall of investments and profits, and vice versa. The financial crisis, thus, turns into a debt deflation, which in Minsky's (1982b) framework is an asset price as well as a profit deflation. The debt deflation will end by making the fulfilment of debt commitments impossible. The consequence will be a wave of bankruptcies, which in its turn will end in a deep depression.

Destruction, however, is creative. Only hedge units (units still able to fulfil debt commitments by profits) survive. Under these circumstances, a phase of tranquillity will suffice to increase confidence and to reactivate the sequence just described. According to Minsky's (1975, 1986) financial instability hypothesis, the system will again experience an expansion, a speculative boom, a financial crisis and a debt deflation, along with a deep depression.[11]

Turning to the real world, Minsky (1982a, 1986) finds confirmation of his analysis. The financial instability of the American economy, which he had previously denounced (Minsky, 1963), surfaced in the middle of the 1960s giving rise to the crises of 1966, 1970, 1974–75, 1979 and 1982. Financial instability had, however, also characterized the periods preceding and separating the two world wars. This confirms that financial crises are systemic and not idiosyncratic (Minsky, 1991). Looking ahead, Minsky (1982a) wonders whether 'It' can happen again. 'It' is the Great Depression and Hyman Minsky's answer is affirmative. Starting from these presuppositions, Minsky (1986) assigns a crucial role to economic policy institutions: 'even though all capitalisms are flawed, we can develop a capitalism in which the flaws are less evident than they have been since 1967' (p. 295).[12]

From this point of view, Hyman Minsky does not place much faith in monetary policy. Given that a great part of the money supply is endogenously created by banks and given the innovative capacity of the financial system, the central bank has only a limited control over the supply of money. In any case, its intervention may turn out to be harmful as well as ineffective. As Minsky (1986) argues, 'Monetary policy to constrain undue expansion and inflation operates by way of disrupting financing markets and asset values. Monetary policy to induce expansion operates by interest rates and the availability of credit, which do not yield increased investment if current and anticipated profits are low' (pp. 303–4). Instead of aiming to control the money supply, the central bank should thus focus on its function as a lender of last resort. By enabling the funding of financial institutions and by sustaining asset prices, it might prevent or reabsorb financial crisis, so removing the threat of debt deflations and deep depressions. In any case, 'Fiscal policies are more powerful economic control weapons than monetary manipulations' (Minsky, 1986, p. 304). The task to stabilize the economy falls mainly on the government. This is the main message of Minsky's (1986) famous book: *Stabilizing an Unstable Economy*.

Setting aside the relative importance assigned to monetary or fiscal manoeuvres, Minsky (1975, 1986) proposes a more general rethinking of the final targets of economic policy. Specifically, he questions the orthodox neoclassical model based on investment and growth. Being a determinant of mark up and profits, investment increases the price level.[13] It also represents a highly unstable component of domestic aggregate demand. Above all, it may turn out to be a failure and compromise the stability and growth of the system.[14] It follows that 'an economy that aims at accelerating growth through devices that induce capital-intensive private investment not only may not grow, but may be increasingly inequitable in its income distribution, inefficient in its choices of techniques, and unstable in its overall performance' (Minsky, 1986, p. 292).

Fiscal policy in a closed economy

After the Keynesian revolution, the progressive rehabilitation of market mechanisms has not only implied the downsizing of fiscal policy. The dominant theory has also deployed ever-new arguments to show that budget deficits are ineffectual or undesirable. Arestis and Sawyer (2003, 2004) criticize these arguments one by one. In their view, the free market is not in general able to align full-employment savings and investments. Given the tendency for full-employment saving to exceed full-employment investment, a government deficit is necessary to fill the gap.[15]

Drawing on the same Keynesian tradition, Minsky (1975, 1982a, 1986) further extends the role of the government. Once the general equilibrium framework is abandoned and room is made for the endogenous instability of capitalism, laissez-faire becomes 'a prescription for economic disaster' (Minsky and Whalen, 1996, p. 161). Government intervention is not only necessary to reach and maintain full employment. It is indispensable to avoid the worst: 'The most significant economic event of the era since World War II is something that has not happened: there has not been a deep and long-lasting depression' (Minsky, 1982a, p. xi). Indeed, 'Big government capitalism is more stable than small government capitalism' (1986, p. 292).

Not only does Hyman Minsky extend the role of fiscal policy; he also extends its effects. To the traditional impact on the goods market, Hyman Minsky adds the repercussions that government budget has on the robustness of the financial system. Specifically, the effects that Minsky (1986) assigns to fiscal policy fall into three categories: 'The first effect is familiar and is dealt with in models that set out how GNP is determined. The second and third effects are often ignored; they are important, however, because the economy is both an income-producing and distributing system and a complicated, interdependent, and sophisticated financial system' (p. 21). The three kinds of effects that Hyman Minsky assigns to fiscal policy are the following:

1. The traditional income and employment effect, which consists in stimulating aggregate demand, output and employment up to their full employment levels. In an advanced society, all those wishing to participate in the productive process should have the opportunity to do so. Given the unreliability of market mechanisms, the State has to take on the function of 'employer of last resort' (Minsky and Whalen, 1996, p. 163).[16] Specifically, it has to give rise to a perfectly elastic public-sector demand for labour at a wage significantly lower than in the private sector (Minsky, 1986, p. 308). Public-sector workers should be employed to increase the physical and intellectual infrastructures.[17] From this point of view, 'The overall policy perspective is to substitute resource creating public spending for the multitude of transfer payments and entitlements that now make up a major part of non-military spending' (p. 300). In this way, the burden for the government budget of the employment of last resort strategy is likely to be small.

2. The cash flows effect, which operates by affecting the sectoral surpluses and deficits. In his works, Minsky (1986, 1992) adopts a conception à la Kalecki-Kaldor-Levy according to which income distribution mirrors the level and composition of aggregate demand rather than input productivity. In clearing the goods market, income fluctuations align aggregate profits to the sum of investments, government budget, net exports and capitalists' consumption net of workers' savings.[18] In order to guarantee the coherence of a capitalist economy, profits thus determined have to exceed firms' inherited debt commitments. It is here that fiscal policy comes into play. In reabsorbing unemployment, fiscal policy stimulates profits to their full employment level, thus strengthening the economy's financial robustness. The task to contain deviations from full employment, hindering the destabilizing tendencies present in the system, then falls on automatic fiscal stabilizers. Specifically, changes in the government budget have to compensate for investment fluctuations in order to stabilize income and profits. By avoiding the rise in profits due to an investment expansion, automatic fiscal stabilizers might hinder the tendency to a speculative boom and a financial crisis. By sustaining profits above inherited debt commitments during an after crisis investment slow down, automatic fiscal stabilizers might hinder the tendency to a debt deflation and a deep depression.

3. The portfolio effect, which operates through regulating the liquidity and solvency of the financial system. Minsky (1986) denies that the main characteristic of money lies in having a fixed price (the prices of goods and assets from which its purchasing power depends is variable) or in being the medium of exchange (in socialist countries money was the medium of exchange but did not have any special role in the economy). According to Minsky (1986), the peculiarity of money lies, instead, in that payment commitments connected to indebtedness, to productive activity, to taxation are denominated in money itself. By allowing the fulfilment of such payment commitments, money offers 'insurance services against bankruptcy' (p. 181). Government bonds can be easily converted into money. Thus, they too offer insurance services against bankruptcy. Together with money, they increase the robustness of the financial system.[19]

The soundness of public finance and the soundness of the whole economy

With the explosion of the government debt relative to gross domestic product over the Reagan-Bush administration, Hyman Minsky started worrying about the credibility of government bonds.[20] As Minsky (1991) puts it, 'The government is no different than any other organization in that it needs revenues to validate its debts' (p. 28). 'A government can run a deficit during a recession without suffering a deterioration of its creditworthiness if there is a tax and spending regime in place that would yield a favourable cash flow (a surplus) under reasonable and attainable circumstances' (Minsky, 1986, p. 302). Hyman Minsky's conclusion is that, save for exceptional situations, full employment government budget must be balanced or in surplus. To put it in his own words, 'Any deviation from a government budget that is balanced or in surplus must be understood as transitory – the war will be over, the resource development program will be finished, or income will be at the full employment level' (1986, p. 304; see also Minsky, 1992). As we shall see, however, this acknowledgement to sound finance risks being inconsistent with each of the three functions that Hyman Minsky keeps assigning to fiscal policy.

The traditional income and employment effect is consistent with the full-employment government balanced budget or surplus only in a particular case. We refer to an economy in which a positive interest level exists able to align full-employment saving and investment. Certainly, it is not the economy with a chronic excess of full-employment saving over investment that Keynes considered in *The General Theory* and that nowadays seems to characterize many European countries. In this case, full-employment would imply a chronic government deficit.

Coming to the budget effect, it is useful to reconsider the issue by consolidating the balance sheets of households and firms (Wray, 2006). As is well known, goods market equilibrium requires that desired sectoral surpluses and deficits offset each other. This means that, in a closed economy as the one under examination, government surplus has to be offset by an equivalent private sector deficit that in its turn implies a growing private net indebtedness. A government budget surplus would thus strengthen the tendency towards firms' overindebtedness that, according to Hyman Minsky, exposes modern capitalism to systemic financial crises followed by debt deflations and debt depressions. On the other hand, Minsky (1975, 1982a, 1986) himself insistently claimed that a growth led by government spending would generate less instability than a growth led by private investments.

As far as the portfolio effect is concerned, one of the novelties of Hyman Minsky's approach lies precisely in reminding us that government bonds are assets to the private sector representing an important source of liquidity and solvency and therefore of financial stability. If wealth grows with the passing of time giving rise to a growing demand for government bonds, financial market equilibrium requires a growing government bonds supply. Such an equilibrium is thus incompatible with a government balanced budget or surplus, be it referring to full employment or not. From this point of view, a growing economy requires an increasing government deficit.

Hyman Minsky seems to be an author more sensitive to the development of the original insights inspired by the observation of the real world than to the logical consistency of his analysis. His acknowledgement to sound finance, however, risks being inconsistent with each of the three functions he keeps assigning to fiscal policy. On this basis, Wray (2006) argues that Hyman Minsky is making a mistake. To keep his analysis consistent, he should have stuck to other approaches he had often given his assent to. We refer to the functional finance[21] and to the chartalist approach,[22] according to which government deficit and debt do not present a problem for the economy.

The present work suggests a different interpretation from Wray's (2006). In the 'Agenda for Reform' that closes his famous Minsky (1986) book, he implicitly takes the compatibility between the so-called sound public finance (p. 302) and the fiscal stabilization (p. 297) and support (p. 308) of the economy for granted. In our opinion, Hyman Minsky must have had his reasons to so do. To identify these reasons, we shall start from the differences between an economy à la Keynes and an economy à la Minsky and show that the compatibility between the so-called soundness of public finance and the soundness of the entire economy may be a problem in the first case, but not in the second. This might explain why Hyman Minsky is not concerned about it.

The literature generally classifies Hyman Minsky as one of the main exponents of the Post Keynesian School. Minsky (1975, pp. 79–80) himself presents his financial instability hypothesis as an authentic interpretation or a legitimate extension of *The General Theory*. His purpose is to bring back Keynes's (1936) theory to its cyclical perspective. In his reinterpretation of Keynes, however, Minsky (1975, 1978, 1980, 1982a, 1986) introduces an upward instability, which seems entirely extraneous to *The General Theory*. From this perspective, the two authors may be considered as two faces of the same coin looking in opposite directions. Hyman Minsky considers a vibrant economy, naturally inclined to over-investment and over-indebtedness. Keynes, on the contrary, considers a depressed economy tending to chronic under-investment and under-consumption and thus prone to high and long-lasting unemployment. Looking at the past 15 years, useful examples might be the USA and the UK economies in the first case and the European economy in the second. Starting from these premises, Hyman Minsky may be considered an author who has extended the economics of Keynes to a vibrant and euphoric economy, making it even more general and modern.

The previous considerations find confirmation in a careful reading of the two authors. While both are at the mercy of waves of optimism and pessimism, Minsky 'fights' against the upswing while Keynes 'fights' against the downswing. With very few exceptions, Hyman Minsky's writings focus on the inconveniences of the boom, taking the consequent disaster and (above all) the subsequent recovery for granted. Minsky (1986, p. 173) himself writes: 'The spectacular panics, debt deflations, and deep depressions that historically followed a speculative boom as well the recovery from depressions are of lesser importance in the analysis of instability than the developments over a period characterized by sustained growth that leads to the emergence of fragile and unstable financial structures'. On the contrary, Chapter 22 of *The General Theory* stresses the precariousness of the recovery, the need to support it at all costs, the systemic inadequacy of the level of investments with respect to the target of full employment, and the precariousness of a full-employment situation supported by investments arising from the depressive effect of accumulation on the marginal efficiency of capital.

On this basis, let us now return to fiscal policy. According to the previous analysis, it seems plausible to assume that the most important phase in terms of intensity and length is the downswing in the economics of Keynes and the upswing in the economics of Minsky. In the latter case, it is then plausible that the government surplus required to prevent the increase in income and profits during the upswing offsets (or more than offsets) the government deficit required to prevent the fall in income and profits during the downswing. Thus, in Hyman Minsky's vibrant economy where the upswings prevail, the fiscal stabilization of the business cycle does not necessarily represent a burden in terms of government budget and debt. Let us now consider the fiscal support to the economy. The growth of the economic system is also a product of the cycle. *Ceteris paribus*, an economy dominated by the upswing *à la* Minsky grows more, thus reaching higher income levels. In this case, a fiscal policy oriented toward full-employment is again less onerous in terms of government budget and debt. To sum up, Minsky (1986) seems to have had his reasons to believe that a 'good' fiscal policy (not misdirected, inefficient and corrupted) is compatible with the so-called soundness of public finance

The previous considerations obviously apply to an economy à la Minsky, where the upswings prevail. What would Hyman Minsky have proposed with regard to an economy *à la* Keynes, for instance the European economy of the past 15 years? To start with, he would have turned to the concrete experience. As known, the European Monetary Union decided to provide its central bank with complete independence. In order to be able to focus entirely on price control, the European central bank was forbidden to directly finance national public sectors. European national government deficits have thus to be funded exclusively by bond issues. To avoid upward pressures on the European interest rates that might damage the other member countries, the Stability and Growth Pact of 1996 introduced the target of a medium-term balanced government budget for the member countries of the Union. Thus, while the Stability and Growth Pact induced the European Union to intensify the fiscal stabilization process started with the Maastricht Treaty of 1992,[23] the American recession started in 2001 led to the transition from the federal budget surplus of 1.7% of GDP in 2000 to the federal budget deficit of 3.5% in 2003. The result was that, while the euro-area growth rate fell from 3.5% in 2000 to 0.4% in 2003, the US recession was surprisingly short and mild. In view of the bad performance of the European economy, in 2005 the Stability and Growth Pact was partially modified. The European Union experience suggests that a government bridled by budget constraints is not only unable to support and stabilize the economy; it can also end with performing a pro-cyclical role, accentuating the recessionary impulses present in the system.

Given the unsatisfactory performance of the European economy in terms of employment and growth, Hyman Minsky would have privileged the soundness of the economy over the soundness of public finance, fiercely opposing the Growth and Stability Pact and prescribing an active use of fiscal policy. To the objection that the issuing of more and more government bonds might become a problem, Hyman Minsky would have probably answered that, given the increasingly unbalanced income distribution, the burden of securing the soundness of public finance must be shouldered by the rich through raising tax rates on them. In addition, he might have suggested the introduction of a constraint on financial intermediaries, which would compel them to invest a given fraction of their portfolio in government bonds. As he puts it (1986): 'finance cannot be left to free markets' (p. 292). However, these last considerations are mere conjectures, even if based on a careful reading of Hyman Minsky's writings.

Sawyer (2001) too criticizes the European single currency from a Minskyan perspective. Hyman Minsky's approach would have implied rather different policy arrangements. The primary task of the European central bank would have been financial (rather than price) stability. The importance of lender of last resort interventions would have been admitted instead of being ignored. The role of fiscal policy in ensuring financial stability and in supporting the economy would have been recognized. The scope of fiscal policy would have been expanded through the institution of a European federal budget instead of being limited through the introduction of constraints on national government budgets.

Fiscal policy in an open economy

With few exceptions, Minsky (1979), the financial instability hypothesis was developed in the context of a closed economy. Its extension to the open economy, however, gave rise to stimulating interpretations of the crisis that took place in Southeast Asia in 1997–98. According to Arestis and Glickman (2002), the possibility of borrowing abroad fuels both growth and the tendency towards financial fragility of open, liberalized, developing economies. In the absence of capital controls – and especially if interest rates are low in the major financial centres – liquid funds will switch into these economies, reinforcing their expansion. Through the increase in domestic deposits and in domestic security prices, however, capital inflow will also stimulate both the availability of credit and the propensity to borrow, strengthening the tendency to a higher indebtedness. In addition, units which borrow abroad will have to fulfil their debt commitments in foreign currency and thus will also become vulnerable to movements in the exchange rate. To sum up, the increase in indebtedness, together with the denomination in foreign currency of part of it, will strengthen the tendency towards financial fragility. As we shall see below, the economy will thus become prone: i) to a crisis that is domestic in origin but impacts on its external situation (call it a *'d to e'* crisis); ii) to a crisis that is external in origin but impacts on its domestic situation (call it an *'e to d'* crisis); and iii) to deviation-amplifying interactions between (i) and (ii).

The *'d to e'* crisis is essentially the one described in the section discussing Minsky's financial instability hypothesis. Once more, however, the openness of the economy accentuates the problems. When the crisis evolves into a debt deflation and a big depression, a flight towards liquidity will break out. Some investors will seek to diversify the now larger liquidity by shifting into other currencies. Others will act in anticipation of behaviours of this kind. The domestic currency will be sold heavily and this will trigger an exchange rate crisis. The devaluation will increase the difficulties of the units with debt commitments in foreign currency and cash receipts in domestic currency, thus intensifying the crisis.

The opening of the economy introduces also the possibility of an *'e to d'* crisis. Capital inflow sustains the domestic exchange rate and thus worsens the current account. As the ratio between foreign indebtedness and foreign reserves grows, speculators may begin to doubt the ability of the state to support the currency and move, possibly on a massive scale, against the currency concerned. As a consequence of the devaluation, units with debt commitments in foreign currency and cash receipts in domestic currency will experience more difficulties in fulfilling their debt commitments. Capital outflow will imply a decrease in domestic deposits as well as the sale of domestic assets and thus the fall in their prices. As a consequence, the rolling over of domestic debts will also become more difficult. In a situation of financial fragility, the devaluation can thus trigger a financial crisis. Under the pressures emanating from the international financial system, during both the *'d to e'* and the *'e to d'* crises, the central bank will raise interest rates in order to bolster the exchange rate. In an open economy, monetary policy thus ends up accentuating the debt-deflation processes instead of mitigating them as Hyman Minsky suggested.

According to Arestis and Glickman (2002), the crisis experienced in Southeast Asia in 1997–98 is an *'e to d'* crisis. Its distinctiveness is that the crisis experienced by the various countries coincided with the spread of financial liberalization processes. Financial liberalization sweeps away the rules and conventions which previously governed the financial system, speeding up the process by which debt ratios rise. It also weakens the barrier of financial conservatism which, in Hyman Minsky's view, acts to contain speculative behaviours. From a Minskyan perspective, the connection between liberalization, financial instability and financial crises is thus perfectly understandable. As Hyman Minsky claimed, controls on domestic financial systems and on capital movements preserve the stability of the financial system.

Kregel (2001) also offers a Minskyan interpretation of the Asian financial crisis. Both directly and through its effects on the exchange rates, a rise in foreign interest rates increases the debt commitments in the indebted developing countries. If foreign banks are unwilling to extend foreign currency lending, the result may be a Minskyan debt-deflation process. Firms and banks will try to liquidate their stocks of goods and assets in order to fulfil their debt commitments and reduce their domestic and foreign debts. The consequent fall in the price of their products, in the price of their assets and in the value of the domestic currency, however, will further diminish their ability to fulfil debt commitments and to reduce debts.

Mistaking the crisis for a traditional balance of payments crisis, the IMF required a reduction in government expenditure and tight monetary targets. This, however, was the opposite of what was required from the point of view of stopping a Minskyan debt-deflation crisis.[24] A slowdown in domestic demand could only decrease the cash receipts of firms, while the increase in interest rates could only raise their financing costs. A more reasonable response would have been to attempt to slow down the withdrawal of foreign lending and to ease the conditions of payment. From this perspective, expansionary monetary and fiscal policies should have been adopted in order to reinforce the financial system and hinder debt deflation.

In the context of the Asian crisis of 1997–98, the experience of Malaysia is especially worth commenting upon. Against the prevailing Washington Consensus, Malaysia did close its frontiers to capital movements. Giving the domestic authorities the necessary room for manoeuvre to employ monetary and fiscal policies to tackle the crisis of the country at that time, that policy initiative was a resounding success. More generally, Stiglitz (2007b) shows that those countries affected by the Asian financial crisis that followed different policies from the ones recommended by the IMF and of the Washington Consensus policy prescriptions have subsequently done very well.

Arestis (2001) compares the Southeast Asia crises of 1997–98 with the successive crises of the period 1977–96 – a period over which financial instability was mainly due to financial liberalization attempts by a significant number of countries around the world. All these crises have some features in common. Specifically, they were preceded by a process of financial deregulation that prompted a climate of euphoria and speculation. However, those of 1997–98 were currency speculative-induced crises while those of 1977–96 were balance of payments speculative-induced crises. The crisis of 1997–98 was triggered by the devaluation caused by the reversal of capital flow due to the rise of the ratio between foreign indebtedness and foreign reserves. The origin of the crises of the period 1977–96 was, instead, the balance of payments deficit due to an unsustainable speculative consumption boom. In any case, both kinds of crises are perfectly understandable from a Minskyan perspective.

The previous survey of the literature inspired by Hyman Minsky, as well as the careful reading of Hyman Minsky's writings, allow the following generalizations about an open economy. In the past decades, the financial transactions influenced by differential interest rates and by the prospects of exchange rate movements have grown relative to the exchange transactions related to international trade. This phenomenon is probably not unconnected with the volatility of exchange rates (real as well as nominal) observed in post Bretton Woods era. This volatility obviously introduces an additional source of uncertainty. From a Minskyan perspective, the opening of the economy thus fuels economic instability in the following ways:

1. For many countries, international trade accounts for a quarter or more of GDP. Under these circumstances, exchange rate volatility implies a high volatility of net exports and domestic incomes.
2. Given the Kalecki–Kaldor–Levy equation (Minsky 1986, 1992), the volatility of domestic incomes also implies the volatility of domestic profits. The fulfilment of debt commitments thus becomes more uncertain.
3. In the presence of borrowing in foreign exchange, the exchange rate volatility turns into the volatility of debt commitments denominated in foreign currency. The financial system becomes vulnerable to exchange rate in addition to the interest rate fluctuations. In a Minskyan perspective, it thus becomes more fragile.

4. Debt commitments on loans incurred in a particular currency have to be repaid in that currency. Thus, not only there have to be sufficient profit flows to fulfil debt commitments; those profit flows have also to be, or to be able to be, converted into the relevant currency. There are numerous examples of countries indebted in foreign currency (e.g. many Eastern European countries in the second half of the 1980s and some Asian economies in the late 1990s) where a trade surplus did not emerge and access to capital inflows faltered, threatening the ability to repay foreign loans.
5. Given the high and increasing international financial integration, and as shown by the recent financial turmoil, financial crises tend to spread from one country to the others, thus increasing the overall instability.
6. Orthodox market-based prescriptions (in terms of financial liberalization and of economic policy in open economies) can accentuate, rather than solve, the problems.

To conclude on this point, Hyman Minsky's approach suggests that the opening up of the economy may accentuate its coordination problems and increase its fragility. Under these circumstances, the stabilizing role of the government becomes even more important. The same holds for the necessity to regulate the balance sheets of firms and financial intermediaries, including foreign indebtedness.

Fiscal policy and the evolution and prospects of capitalism

Minsky and Whalen (1996) argue that 'Capitalism is a dynamic, evolving system that comes in many forms. Nowhere is this dynamism more evident than in its financial structure' (p. 3). With regard to the evolution of the financial structure of the American economy, Minsky and Whalen (1996; see also Minsky, 1993) identify the following phases:

1. *Commercial capitalism.* This was the initial phase of capitalism, during which external finance was used mainly for trade and manufacturing.
2. *Industrial capitalism.* This was the phase of the first decades of the previous century, during which external finance was used mainly to finance long-term capital development. The nineteenth century was the first great era of capitalism, which required expensive and durable capital assets. The funds were made available through commercial banks, investment banks and the flotation of stocks and bonds. The great crash of 1929–33 brought this second stage to an end.

3. *Paternalistic capitalism.* The New Deal restructuring ushered in the paternalistic era, based on: countercyclical fiscal policy sustaining profits when the economy faltered; on the low interest rates due to a Federal Reserve unconstrained by gold-standard considerations; on deposit insurance for banks and thrifts; on the establishment of a temporary national investment bank (the Reconstruction Finance Corporation) in support of transportation, industry and finance; and on interventions by organizations created to address sectoral concerns (such as those in housing and agriculture). As we have seen, in this period the government took over the responsibility for the adequacy of profits. As a consequence, internal cash flows of firms could finance their investments; firms rather than bankers were the masters of the private economy. The stabilization of profits spread optimism and thus boosted speculative behaviours.

4. *Money-manager capitalism.* This is the current stage of capitalism, resulting from the evolution of speculative financial practices and from the emergence of plans that have supplemented social security with private pensions. As the label money-manager capitalism suggests, in such a system money managers dominate financial markets.[25] Their aim is the maximization of the value of the investments made by the fund holders, i.e. the maximization of the total return on assets (the combination of dividends and interest received and the appreciation in per share value). Today's money-managers are but little concerned with the development of the capital assets of an economy. They do not conform to Schumpeter's (1912) vision of bankers as the ephors of capitalism, who assure that finance serves progress. Today's financial structure is more akin to Keynes' (1936) characterization of the financial arrangements of advanced capitalism as a casino.

When one considers the pressure due to the rapidly evolving financial system and to the economy's other structural changes, it is not surprising that current economic insecurity is so widespread. Looking ahead, Minsky and Whalen (1996) envisage two different futures for American capitalism. *Fortress capitalism,* a system with declining fortunes for all but a few who must seek protection behind walled and gated communities; this is the result of a return to laissez-faire. The alternative is a *shared-prosperity capitalism,* characterized by public intervention in the economy.

In the current era, economic success does not only require economic growth, low unemployment and minimal inflation. It also requires that economic insecurity be reduced and that prosperity be available to the whole of society. The task of big government is to reduce inequality and insecurity. It has to act in such a way as to provide full employment, and to promote a high performance path to competitiveness (as an alternative to the low-wage path). This requires not only incentives for private investment, but also public investment in education and training, science and technology, and infrastructure.

Summary and conclusions

In Hyman Minsky's view, the dominant theory has been able to adopt an equilibrium framework since it has amputated crucial aspects of the reality as uncertainty, its connections with finance, the financial instability of capitalism and the crucial role of institutions. The originality and the importance of Hyman Minsky's contributions lies precisely in recovering these issues and placing them at the centre of his financial instability hypothesis. According to such a hypothesis, modern economies endogenously assume a cyclical behaviour that culminates in financial crises followed by debt deflations and deep depressions.

Contrary to the dominant theory, Minsky (1975, 1986) believes that fiscal policies are the most powerful economic control weapons. In his view, government intervention is not only necessary to reach and maintain full employment; it is also indispensable to contain capitalism's instability thus avoiding disaster. The effect of fiscal policy is not only to underpin and stabilize aggregate demand, income and employment. It has also the task of protecting the robustness of the financial system by stabilizing profits and by issuing government bonds. Finally, big government has the function of reducing inequality and insecurity and of promoting a high performance path to competitiveness (as an alternative to the low-wage path). Although Hyman Minsky's analysis mainly refers to a closed economy, it can be readily extended to an open economy. The opening of the economy increases its fragility in many ways. As a consequence, the stabilizing role of the government becomes even more important.

This last conclusion is particularly pertinent both in view of the resounding turmoil that, starting from the USA, has recently hit the international financial markets and in view of the fiscal expansion adopted by Bush against it. Minsky's (1986) vision that 'the *normal* functioning of our economy leads to financial trauma and crises' and that 'financially complex capitalism is inherently flawed' (p. 287; italics in original) applies to this recent crisis very well indeed. Minsky's (1986) prescription according to which a big government is necessary to stabilize our unstable economy is also confirmed by recent events. It provides at the same time a great deal of support to an active fiscal policy so much missed in recent economic policy debates.

Can the recent financial turmoil be defined as a 'Minsky moment'?[26] In our opinion, the answer is ambiguous.[27] In Minsky's financial instability hypothesis, it is the expansion of the real sector that leads to optimism and financial fragility. As we have seen earlier, it is basically the deviation-amplifying link of greater investments-greater profits-greater investments to sustain the high and increasing profit expectations, which leads to over-indebtedness. In the beginning of the 2000s, American growth experienced a standstill. To reactivate it was the debt financed boom of household expenditure on houses and consumption goods, in addition to the increased government deficit. The increasing indebtedness of American households, however, was not supported by the optimistic expectations concerning the real economy. Rather than being based on high and increasing available income expectations, this increasing indebtedness relied on the low interest rates and on the expected capital gains on houses. Given its financial/speculative (rather than real) origin, the recent financial turmoil seems thus to be more faithful to the spirit than to the letter of Hyman Minsky's financial instability hypothesis.[28] It could be referred to as the money-manager capitalism that Hyman Minsky did not have the time to develop.

Acknowledgement

We are extremely grateful to the editors of this book, Jérôme Creel and Malcolm Sawyer, for very helpful comments. The usual disclaimer applies of course.

Notes

1. See Velupillai (2005a, 2005b) for a technical and illuminating critique of general equilibrium.
2. The definition of Monetarism Mark 1 and 2 is based on the fact that, in both cases, what determines economic fluctuations are the shocks concerning money supply. The main references are Friedman 1968 for Monetarism Mark 1 and for Monetarism Mark 2 Lucas and Rapping 1969 and Lucas 1972, 1973.
3. Contrary to Monetarism Mark 1 and 2, these time shocks are real and concern productivity. See Kydland and Prescott 1982.
4. The survey of the evolution of orthodox macroeconomic theory is inspired by Leijonhufvud's Swedish flag. See Leijonhufvud (2000, pp. 33–51).

5. To quote Tobin (1989): 'He is right to stress that monetary and financial institutions and market make a big difference and to reject the Modigliani-Miller
   theorem that assets and debts which wash out in accounting aggregations
   wash out in economic effects as well' (p. 107).
6. As a consequence, the robustness of the financial system cannot be taken for
   granted.
7. In Minsky's (1975) view, since Keynes lived through the experience of the
   Great Depression he dwelled upon the particular case of an economy, which,
   as a consequence of a financial crisis, followed by a debt deflation, fell into a
   deep depression. Despite not developing it, however, in Minsky's view Keynes
   had in mind a cyclical perspective.
8. This might be the reason why Minsky (1975, 1986) prefers to speak of a
   financial instability 'hypothesis' rather than of a financial instability 'theory'.
   This aspect is developed in De Antoni (2007).
9. According to Minsky (1986, pp. 206–7 in particular) a robust financial system is dominated by hedge units, which by definition are able to fulfil their
   debt commitments by profits. A fragile financial system is instead dominated
   by speculative and ultra-speculative (or Ponzi) units. Having to fulfil their
   debt commitments by indebtedness, speculative and Ponzi units are more
   vulnerable to the conditions prevailing in financial markets.
10. Minsky (1978) puts it as follows: 'However, the internal workings of the bank-
    ing mechanism or Central Bank action to constrain inflation will result in the
    supply of finance being less than infinitely elastic leading to a rapid increase
    in short-term interest rates' (p. 45).
11. According to De Antoni (2007), however, the recovery is not as granted as
    Minsky argues.
12. The task Minsky (1992) assigns to economic policy institutions is anything
    but easy. They must be continuously revised and kept up to date, since
    the flaws of capitalism are always evolving. It follows that Minsky strongly
    disagrees with the adoption of fixed rules in economic policy.
13. From a Kaleckian perspective, aggregate investment determines aggregate
    profits but not the mark-up. On this issue, Minsky seems more akin to Eichner
    (1991).
14. Bad investments may generate profits lower than debt commitments and
    thus foster a wave of bankruptcies that depress expectations, confidence and
    economic activity.
15. Whenever full-employment investment exceeds full-employment saving,
    a government surplus is obviously necessary to ensure the simultaneous
    equilibrium of the goods and labour markets.
16. Recent years have seen a flourishing of the debate on the employment of
    last resort strategy. See for instance Aspromourgos (2000), Forstater (1998),
    Gordon (1997), Mitchell (1998, 2000), Mitchell and Watts (1997), Mosler
    (1997), Sawyer (2003), Wray (1998a, 1998b, 2001).
17. While being a great supporter of the government, Minsky (1975, 1982a,
    1986) is perfectly aware of its limits. Like investments, government deficit is
    a determinant of mark up and therefore sustains the price level. Government
    intervention is often inefficient. By stabilizing the economy, government
    may legitimize speculative behaviours. To avoid the aforementioned draw-
    backs, Minsky (1986) suggests intervening in two directions. First, it is

necessary to qualify government intervention in order to increase investments in the physical and intellectual infrastructures, thus stimulating the productivity and efficiency of the system. Second, he suggests reducing financial fragility by carefully regulating the balance sheets of firms and financial intermediaries as well as the financial transactions.

18. Aggregate saving S is the sum of workers' saving (Sw) and capitalists' saving (Sc), equal in its turn to the difference between capitalists' profits (Π) and capitalists' consumption (Cc). This means that $S = Sw + (\Pi - Cc)$. By substituting into the goods market equilibrium condition, $I + DF + NX = S$, and rearranging we get: $\Pi = I + DF + NX + Cc - Sw$. Aggregate profits Π are therefore determined by investments I, government deficit DF, net exports NX plus capitalists' consumption Cc net of workers' saving Sw. The relationship connecting profits to investments obviously holds only at an aggregate level. At a microeconomic level, profit generated by investment does not usually go the investing firm.

19. This puts forward an additional argument in favour of automatic fiscal stabilizers. Through the government budget anti-cyclical behaviour, they imply an increase (decrease) in government bond issues during recessions (expansions). By so doing, they also hinder the endogenous decrease (increase) in bank credit and thus in money supply due to the fall (rise) in the business demand for loans. In both ways, automatic fiscal stabilizers also stabilize the financial system.

20. To quote Minsky (1996), 'The explosion of the government debt relative to gross domestic product over the 12 years of Reagan-Bush was largely due to an irresponsible fiscal policy... In the present circumstances, the role of tax policy is to assure that a downward trend in the ratio of Federal Debt to Gross Domestic Product rules, so that over a span of years the ratio of debt to income is lowered from the present 65% to about 50%' (p. 4).

21. According to Lerner (1943), fiscal variables have to be evaluated on the basis of their effects on the economy rather than on the basis of a priori criteria of sound finance. In this perspective, government expenditure and revenues have to be considered as aggregate demand control weapons whose task is to align the latter to its full employment level. Government bond sales have in their turn to guarantee the desired level of the interest rate (and thus of investments). The remaining part of the government deficit (including the interest payments on government debt) can simply be financed by money. Below full employment, there is no inevitable link between the latter and the price level. In Lerner's view, government deficit and debt thus present 'no danger to society' (p. 42).

22. According to the state money or chartalist approach, fiscal authorities first define what money is by stating that which is necessary to pay taxes and second create (destroy) money through the government deficit (surplus). The US federal government funds itself by writing cheques on its central bank account, which once deposited turn into new bank reserves (Wray, 1998b; Bell and Wray 2002–03). Contrary to the dominant view, federal deficit thus tends to reduce the interest rate and to stimulate investment. Bond sales by either the central bank or the treasury are properly seen as part of a 'horizontally' oriented monetary policy designed to avoid the fall of the interest rate below its target value. Bonds are not sold to borrow but to drain excess

reserves. If markets do not want government bonds, then bonds have simply not to be sold.

23. The Maastricht Treaty dictated the ceilings of 3 and 60 per cent for the ratios, respectively, of government deficit and government debt to GDP.

24. Stiglitz (2007a, 2007b) also criticizes the cures proposed by the IMF at the time of the Asian financial crisis. He points out that the two countries (India and China) which resisted capital market liberalization, unsurprisingly, were not affected by the Asian financial crisis.

25. Money-manager capitalism introduces a new layer of intermediation into the financial structure. The largest proportion of the liabilities of corporations is held either by financial institutions, such as bank trust companies or by pensions or mutual funds. Individual wealth holdings increasingly take the form of ownership of the liabilities of the managed funds.

26. This definition is adopted, for instance, by Whalen (2007).

27. We are grateful to Jérôme Creel for suggesting that we touch upon this theme. To analyse properly the Minskyan features of the recent financial crisis, however, a deeper analysis is necessary. The issue would require a study entirely devoted to it.

28. For a different interpretation of the reasons why the recent financial turmoil may not be of a Minskyan type, see Davidson (2008) and Kregel (2008).

References

Arestis, P. (2001) 'Recent banking and financial crises: Minsky versus the financial liberalizations', in R. Bellofiore and P. Ferri (eds), *Financial Keynesianism and Market Instability; the Economic Legacy of Hyman Minsky – Vol. 1*, Cheltenham, UK/Northampton, USA: Edward Elgar, pp. 159–79.

Arestis, P. and Glickman, M. (2002) 'Financial crisis in South East Asia: Dispelling illusion the Minskyan way', *Cambridge Journal of Economics*, 26(2), 237–60.

Arestis, P. and Sawyer, M. (2003) 'Reinventing fiscal policy', *Journal of Post Keynesian Economics*, 26(1), 3–25.

Arestis, P. and Sawyer, M. (2004) *Re-examining Monetary and Fiscal Policy for the 21st Century*, Cheltenham, UK/Northampton, USA: Edward Elgar.

Arestis, P. and Zezza, G. (eds) (2007) *Advances in Monetary Policy and Macroeconomics*, New York: Palgrave Macmillan.

Aspromourgos, T. (2000) 'Is an employer of last resource policy sustainable? A review article', *Review of Political Economy*, 12(2), 141–55.

Bell, S. and Wray, L.R. (2002–03) 'Fiscal impacts on reserves and the independence of the Fed', *Journal of Post Keynesian Economics*, 25(2), 263–71.

Davidson, P. (2008) 'Is the current financial distress caused by the subprime mortgage crisis a Minsky moment? Or is it the result of attempting to securitize illiquid non commercial mortgage loans?', *mimeo*, Bernard L. Schwartz Center for Economic Policy Analysis, New School University, New York.

De Antoni, E. (2007) 'Minsky's vision and its relationship with *The General Theory*', in Arestis, P. and Zezza, G. (eds) *Advances in Monetary Policy and Macroeconomics*, New York: Palgrave Macmillan, pp. 174–91.

Eichner, A.S. (1991) *The Macrodynamics of Advanced Market Economies*, Armonk, NY: M.E. Sharpe Inc.

Forstater, M. (1998) 'Flexible full employment: Structural implications of discretionary public sector employment', *Journal of Economic Issues*, 32(2), 557–63.

Friedman, M. (1968) 'The role of monetary policy', *American Economic Review*, 58(1), 1–17.

Gordon, W. (1997) 'Job assurance – the job guarantee revisited', *Journal of Economic Issues*, 31(3), 826–33.

Hicks, J.R. (1937) 'Mr Keynes and the classics: A suggested interpretation', *Econometrica*, 2(5), 1–9.

Keynes, J.M. (1936) *The General Theory of Employment, Interest and Money*, London: Macmillan.

Kregel, J. (2001) 'Yes, "it" did happen again – the Minsky crisis in Asia', in R. Bellofiore and P. Ferri (eds) *Financial Keynesianism and Market Instability; the Economic Legacy of Hyman Minsky – Vol. 1*, Cheltenham, UK/Northampton, USA: Edward Elgar, pp. 194–213.

Kregel, J. (2008) 'Minsky's cushions of safety: Systemic risks and the crisis in the U.S. subprime mortgage market', *Public Policy Brief No. 93*, Levy Economics Institute of Bard College.

Kydland, F.E. and Prescott, E.C. (1982) 'Time to build and aggregate fluctuations', *Econometrica*, November.

Leijonhufvud, A. (2000) *Macroeconomic Instability and Coordination*, Cheltenham, UK/Northampton, USA: Edward Elgar.

Lerner, A.B. (1943) 'Functional finance and the federal debt', *Social Research*, 10(1), 38–51.

Lucas, R.E. Jr. (1972) 'Expectations and the neutrality of money', *Journal of Economic Theory*, 4(2), 103–24.

Lucas, R.E. Jr. (1973) 'Some international evidence on output–inflation tradeoffs', *American Economic Review*, 63(3), 326–34.

Lucas, R.E. Jr. and Rapping, L.A. (1969) 'Real wages, employment and inflation', *Journal of Political Economy*, 77(5), 721–54.

Minsky, H.P. (1963) 'Can "it" happen again?', in D. Carson (ed.), *Banking and Monetary Studies*, Homewood, IL: R.D. Irwin, pp. 101–11.

Minsky, H.P. (1975) *John Maynard Keynes*, New York: Columbia University Press.

Minsky, H.P. (1978) 'The financial instability hypothesis: A restatement', *Thames Papers in Political Economy*, *North East London Polytechnic*. Reprinted in Arestis, P. and Skouras, T. (eds) (1985) *Post Keynesian Economic Theory*, Armonk, NY: M.E. Sharpe.

Minsky, H.P. (1979) 'Financial interrelations, the balance of payments and the dollar crisis', in J.D. Aronson, (ed.), *Debt and the Less Developed Countries*, Westview Press, Boulder Co, 103–22.

Minsky, H.P. (1980) 'Capitalist financial processes and the instability of capitalism', *Journal of Economic Issues*, XIV(2), 505–22.

Minsky, H.P. (1982a) *Can 'It' Happen Again? Essays on Instability and Finance*, Armonk, NY: M.E. Sharpe.

Minsky, H.P. (1982b) 'Debt deflation processes in today's institutional environment', *Banca Nazionale del Lavoro, Quarterly Review*, December, 265–77.

Minsky, H.P. (1986) *Stabilizing an Unstable Economy*, New Haven: Yale University Press.

Minsky, H.P. (1991) 'Financial crises: Systemic or idiosyncratic?', *Working Papers Series No. 51*, Levy Economics Institute of Bard College.

Minsky, H.P. (1992) 'Profits, deficits and instability: A policy discussion', in D.B Papadimitriou (ed.), *Profits, Deficits and Instability*, London: Macmillan.

Minsky, H.P. (1993) 'Shumpeter and finance', in S. Biasco, A. Roncaglia, and M. Salvati (eds). *Market and Institutions in Economic Development: Essays in Honor of Paolo Sylos Labini*, New York: St Martin's Press/London: Macmillan Press, 103–15.

Minsky, H.P. (1996) 'Uncertainty and the institutional structure of capitalist economics', *Working Papers Series N. 155, Levy Economics Institute of Bard College.*

Minsky, H.P. and Whalen, C.J. (1996) 'Economic insecurity and the institutional prerequisites for successful capitalism', *Working Papers Series No. 165*, Levy Economics Institute of Bard College.

Mitchell, W.F. (1998) 'The buffer stock employment model and the path to full employment', *Journal of Economic Issues*, 32(2), 547–55.

Mitchell, W.F. (2000) 'The job guarantee in a small open economy', in E. Carlson, and W.F. Mitchell (eds), *The Path to Full Employment, Economic and Labour Relations Review*, pp. 89–116.

Mitchell, W.F. and Watts, M. (1997) 'The path to full employment', *Australian Economic Review*, 31(4), 436–44.

Mosler, W. (1997) 'Full employment and price stability', *Journal of Post Keynesian Economics*, 20(2), 167–82.

Patinkin, D. (1956) *Money, Interest and Prices*, Evanston, IL: Row-Peterson & Co.

Robinson, J. (1971) *Economic Heresies*, London: Macmillan.

Sawyer, M. (2001) 'Minsky's analysis, the European single currency and the global financial system', in R. Bellofiore and P. Ferri (eds), *Financial Keynesianism and Market Instability*, Aldershot: Edward Elgar, pp. 179–93.

Sawyer, M. (2003) 'Employer of last resort: Could it deliver full employment and price stability?', *Journal of Economic Issues*, 37(4), 881–907.

Schumpeter, J. (1912) *The Theory of Economic Development*, Cambridge, MA: Harvard University Press.

Stiglitz, J.E. (2007a) 'The Asian crisis ten years after', *Project Syndicate*, available from: http://www.project–syndicate.org/commentary/stiglitz89

Stiglitz, J.E. (2007b) 'Financial hypocrisy', *Project Syndicate*, available from: http://www.project–syndicate.org/commentary/stiglitz93

Tobin, J. (1989) 'Book review of *Stabilizing an Unstable Economy* by Hyman P. Minsky', *Journal of Economic Literature*, 27(March), 105–108.

Velupillai, K. (2005a) 'The unreasonable ineffectiveness of mathematics in economics', *Cambridge Journal of Economics*, 29(6), 849–72.

Velupillai, K. (2005b) 'The foundations of computable general equilibrium theory', *Discussion Paper No. 13*, Department of Economics, University of Trento.

Vercelli, A. (2001) 'Minsky, Keynes and the structural instability of a sophisticated monetary economy', in R. Bellofiore and P. Ferri (eds), *Financial Fragility and Investment in the Capitalist Economy; the Economic Legacy of Hyman Minsky – Vol. 2*, Cheltenham, UK/Northampton, USA: Edward Elgar, pp. 33–53.

Whalen, C.J. (2007) 'The US credit crunch of 2007: A Minsky moment', *Public Policy Brief No. 92*, Levy Economics Institute of Bard College.

Wray, L.R. (1998a) 'Zero unemployment and stable prices', *Journal of Economic Issues*, 32(2), 539–45.

Wray, L.R. (1998b) *Understanding Modern Money: The Key to Full Employment and Price Stability*, Cheltenham: Edward Elgar.

Wray, L.R. (2001) 'Government as employer of last resort: Full employment without inflation', *Working Papers Series No. 213*, Levy Economics Institute of Bard College.

Wray, L.R. (2006) 'Extending Minsky's classification of fragility to government and the open economy', *Working Papers Series No. 450*, Levy Economics Institute of Bard College.

5
The Continuing Relevance of Fiscal Policy

Malcolm Sawyer

Introduction

The purpose of this chapter is to review some of the arguments on fiscal policy and budget deficits. It is useful to begin by drawing a distinction between two approaches to fiscal policy (though in practice there is some blurring between the two). First, what may be termed the Keynesian approach for which we use the label 'functional finance'. In that analysis, there is the underlying assumption that a market economy tends to operate with low private aggregate demand which is not adequate to support a high level of economic activity, and the purpose of fiscal policy should be to rectify that inadequacy of demand. Hence, a budget deficit would then only appear when private demand would otherwise be too low to achieve the desired level of economic activity. The second approach tends to ask the question what will happen if the budget deficit is increased without specifying the purpose of the deficit increase. The question is often answered by use of a theoretical or empirical model where there is some presumption that aggregate demand is not, at least on a long term basis, below supply.

In the next section we outline the 'functional finance' approach. We then turn to a critical appraisal of a variety of arguments that have been raised against the use of fiscal policy. These begin with the arguments from 'Ricardian equivalence', and then the notion of a 'supply-side equilibrium' which acts as a strong attractor for the level of economic activity. The two final sections before some brief conclusions relate to some empirical considerations and the debate over fine and coarse tuning. One other set of arguments are raised against the use of budget deficits, namely that, since a deficit adds to public debt and future interest payments, deficits are unsustainable. These arguments are directly addressed in Arestis and Sawyer (Chapter 6 of this book).

Functional finance

The general proposition of the 'functional finance' approach is that the budget position should be used to secure a high level of economic activity in conditions where there would otherwise be a lower level of economic activity. The term 'high level of economic activity' is used rather than 'full employment' or 'supply side equilibrium' level of employment (or output): in this chapter we wish to avoid discussion over the meaning of full employment and the interactions between level of (un)employment and inflation. Further, full employment of labour may be constrained through lack of sufficient productive capacity, and not just lack of demand.

Lerner (1943) put the case for 'functional finance', which 'rejects completely the traditional doctrines of "sound finance" and the principle of trying to balance the budget over a solar year or any other arbitrary period' (p. 355). 'Functional finance' supports the important proposition that total spending should be adjusted to eliminate both unemployment and inflation. In a similar vein, Kalecki (1944a) argued that sustained full employment 'must be based either on a long-run budget deficit policy or on the redistribution of income' (p. 135). Kalecki based his argument on the assumption that there would be a tendency for the level of aggregate demand to fall short of what was required for full employment. Then there was a need for either a budget deficit to mop up the difference between full employment savings and investment or for full employment savings to be reduced through a redistribution of income (from rich to poor).

Musgrave (1985, p. 46) described the evolution of these ideas in the following way:

> The impact of Keynesian economics on fiscal theory profoundly changed its focus. Whereas the problem had been to observe resulting shifts in resource use, concern now was with effects on its overall level. With employment seen to depend on aggregate demand and with budget policy a direct contributor thereto, budget policy became a critical determinant of the level of employment. This new function of budget policy was the more important because departure from full employment was seen no longer as a temporary aberration, but a central tendency of the economy. A continuing tendency towards

oversaving [Keynes, 1936, p. 31)] and stagnation [Hansen, 1938, 1941] was expected to prevail with expansionary fiscal policy called for on a sustained basis in order to maintain high employment in a mature economy.

The case for an unbalanced budget position rests on the proposition that the equality between *ex ante* private savings and *ex ante* private investment at a high level of economic activity cannot be assured, or indeed at any target level of income (or level of income corresponding to full employment or any supply-side equilibrium).[1] If there were some automatic tendency for that equality to be assured then any case for fiscal policy in the form of unbalanced budgets would disappear. But conversely in the absence of any such automatic tendency there is a strong case for an unbalanced budget. Further, if the relevant rate of interest can be manipulated through monetary policy in such a way as to ensure this equality, then again there would be little room for fiscal policy. The basic argument is that there is no assurance that this equality will be satisfied, and hence a need for fiscal policy and for an unbalanced budget. From a 'functional finance' perspective budget deficits are to be applied when there would otherwise be a deficiency of aggregate demand (below that required for the target level of economic activity), and budget surpluses applied when there would otherwise be an excess of aggregate demand. This is not to suggest that fiscal policy is always (or evenly usually) applied in this manner. But it is to argue that the case for fiscal policy and its effects should be evaluated against this background. The evaluation of fiscal policy should not start from the presumption that there would otherwise be adequate effective demand in that all would agree that in the context of adequate private effective demand there is no requirement for budget deficits.

The budget deficit is to be used to mop up 'excess' private savings (over investment), and the counterpart budget surplus used when investment expenditure exceeds savings (at the desired level of economic activity). This can be expressed as the government should set tax and expenditure such that the resulting budget deficit is given by:

$$G - T = S(Y_f) - I(Y_f) + M(Y_f) - X(WY) \tag{5.1}$$

where G is government expenditure, I investment, X exports, T tax revenue, S savings and M imports, Y_f is the target level of income, WY is world income (taken as given here).

The general presumption of Keynesians and others has been that there is likely to be a deficiency of *ex ante* investment relative to *ex ante* savings, rather than the reverse. This does not rule out that there will be occasions (as in the late 1990s in the UK and the USA with conditions of low unemployment) when investment runs ahead of savings. In the former case, a budget deficit is required to mop up the excess savings, while in the latter case a budget surplus results.

The general argument of this chapter is that the case against fiscal policy (and specifically budget deficits) has been based on the view that the equality of savings and investment at some high level of economic activity is assured, at least in the longer term, and/or that there is some way by which the level of economic activity adjusts to the high level of economic activity whether through market forces or through other policy measures (notably the use of monetary policy). In the next sections, we review the best known cases that have been advanced against the use of fiscal policy and budget deficits. We seek to show that they incorporate at some point the assumption on the equality of savings and investment just mentioned.

Ricardian equivalence[2]

The Ricardian equivalence proposition is that the method of financing any particular time path of government expenditure is irrelevant such that the future prospects of taxation to pay for a bond-financed budget deficit reduces consumer expenditure (and increases savings) which may exactly offset the boost to aggregate demand arising from the budget deficit. The overall level of savings (public savings plus private savings) and the share of savings (in a growing economy) remain unchanged.

The Ricardian equivalence proposition has been derived in the context of full employment (or at least a level of income set on the supply side of the economy) and the implicit assumption that private sector aggregate demand will underpin that level of income. Thus, the Ricardian equivalence proposition is essentially irrelevant in the context of the application of the functional finance approach in the sense that if aggregate demand were always sufficient to generate full employment, fiscal policy would not be required. The Ricardian equivalence proposition relates to the question of what happens if a budget deficit were introduced into a situation where *ex ante* investment and savings were equal at full employment (or equivalent). Functional finance is concerned with the policy recommendation of introducing a budget deficit into a situation where there is a difference between *ex ante* savings and *ex ante* investment (usually an excess of savings over investment) at full employment.

The 'Ricardian equivalence' proposition clearly indicates that the level of aggregate demand is invariant to the budget deficit position. But it does not indicate what that level of private demand will be, though there is perhaps the presumption that some form of Say's Law will operate, and that aggregate demand will be sufficient to underpin full employment. However, there is no particular reason for this level of aggregate demand to correspond to any supply-side equilibrium. Specifically, in the event of a shift in the supply-side equilibrium, there is no assurance that there will be a corresponding shift in the level of private demand.

Now consider the approach of Barro (1974, 1989) that revived interest in the Ricardian equivalence proposition and we follow with some amendments the notation used in Barro (1974).

In an overlapping-generation framework, where a generation live during two periods, i.e. 'youth' and 'retirement', generation 1 inherits a bequest of A_0^0 from generation 0, and acquires assets (saves) of A_1^y while they are young; during their old age they consume c_1^0 and leave bequest of A_1^0. Their budget constraint in this retirement period is:

$$A_0^0 + A_1^y = c_1^0 + (1-r)A_1^0 \tag{5.2}$$

where r is the rate of interest. The assets bequested are assumed to be acquired at the beginning of the retirement period and yield interest during the period. There is no 'wealth effect' (in the sense of Musgrave, 1959, 1985) emanating from the bequests, since bequests only produce capital/interest income in addition to labour income.

Generation 2 receive labour income of w, and saves A_2^y (on which they receive interest), and consume c_2^y and their budget constraint is:

$$c_2^y + (1-r)A_2^y = w \tag{5.3}$$

In this economy, there is net savings to provide for an increase in the capital stock which yields interest at rate r, hence it is required that:

$$A_1^0 + A_2^y - A_0^0 - A_1^y = DK \tag{5.4}$$

where DK is the change in the capital stock set by the desire to invest.

This is equivalent to:

$$c_1^0 + c_2^y + DK = w + r(A_1^0 + A_2^y) = y \tag{5.5}$$

where y stands for income.

These equations refer to *ex post* outcomes, but there is nothing, which ensures that this equality will hold when the variables are in notional (*ex ante*) form. Consider the case in *ex ante* terms, and placing an * after a variable to signify that it is in *ex ante* rather than *ex post* term, where

$$c^{*0}_1 + c^{*y}_2 + DK^* < w^* + r^*(A^{*0}_1 + A^{*y}_2) \tag{5.6}$$

i.e. intended expenditure falls short of income, and equivalently:

$$A^{*0}_0 + A^{*y}_1 + DK^* < A^{*y}_2 + A^{*0}_1 \tag{5.7}$$

This would be a deflationary situation with intended expenditure falling short of intended income. Consider the case where income adjusts to bring equality between income and intended expenditure. We assume that consumption is a function of income (labour and capital income) and that return on capital varies proportionally with labour income (though utilization effects). Write w^+ as the labour income which would result at full employment, and r^+ as the rate of return at full employment, and the income and rate of return which results from a lower level of income as $m.w^+$ and $m.r^+$, then:

$$c^{*0}_1(m) + c^{*y}_2(m) + DK^* = m.w^+ + m.r^+(A^{*0}_1 + A^{*y}_2) \tag{5.8}$$

to give a solution for m ($m < 1$).

By assumption in this context, the intention to save will have adjusted so that:

$$A^{*0}_0 + A^{*y}_1 + DK^* = A^{\wedge y}_2 + A^{\wedge 0}_1 \tag{5.9}$$

where a variable followed by $^\wedge$ refers to the ex post value of that variable. In equation (5.7) the left hand side is treated as a given, and the right hand side has adjusted to the indicated level.

Now introduce the use of functional finance such that the budget deficit is set to absorb excess private savings; this would mean that:

$$c^{*0}_1 + c^{*y}_2 + DK^* + B = w^+ + r^+(A^{*0}_1 + A^{*y}_2) \tag{5.10}$$

where B is the budget deficit and the other variables are at the level which corresponds to full employment. Income is higher by $(1 - m^*)$, net private savings are equal to $DK^* + B$, and hence:

$$A^{*0}_0 + A^{*y}_1 + DK^* + B = A^{*y}_2 + A^{*0}_1 \tag{5.11}$$

with

$$A^{*y}_2 + A^{*0}_1 - (A^{\wedge y}_2 + A^{\wedge 0}_1) = B \qquad (5.12)$$

In this model, generation 2 is able to save what they wish and do so in the form of assets and bonds. Their overall savings are higher than it would have been in the absence of a functional finance budget deficit.

What about next period's budget constraint for generation 2? In the absence of functional finance this is:

$$A^{\wedge y}_2 + A^{\wedge 0}_1 = c^0_2 + (1-r)A^0_2 \qquad (5.13)$$

while with functional finance it is:

$$A^{*y}_2 + A^0_1 = c^{*0}_2 + (1-r)A^{*0}_2 \qquad (5.14)$$

and the left-hand side of (5.14) is greater than the left-hand side of (5.13) through equation (5.12).

When fiscal policy is approached in 'functional finance' terms, which is a budget deficit run by the government because there is a difference between savings and investment at the desired income level, then the Ricardian equivalence approach is scarcely relevant. In the absence of a budget deficit, the excess of savings over investment cannot occur (and the discrepancy is dealt with through a fall in income, reducing savings until brought into line with income).

In Arestis and Sawyer (2006) we argued through a simple numerical example and simulation that when fiscal policy is used as an automatic stabilizer and when there are 'disturbances' on private sector savings and investment (thereby generating changes in the observed budget deficit position) that a partial Ricardian equivalence outcome may be observed. That is to say the estimation of a savings function would indicate a negative coefficient on the budget deficit which is significant though somewhat below unity.

A slightly different expression of essentially this argument comes from Eisner when he wrote:

> However, there is one overriding objection [to Ricardian equivalence] that cannot be overstressed. We simply do not live in a Walrasian, market-clearing world, and all our economic agents – as opposed apparently to some economists – know it. Aside then from all the issues of uncertainty as to who might pay any future taxes occasioned by a current deficit, real world economic agents have no reason to assume that there will be any additional tax burden at all. With the

existence of what, in the older vernacular, we used to call simply 'less-than-full-employment' – the so-called 'natural' (God-given?) rate of unemployment belongs perhaps with those who accept the doctrine of creationism – increases in current consumption need not involve any borrowing from the future or from any future resources. With the consumption then will come more, not less investment. The economy will move to a higher growth path. Extra taxes in the future, if these are to be any, may then readily be paid out of higher future incomes. (Eisner, 1989, pp. 73–4)

Supply-side equilibrium

The second form of 'crowding out' discussed arises from the notion that there is some form of supply-side equilibrium (such as the 'natural rate of unemployment' or the NAIRU), which is itself uninfluenced by the level of aggregate demand, and that this supply-side equilibrium is an 'attractor' for the level of economic activity. In effect, there are forces at work that guide the level of demand to this supply-side equilibrium. In the context of an exogenous money supply, this came through the assertion of a 'real balance' effect, with changes in the price level generating changes in the real value of the stock of money, thereby generating changes in the level of aggregate demand.

One of the major theoretical arguments as to how aggregate demand will adjust to ensure high level of economic activity has come from the operation of the real balance effect (the Pigou effect): low demand generates falling prices and a rising real value of the money stock and wealth, which stimulates aggregate demand. This continues until the level of aggregate demand is (eventually) brought into line with the supply-side equilibrium. In many macroeconomic models, the level of demand has been represented by the real value of the stock of money, and in that way the Pigou effect has been given a central role since the real value of the stock of money increases as prices decline.

But it is well known (at least since Kalecki, 1944b) that the real balance effect relies on 'external' money with net worth to the private sector and to the stock of money remaining unchanged in the face of price changes. In a world of largely bank credit money, the amount of 'external' money is relatively small. The empirical relevance of the real balance effect has long been doubted (though it continues to make an appearance in many macroeconomic models, notably those of a new Keynesian form). There are strong reasons to doubt the theoretical relevance of the Pigou effect as well. When money is treated as endogenous credit money then the stock of money is determined by the demand for money, and money does not constitute net worth. If prices were then to fall, then the demand for money would decline, and so would the stock of money, and hence the Pigou effect would not be operational. Further, since money in the form of bank deposits is an asset for its holders, it is a liability for the banks, and hence again there is no net worth for the Pigou effect to 'bite on'. Indeed we can go further and argue that when money is endogenous, a decline in prices would adversely affect those who have taken out loans (the real value of which has risen), which may well undermine rather than increase, aggregate demand. Hence the theoretical reasons for the stock of money influencing the level of aggregate demand disappear.

In the context of endogenous money, the adjustment of aggregate demand to ensure high level of economic activity would come through the adjustment of interest rate by the Central Bank. This could occur if the Central Bank adopted some form of 'Taylor's rule' under which the setting of the key interest rate depends on the 'equilibrium' rate of interest, deviation of inflation from target and deviation of output from trend level (Taylor, 1993). Monetary policy can guide aggregate demand to match supply provided that interest rates are effective in influencing the level of demand and provided that the Central Bank's calculation of the 'equilibrium rate' of interest is accurate.

Fiscal policy has an effect on the level of aggregate demand, and 'crowding out' only occurs if it assumed that the supply-side equilibrium must be attained (in order to ensure a constant rate of inflation) *and* that the level of aggregate demand would anyway be equivalent to the supply-side equilibrium. In the absence of some powerful automatic market forces or a potent monetary policy, which can ensure that the level of aggregate demand moves quickly to be consistent with the supply-side equilibrium, then fiscal policy has a clear role to play.

The supply-side equilibrium can itself be influenced by the path of aggregate demand. The size and distribution of the capital stock is a determinant of the productive capacity of the economy, and a larger capital stock would be associated with the supply-side equilibrium involving a higher level of output and employment. The level of aggregate demand (including the change in economic activity and profitability) has an impact on investment expenditure, and thereby on the size of the capital stock. The supply-side equilibrium may form an inflation barrier at any point in time, but it is not to be seen as something immutable and unaffected by the level of aggregate demand.

The existence of a supply-side equilibrium in an economic model does not ensure that there would be adjustment towards that equilibrium position. In the case of many supply-side equilibria, the position is more complex in that there is no presumed mechanism of adjustment on the supply-side, but rather the adjustment is perceived to come from the demand-side. There is often perceived to be a separation between the supply-side and the demand-side (at its most complete in the classical dichotomy) and the presumption that differences between the supply-side equilibrium and the demand-side equilibrium will be resolved through the demand-side changing. In the present context, the supply-side equilibrium would appear to limit any role for fiscal policy (acting on the demand side of the economy) in that economic activity cannot be raised above the supply-side equilibrium for any length of time. However, this notion of supply-side equilibrium and the dichotomy (separation) between the supply-side and demand-side of the economy (which sometimes corresponds to the separation between the real side and the monetary side of the economy as in the classical dichotomy) raises the question of the mechanism by which aggregate demand adjusts to the supply-side equilibrium. We argued there that the postulated mechanisms of the real balance effect and interest rate were ineffectual, and did not give convincing reasons for demand adjusting to supply.

Eisner (1989, p. 73) argued that:

> [b]udget deficits have not only been related positively to growth of GNP as a whole, but also to growth of its components of both consumption and investment. We may note ... that each percentage point of real high-employment deficit was associated with growth of consumption the next year amounting to 0.642 percentage points of consumption. It was also associated with growth in gross private domestic investment equal to 1.383 percentage points of GNP. The evidence is thus that deficits have not crowded out investment. There has rather been 'crowding in'.

If that is indeed the case, then fiscal policy has the potential to influence future supply and economic activity through its impact on the capital stock. When the size of the capital stock is viewed as a major element in any supply-side equilibrium (Sawyer, 2002), then fiscal policy can have long-lasting effects.

Empirical considerations

Fiscal policy is often viewed in terms of the determination of government expenditure and taxation as undertaken without specific regard to the state of private aggregate demand. The 'crowding out' argument after all assumes that there is something to be crowded out. That approach to fiscal policy suggests either that fiscal policy has no effect on the level of economic activity (since there is crowding out) or that there is a positive link between government expenditure (budget deficit) and the level of economic activity. The investigation of fiscal policy through the means of simulation of macroeconometric models is concerned (usually) with the question of what happens if government expenditure is increased, other things being equal. The results of such simulations, generally, suggest that an increase in government expenditure does have a positive effect on the level of economic activity (Arestis and Sawyer, 2003). Indeed in the context in which these simulations are undertaken, it is somewhat surprising that positive results are obtained since such macroeconometric models generally build in a variety of ways by which there would be crowding out – the most notable one being that imposition of some form of supply-side equilibrium, and an adjustment process by which the economy moves to that supply-side equilibrium.

The effects of fiscal policy depend on why it is introduced and in what economic environment. To state the obvious, fiscal stimulus introduced when the economy is at (or would be at) full employment will lead to 'crowding out' through a variety of routes, but a fiscal stimulus applied when the economy is operating with excess capacity and unemployment of labour will 'crowd in'.

Fine and coarse tuning

The general view that there can be fluctuations in the level of private aggregate demand which would lead to fluctuations in the level of economic activity (and particularly where those fluctuations involve substantial downturns in economic activity) but which can be offset by policy measures raises a set of issues such as knowledge of the future, lags in policy implementation and frequency of policy decisions and changes. In the context of fiscal policy, Keynesian fiscal policy became associated (rightly or wrongly) with 'fine tuning'. This raised many well-known problems which are still largely relevant. The lags involved, a recognition lag (including arising from collection and interpretation of the relevant and accurate statistics), decision lag, implementation lag, and lags in the policy change impacting on the economy are well-known. These lags, which cumulatively could amount to many quarters, could lead to some destabilizing of the economy: fiscal policy designed to address a slow-down may come through as the economy is picking up:

Third, the combination of fiscal policy lags (recognition lags, implementation lags, and lags in the effect of spending and taxes on aggregate demand) and the substantial uncertainty about the magnitude of the economic response to fiscal changes increase the risk that well intentioned fiscal policy will be destabilizing, a point emphasized many years ago by Milton Friedman (1953). With the average recession lasting just 11 months from peak to trough, it takes remarkably good luck to add fiscal stimulus at just the right time. (Feldstein, 2002, p. 153)

The other two were that 'the powerful multiplier effect assumed in the early textbook Keynesian models was dramatically reduced when economists recognized that the marginal propensity to save out of temporary tax cuts is likely to be relatively high' and that 'tax reductions or expenditure increases can actually depress economic activity' (Feldstein, 2002, p. 153). But with one (and rather important) exception, these issues also apply to monetary policy: the exception being the administrative ease of changing the policy instrument (interest rate) in the case of monetary policy as compared with fiscal policy, and the associated length of the decision-making and implementation process.

These type of considerations lead us (Arestis and Sawyer, 1998) to argue for 'coarse tuning' rather than 'fine tuning'. The 'natural' rhythm of fiscal policy is an annual round of tax and expenditure decisions. In one sense, 'coarse tuning' is generally applied: budgets rarely leave tax and expenditure decisions 'on hold'. It is more a question of what are the objectives currently pursued by fiscal policy as clearly the 'functional finance' approach postulates an objective of the optimum sustainable level of economic activity. It may also be a matter of whether governments would be willing to run the scale of deficits which may be required to reach the desired level of economic activity. For example, in the context of the UK in the early 1990s when budget deficit reached around 8 per cent of GDP in the face of a large upswing in savings and decline in investment, a budget deficit to sustain a high level of economic activity would have been well into double figures (as a per cent of GDP).

A coarse tuning approach would involve aiming to achieve a budget position to achieve a high target level of economic activity, which is given in equation (5.1). The budget deficit required to achieve Y_f can be clearly seen to depend on propensities to save, invest, import and the ability to export, and these over country and across time. The underlying budget position should then be set in accordance with the perceived underlying values of the propensities to save, invest, import and export (see Sawyer, 2007). This approach to fiscal policy can be said to incorporate a clear rule: set the underlying budget deficit compatible with the desired level of output. But it is clear that the estimation of the relevant budget stance would involve substantial difficulties and disputes (though whether the difficulties are any greater than the estimation of key variables in the current orthodoxy such as the 'equilibrium rate of interest' and the 'non-accelerating inflation rate of unemployment' is open to debate).

The ultimate in fine tuning would arise when the budget stance was continuously changed in response to variations in economic activity (arising from variation in the behaviour of S, I, X or M). This would be comparable to the fine tuning that is currently attempted through interest rate changes, with decisions on interest rates being made on a frequent (e.g., monthly) basis, even if the decision made is no change. The problems of fine tuning are well-known in terms of the various lags involved including those of recognition, decision making, implementation and effect. However, the automatic stabilizers of fiscal policy already perform part of that task in the sense that a downturn is met by reduced tax and increased expenditure which modify but do not eliminate the degree of fluctuations in economic activity. The tax and expenditure regime could be designed in a manner to increase the extent of stabilization and a more progressive tax system would enhance the stabilization properties but that should be argued for on grounds of equity and income distribution, albeit that there would be the additional benefits for stabilization.[3]

The question to be addressed is whether discretionary fiscal policy can and should also be used to help stabilize the economy. A Fiscal Policy Committee (FPC) analogous with a Monetary Policy Committee (MPC) has been suggested in a number of forms. If interest rates can be varied to seek to fine tune the economy, then cannot fiscal policy be used in a similar way? There can be seen to be a basic similarity between interest rate policy and fiscal policy in this respect. For example, it has been argued that 'the literature stemming from Barro and Gordon that is often cited by economists as justifying ICBs [Independent Central Banks], does not specify what instrument is used to control output and inflation, and so it applies equally to fiscal countercyclical policy' (Leith and Wren-Lewis, 2005, p. 595). In the approach here, an FPC would be concerned with the short-term level of demand, and an MPC would no longer be needed for that purpose, and as argued below the Central Bank would pursue an interest rate policy directed to other aims.

It is often objected that the politically sensitive nature of tax and expenditure decisions and the need for those to be taken by Parliament prevents this. Further, while lowering taxes and raising transfers may be an acceptable way of responding to a downturn, it is unlikely to be acceptable way of dealing with an upturn – 'your benefit has been cut this week as the economy is growing too fast' would not be well received!, though, of course, a similar argument is put in the case of interest rates – 'your mortgage payments will rise because the economy is growing too fast.' But there are taxes, such as value added tax, social security contributions which could be varied in this manner. The role of the FPC would be to judge on say a six-monthly basis whether a change in tax rates would be warranted. It would require institutional arrangements that would enable these decisions to be taken in a timely manner under operating procedures agreed through the democratic process. The key role of the FPC would be to use their discretion to adapt the fiscal stance in the face of significant short-run movements in the economy:

> The critical question for an active fiscal stabilization policy is the ability to adjust the intervention appropriately given the nature of shocks and the structure of the economy. It is much easier to establish a principle case for an active stabilization policy than to implement it in practice. There are thus good reasons to be very cautious in the use of fiscal stabilization policy in the sense of only resorting to such measures in 'exceptional' situations. In 'normal' cases stabilization should be left to the automatic stabilizers. However, automatic stabilizers are what they are more by chance than by design, that is, they are the net result of policy decisions in various areas, which rarely are made with a consideration of their effect for the overall strength of the automatic stabilizers. More research on these issues is needed for several reasons. First, to consider whether it is possible to amend the automatic stabilizers through other means, e.g. buffer funds. Second to take into account the trade off between insurance and incentive when considering policy reforms in other areas. Finally, to consider the scope for refining the automatic stabilizers so that they work more appropriately for various types of shocks. Given the reliance on automatic stabilizers, the marginal value of further insights on these issues is potentially large. (Anderson, 2005, p. 536)

There is a sense in which fiscal policy by its nature is discretionary. At least under present decision-making arrangements, tax and expenditure plans are settled on an annual basis in the budget round. At the time of the budget, forecasts are available for the level of economic activity in the forthcoming years, and some decisions will surely be influenced by those forecasts. This is not to say that fiscal policy is then operated in a counter-cyclical fashion for apart from the issues over lags noted above there are a range of (from a level of economic activity point of view) extraneous factors that impinge on taxation and public expenditure decisions.

Concluding comments

Fiscal policy is often viewed in terms of the determination of government expenditure and taxation as undertaken without specific regard to the state of private aggregate demand. The 'crowding out' argument after all assumes that there is something to be crowded out. That approach to fiscal policy suggests either that fiscal policy has no effect on the level of economic activity (since there is crowding out) or that there is a positive link between government expenditure (budget deficit) and the level of economic activity. The investigation of fiscal policy through the means of simulation of macroeconometric models is concerned (usually) with the question of what happens if government expenditure is increased, other things being equal. The results of such simulations, generally, suggest that an increase in government expenditure does have a positive effect on the level of economic activity (Arestis and Sawyer, 2003). Indeed in the context in which these simulations are undertaken, it is somewhat surprising that positive results are obtained since such macroeconometric models generally build in a variety of ways by which there would be crowding out – the most notable one being that imposition of some form of supply-side equilibrium usually in the form of a NAIRU (non accelerating inflation rate of unemployment), along with a mechanism which steers the economy towards that equilibrium position. If the economy operates around the supply-side equilibrium, there is, by definition, little room for manoeuvre and indeed little need for fiscal policy.

We would argue that the impact of fiscal policy has to be examined, both empirically and theoretically, in a framework that permits insufficiency of aggregate demand relative to supply. If the world were one where inadequate (private) aggregate demand was never an issue, then we would all agree that fiscal policy and budget deficits would have no role to play.[4]

Acknowledgements

I am grateful to Jérôme Creel for comments on an earlier draft and to Philip Arestis for fruitful collaboration in many areas including fiscal policy.

Notes

1. This discussion is cast in terms of a closed economy. Adjustments to account for an open economy can be readily made without undermining the basic approach pursued here.
2. This section draws very heavily on Arestis and Sawyer (2006).
3. See Creel and Saraceno (ch. 7, this volume) for the argument that the automatic stabilizers in EU countries have been diminished over the past years.
4. We could, though, add the caveat that in a growing economy (in nominal terms) there is some requirement for expansion of the stock of government money, and hence a budget deficit may be required as a means of ensuring such an expansion.

References

Andersen, T.M. (2005) 'Is there a role for an active fiscal stabilization polcy?' *CESifo Economic Studies*, 51(4), 511–47.
Arestis, P. and Sawyer, M. (1998) 'Keynesian policies for the New Millennium', *Economic Journal*, 108, 181–95.
Arestis, P. and Sawyer, M. (2003) 'Reinventing fiscal policy', *Journal of Post Keynesian Economics*, 26(1), 4–25.
Arestis, P. and Sawyer, M. (2006) 'Fiscal policy matters', *Public Finance*, 54(3), 133–53.
Barro, R.J. (1974) 'Are government bonds net wealth?', *Journal of Political Economy*, 82(6), 1095–117.
Barro, R.J. (1989) 'The Ricardian approach to budget deficits', *Journal of Economic Perspectives*, 3(2), 37–54.
Eisner, R. (1989) 'Budget deficits: Rhetoric and reality', *Journal of Economic Perspectives*, 3(2), 73–93.
Feldstein, M. (2002) 'Commentary: Is there a role for discretionary fiscal policy?' in *Rethinking Stabilization Policy*, Federal Reserve Bank of Kansas City Papers and Proceedings, pp. 151–62.
Friedman, M. (1953) 'The effects of full employment policy on economic stability: A formal analysis', in *Essays in Positive Economics*, Chicago: University of Chicago Press, pp. 117–32.
Hansen, A.H. (1938) *Full Recovery or Stagnation?*, London: Macmillan.
Hansen, A.H. (1941) *Fiscal Policy and Business Cycles*, New York: W.W. Norton.
Kalecki, M. (1944a) 'The white paper on employment policy', *Bulletin of the Oxford University Institute of Statistics*, 6(1), 137–144.
Kalecki, M. (1944b) 'Professor Pigou on "The classical stationary state": A comment', *Economic Journal*, 54(1), 131–2.

Keynes, J.M. (1936), *The General Theory of Employment, Interest and Money*, London: Macmillan.

Leith, C. and Wren-Lewis, S. (2005) 'Fiscal stabilization policy and fiscal institutions', *Oxford Review of Economic Policy*, 21(4), 584–97.

Lerner, A. (1943) 'Functional finance and the Federal debt', *Social Research*, 10, 38–51; reprinted in W. Mueller (ed.), *Readings in Macroeconomics*, New York: Holt, Rinehart and Winston, pp. 353–60 (page numbers refer to the reprint).

Musgrave, R.A. (1959) *The Theory of Public Finance*, London: McGraw-Hill.

Musgrave, R.A. (1985) 'A brief history of fiscal doctrine', in P. Auerbach and M. Feldstein (eds), *Handbook of Public Economics*, New York: North-Holland, pp. 1–60.

Sawyer, M. (2002) 'The NAIRU, aggregate demand and investment', *Metroeconomica*, 53(1), 66–94.

Sawyer, M. (2008) 'Re-thinking macroeconomic policies' in C. Gnos and L.-P. Rochon (eds), *Credit, Money and Macroeconomic Policy: A Post-Keynesian Approach*, Aldershot: Edward Elgar, forthcoming.

Taylor, J. (1993) 'Discretion versus policy rules in practice', *Carnegie-Rochester Conference Series on Public Policy*, 39, 195–214.

6
The Intertemporal Budget Constraint and the Sustainability of Budget Deficits

Philip Arestis and Malcolm Sawyer

Introduction

The use, and particularly the continuing use, of budget deficits as a means of promoting economic activity has encountered many objections (see, for example, Arestis and Sawyer, 2003). In this chapter, we investigate two related objections. The first arises from the idea that the government faces an intertemporal budget constraint such that, in effect, the net wealth position of the government is constrained to be zero, and hence that the sum of initial outstanding debt plus discounted future budget positions sum to zero. For a government with outstanding debt, this requires that at some stage (primary) budget surpluses would have to be run. The second is that a continuing budget deficit would be unsustainable, as the borrowing adds to the government debt with debt and interest payments rising over time without limit.

We argue that these objections have been overstated and indeed that the objections themselves are unsustainable. More specifically, we argue that the sustainability of a budget deficit has to be considered from the perspective of the purpose for which a budget deficit is incurred and the effects of the public expenditure that is undertaken.

Outline of the intertemporal budget constraint

The basic idea of the intertemporal budget constraint is, as the name suggests, that the government, like any other economic agent, faces a budget constraint, which is such that borrowing can be undertaken in some periods, but not in all, and that overall the debt position of the government sums to zero.

The general approach can be viewed as starting from the view that households seek to maximize their lifetime utility.[1] Households pursue consumption smoothing over time, and in pursuing this objective, they can borrow and lend and could enhance their economic welfare by borrowing to increase their consumption above their income. It is, though, paramount to introduce an additional condition 'that prevents families from choosing such a path, with an exploding debt relative to the size of the family. At the same time we do not want to impose a condition that rules out temporary indebtedness. A natural condition is to require that family debt does not increase asymptotically faster than the interest rate:

$$\lim_{t \to \infty} a_t \exp \left[-\int_0^t (r_v - n)dv \right] \geq 0 \qquad (6.1)$$

This condition is sometimes known as a no-Ponzi-game (NPG) condition. Although equation (6.1) is stated as an inequality, it is clear that as long as marginal utility is positive, families will not want to have increasing wealth forever at rate $r - n$, and that the condition will hold as an equality' (Blanchard and Fischer, 1989, pp. 49–50). Here a is non-human wealth, n population growth and r the rental price of capital.

A similar argument is applied in the case of the government. Blanchard and Fischer (1989) suggest that 'Integrating this budget constraint and imposing the NPG condition this time on the government (that debt not increase faster asymptotically than the interest rate) gives an intertemporal budget constraint for the government

$$b_0 + \int_0^\infty g_t R_t dt = \int_0^\infty \tau_t R_t dt \qquad (6.2)$$

The present values of taxes must be equal to the present value of government spending plus the value of the initial government debt b_0, given the NPG condition. Equivalently, the government must choose a path of spending and taxes such that the present value of $g_t - \tau_t$, which is sometimes referred to as the primary deficit, equals the negative of initial debt, b_0; if the government has positive outstanding debt, it must anticipate running primary surpluses at some point in the future' (p. 55). Here g is government expenditure (other than interest payments), τ tax revenue, and R the discount factor.

Blanchard and Fischer (1989) go on to argue that 'integrating this budget constraint subject to the NPG condition gives the following intertemporal budget constraint:

$$\int\limits_{0}^{\infty} c_t R_t dt = k_0 - b_{p0} + b_0 + \int\limits_{0}^{\infty} w_t R_t dt - \int\limits_{0}^{\infty} \tau_t R_t dt \qquad (6.3)$$

The present value of consumption must be equal to the sum of nonhuman wealth, which is the sum of $k_0 - b_{p0}$ and b_0, and of human wealth, which is the present value of wages minus taxes. The government budget constraint shows that for a given pattern of government spending (and given b_0), the government has to levy taxes of a given present value: equivalently, the government need not run a balanced budget at every moment of time' (p. 55).

Re-writing equations (6.2) and (6.3) gives:

$$b_0 = \int\limits_{0}^{\infty} \tau_t R_t dt - \int\limits_{0}^{\infty} g_t R_t dt \qquad (6.4)$$

$$b_0 = \int\limits_{0}^{\infty} c_t R_t dt - k_0 + b_{p0} - \int\limits_{0}^{\infty} w_t R_t dt + \int\limits_{0}^{\infty} \tau_t R_t dt \qquad (6.5)$$

so that the discounted value of the budget surplus is equal to the discounted value of the private sector deficit. This is essentially the dynamic equivalent of $S - I = G - T$ (S savings, I investment, G government expenditure and T tax revenue) in an *ex ante* sense. In the present context of a closed economy, a similar looking equation would hold as an *ex post* accounting identity. But here it is clearly presented as an *ex ante* result, albeit derived from the assumption of a budget constraint imposed on the government.

In a closed economy, the counterpart to an intertemporal government budget constraint is an intertemporal private sector budget constraint, of the form that the present value of the difference between private savings and investment summed over the future would also be zero (noting that the same discount rate would have to be used for both constraints). The fulfilment of the intertemporal private sector budget constraint requires the equality (over time) between *ex ante* savings and investment. It is possible that savings and investment would be equal at a rate of interest linked with the rate of discount used and compatible with a high level of economic activity. In effect if the private sector imposed upon itself the intertemporal budget constraint, then the government would be faced with a corresponding constraint. Similarly, if the private sector operated with a constraint of the form that discounted future investment is greater or equal to discounted future savings, the constraint on the government is that discounted tax revenue would be greater than or equal to government expenditure. But conversely if the private sector did not perform according to that constraint, and specifically if investment tended to fall short of savings, then the budget constraint on the government would have to be amended accordingly. But further the private sector constraint is intended to apply to *ex ante* savings and investment and at the supply side equilibrium level of economic activity.

One of two arguments would usually be invoked to support the view that *ex ante* investment is at least equal to *ex ante* savings. The first would correspond to an appeal to Say's Law to the effect that 'supply creates its own demand'. The second would be to argue that the interest rate was also set such that the condition held. However, in any other circumstances (that is when *ex ante* savings tends to exceed *ex ante* investment at full employment), then adherence to the intertemporal budget constraint would impose on the private sector a requirement (over time) of *ex post* savings equals to *ex post* investment. This would entail low levels of economic activity to reduce savings (below the full employment *ex ante* level), and significant levels of unemployment would be the consequence of meeting the intertemporal budget constraint.

If the private sector seeks to save more than it invests (in a single period or more generally) then the private sector is not imposing (on itself) a budget constraint (intertemporal or otherwise) in terms of equality between savings and investment. If it were indeed the case that (*ex ante*) savings and investment were equal, then that equality would be in effect the budget constraint for the private sector, and hence there would be a budget constraint on the public sector. If there is an intertemporal equality between savings and investment, then similarly there would be an intertemporal budget constraint on the public sector. But then the question arises as to whether households behave in the manner portrayed by the intertemporal budget constraint thesis. We examine this question in the section that follows.

Is household behaviour consistent with the intertemporal budget constraint thesis?

In attempting to answer the question posed, it is necessary to examine the household budget constraint, which is the counterpart of the government's intertemporal budget constraint. The basis of the argument is straightforward. Each (representative) household maximizes life-time utility, which depends on consumption. The household will spend up to budget constraint under a non-satiation assumption. In effect there is a life-time marginal propensity to consume of 1. A 'bequest effect' (specifically desire to leave more than inherited) would imply overall life time savings.

The use of intertemporal optimization can be objected to along the lines of 'unrealism' in terms of the information and computational requirements. It can also be pointed out that the analysis makes no allowance for uncertainty about the future, where here uncertainty is fundamental uncertainty in the sense of Knight and Keynes, rather than risk with known probabilities on future outcomes. There is clearly no allowance for learning nor for changes in tastes and preferences in light of experience, nor any consideration of changes in household membership in essentially a world without separation and divorce. In terms of the considerations of this chapter, a particularly important aspect of this approach is the perfect capital market assumption. More specifically, the absence of credit rationing (which would mean that some individuals were credit constrained) and the assumption of a single interest rate are important considerations. Furthermore, there is no mention of banks in this analysis, and since banks play an important role in terms of credit rationing their omission is noteworthy.

Insofar as *ex ante* income and expenditure are equated with each other (perhaps through suitable variations in the rate of interest), any role for fiscal policy would be negated. As we have shown elsewhere (Arestis and Sawyer 2004a, 2004b, 2006), the need for fiscal policy (in the sense of the absence of a balanced budget) arises where *ex ante* savings and investment are not equal to one another at a desirable level of income (often taken to be high level of employment). In a closed economy, it is well known that there is equality between net private savings and the budget deficit, and the purpose of a budget deficit can be seen to be the absorption of 'excess savings'. The imposition of the condition that income is equal to expenditure is equivalent to imposing the condition that savings is equal to investment, which is the re instatement of Say's Law. In this context the relevance of fiscal policy is ruled out by assumption.

The obvious interpretation of the 'no Ponzi' condition is that an economic agent cannot continue to borrow for ever, and that those who lend to that economic agent would not be willing to continue to lend. But an excess of private savings over private investment requires some outlet, and reveals a willingness by the private sector to continue to acquire public debt.

For the individual it would be anticipated that the assumption of being able to borrow as much as they wish at the prevailing rate of interest would not hold, and in effect the individual would face some form of credit rationing. In the case of government, its ability to borrow would be constrained by the willingness of the private sector to lend since the budget deficit is equal to private net savings. If the government sought to borrow more than the maximum amount of private net savings, then it would indeed be faced by a borrowing constraint. However, if the government practices 'purposeful fiscal policy' and seeks to run a budget deficit equal to private net savings (at the target level of economic activity), then it would not face this borrowing constraint.[2]

Liabilities and assets and their importance to the budget constraint

The intertemporal budget constraint as discussed above is cast in terms of the financial position of the government. The liabilities of the public sector in the form of public debt are included but there is no mention of any assets. But the public sector does own a wide range of assets often in the form of infrastructure such as roads, other transport facilities, buildings etc. At least for the UK, public sector net worth is estimated to be positive, equivalent to around 25 per cent of GDP in 2003–04, which can be compared to the net debt position of around 33 per cent of GDP (Treasury, 2005, Table C24).

The intertermporal budget constraint is written by Buiter (2001) in the following forms:

$$\dot{B} = iB + P(G^C + G^I - \theta K^G - T) \tag{6.6}$$

where G^C, G^I are government expenditure on current goods and services and investment respectively, K^G is the government capital stock and θ is the extent to which the capital stock contributes to government revenue (e.g. through charges).

The net liability position of the government is then given by

$$L = B - PK^G \tag{6.7}$$

and the rate of change by

$$\dot{L} = iL + P(G^C - T) + [r - (\theta - \delta)]PK^G \tag{6.8}$$

and hence

$$L(t) = \int_t^\infty P(s)[T(s) - G^C(s)]e^{-i(s-t)}ds + \int_t^\infty [r(s) - (\theta - \delta)P(s)K^G(s)e^{-i(s-t)}ds \tag{6.9}$$

where for simplicity the discount rate is assumed constant over time.

There are two interesting aspects of this formulation. First, the intertemporal budget constraint is now expressed in terms of net liability position of government, which can give a different complexion to that constraint. From equation (6.8) it can be seen that the net liability position is equal to the discounted future budget surplus plus discounted return on public assets. Clearly the net liability position may be positive or negative. In the case where there is positive public sector net worth (and taking the second term on the right hand side as small or zero), then this constraint indicates that with net liabilities negative then the sum of future surpluses would also be negative.

Second, Buiter (2001, p. 3, fn. 4) postulates some financial return to public sector assets. The argument is that these 'cash returns . . . include not only user charges and other revenues obtained by extracting fees from private beneficiaries of the services provided by the public sector capital stock, but also any additions to tax revenues resulting from the positive effects of the public sector capital stock on the tax base', that is, by raising national income. In one sense this would appear to involve double counting as the tax revenues are already included in the equations above. However, it would mean that future tax revenues are not independent of the current level of public expenditure. The nature of the budget constraint facing the government is thereby changed in that public expenditure now which raises future income and taxation thereby shifts out the budget constraint on the government. It would also change the budget constraint facing the private sector in that the level of income in the future would be higher than otherwise.

The distinction drawn between current expenditure and capital expenditure is not particularly useful in the context of fiscal policy in the following sense. Both forms of expenditure impact on aggregate demand

and on the use of resources in essentially similar ways. Further, in so far as the use of public sector assets do not generate user fees, then the direct effects of both forms of expenditure on future revenue streams are also essentially similar (i.e. negligible). Note, though, that this relates to direct effects, and we return to indirect effects shortly.

The definition of capital expenditure in this context relates to gross fixed capital formation, and to the purchase of capital which remains in the ownership of the public sector. A broader definition of capital formation would relate to any expenditure, which leads to a stream of future benefits, and the asset thereby created does not necessarily remain in the ownership of the public sector. In the context of public expenditure, that on education forms an obvious example of where public expenditure helps to create a stream of future benefits, but where the 'ownership' of the asset (what may be termed human capital) resides with the individual. This corresponds to the widely used term of 'investment in education' (but which is not currently included in the investment or capital expenditure of government). The future benefits may largely arise at the level of the individual but of relevance in this context are the effects on future tax revenue and on future growth of income.

This suggests a three-way division of public expenditure into:

1. 'pure' consumption expenditure which has no effect on future benefits or costs, G_A;
2. capital expenditure where government retains ownership of the asset (generally physical assets), G_B; and
3. expenditure, which creates a stream of future benefits, G_C, but where the government does not retain ownership.

This is a conceptual division, and the definition and measurement of the three forms of expenditure would in practice be fraught with difficulties. The particular point, which we wish to make here, is that the growth rate and time path of the economy will be influenced by the structure of public expenditure. Consequently, the time path along which the economy moves cannot be specified without consideration of the level and form of public expenditure. Hence, if there is an intertemporal budget constraint, then it cannot relate to a growth rate and time place which is independent of actions including fiscal policy. For example, if fiscal policy in the present enables aggregate demand to be higher (than otherwise), leading to higher levels of investment and savings then the growth path of the economy will be influenced. Similarly if public investment is undertaken which directly or indirectly aids growth then the path of the economy is influenced.

The sustainability of deficit

As one year's budget deficit adds to the public debt and leads to future interest payments, the question arises as to the sustainability of a budget deficit that is without involving continuously rising public debt. The continuation of a primary budget deficit (deficit excluding interest payments) involves the build up of interest payments, and further borrowing to cover those interest payments and the continuing primary deficit. Although the budget deficit is growing (when interest payments are included) and the public debt is also growing, their relationship with GDP depends on the growth of the economy as well as on the level of interest rates. Domar (1944) provided an early analysis of this and saw 'the problem of the debt burden [as] essentially a problem of achieving a growing national income' (p. 822); when numerical values for the key variables were used in the analysis, rates of interest of 2 per cent and 3 per cent were assumed. Kalecki (1944) argued that an increasing national debt did not constitute a burden on society as a whole since it is largely an internal transfer, and further noted that in an expanding economy the debt to income ratio need not rise if the rate of growth is sufficiently high.

It is well-known that a continuing primary budget deficit equivalent to a proportion d of GDP will lead to a debt to GDP ratio stabilizing at $b = d/(g - r)$ (where g is the growth rate and r interest rate, either both in real terms or both in nominal terms).[3] It is evident that the stabilization of the debt to income ratio (with a given primary deficit) requires that $g > r$. In a similar vein, a continuing total budget deficit of d' (including interest payments) leads to a debt to GDP ratio stabilising at d'/g where here g is in nominal terms. But this implies that $b + rd = gd$, i.e. $b = (g - r)d$ and hence if g is less than r the primary budget deficit is negative (i.e. primary budget is in surplus).

The budget deficit, which is generally reported and commented upon, and indeed the one which would seem appropriate for fiscal policy and stimulation of aggregate demand, is the total budget position rather than the primary deficit (or surplus). To the extent that a budget deficit is required to offset an excess of private savings over investment, then it is the overall budget deficit which is relevant. Bond interest payments are a transfer payment and add to the income of the recipient, and is similar in that respect to other transfer payments (though the propensity to consume out of interest payments is likely to be less than that out of many other transfer payments). In an earlier paper (Arestis and Sawyer, 2006) we considered the empirical case with regard to interest rate and growth rate. We concluded in that study that when allowance is made for taxation on interest payments, it has often, but not always, historically been the case that the growth rate has exceeded the rate of interest.

The growth rate is taken to be the trend growth of GDP, in which case the key question with regard to the sustainability question is whether fiscal policy has any impact on the growth rate. The usual presentation treats the growth rate as a given, in effect set by the growth of supply; and as Blanchard and Fischer (1989, p. 58) argue 'In the closed economy model used so far, there was no cost to installing capital; whatever was saved could be added to the capital stock at no cost, and investment was purely passive.' Their relevant equation 'contains a very strong result, namely, that the rate of investment (relative to the capital stock) is a function only of q_t, which is the shadow price in terms of consumption goods of a unit of installed capital' (Blanchard and Fischer, 1989, p. 62). Fiscal Policy (budget deficits) may impact on the rate of growth in the following way. The impact in question concerns the relationship between the size of the deficit and investment (and hence increases in the capital stock), and also the effects of the composition of public expenditure on growth. With regard to the first, the 'crowding out' view of fiscal deficits would suggest that investment would be reduced through budget deficits and their effect on the rate of interest. In so far as that is right, then budget deficits would tend to slow the rate of growth, or at least slow capital formation. But when budget deficits are used in the manner, which we above labelled 'purposeful fiscal policy', that is to, in effect, mop up excess private savings, they lead to 'crowding in' and a higher level of economic activity than otherwise. When investment expenditure is sensitive to the level of economic activity, then fiscal policy leads to a higher level of investment, and thereby a larger capital stock. A number of views of the growth process (e.g., endogenous growth, demand-led growth), envisage that higher rates of capital formation are associated with faster growth of productivity. Thus, it may be argued that fiscal policy (of the 'purposeful' type) raises the growth rate of the economy.

There is now a substantial body of literature (see, for example, Aschauer, 1989; Easterly and Rebelo, 1993; Erenburg and Wohar, 1995; Martinez Lopez, 2006), which argues that public investment, notably on infrastructure, can have a positive supply-side effect on private capital formation and the supply rate of growth. This simple analysis of the budget deficit makes no allowance for any reaction in the willingness and desire of the private sector to hold the public debt. When 'purposeful' fiscal policy is employed to mop up excess private savings, then the bonds are willingly accepted as part of the asset portfolio of the private sector, and the wealth of the private sector increases (since savings are the addition to wealth). Rising wealth may have the effect of diminishing the appeal of savings, which has the beneficial effect of stimulating aggregate demand.

The analysis of Godley and Rowthorn (1994) incorporates aspects of that notion and includes a (pre-determined) wealth to income ratio for the private sector and a bond to wealth ratio which depends on the (exogenous) interest rate and the rate of inflation: hence there is a desired bond to income ratio. There is a sense in which the deficit of the public sector is then constrained by that bond to income ratio, and hence the non-monetized debt to income ratio. But this constraint may be of little relevance in the sense that the government is not seeking to run a deficit for the sake of it. It is more significant whether there is a constraint on the level of public expenditure and whether there are other constraints on the economy. On the former, we can note that in the Godley and Rowthorn (1994) model, an expansion in the level of public expenditure sets off an expansion of output and hence of tax revenue (and other changes) such that there is not an explosion in the debt to GDP ratio (and this does not rely on the rate of growth being greater than the rate of interest). This would suggest that there may be reactions from the private sector (arising from a reluctance to hold ever increasing amounts of government debt) which make the conditions for the sustainability of a deficit position less constraining than it first appeared.

Eisner and Hwang (1993, p. 255) express the argument in this way:

> Simply enough, real deficits add to the permanent income and/or real wealth perceived by private agents in the form of public debt or the monetary and nonmonetary assets the debt may back. This increase in perceived wealth increases current and planned future consumption. These increases in turn raise the demand for physical capital and hence increase investment.

A similar argument was put forward by Lerner (1948). This was summarized by Ackley (1951, p. 161) as the 'Lerner effect', which was:

> that, under stagnation conditions, deficit finance to maintain full employment might be self-limiting, because the necessary deficits would be financed by the creation of consumer assets (debt or money) which would eventually so saturate the desire to save as to

eliminate any tendency for saving to outrun private investment at full employment.

Ackley continued by arguing that this 'Lerner effect' would require these assets to grow relative to national income (at full employment), which would itself be growing.

Authors such as Christ (1968), Blinder and Solow (1973) and Turnovsky (1977), Chapter 4 clearly indicate that the imposition of an overall government budget restraint does not invalidate the finding that an increase in government expenditure can generate increases in output. The overall result of an increase in government expenditure does depend on the method of finance, and the use of bond finance can generate further increases in demand following from interest payments.

Real terms calculations

It should be noted that, generally implicitly, the above arguments are posed in real terms, and specifically it is the budget deficit in real terms, which is of relevance for the argument. It is well known that inflation tends to boost interest rates, and thereby payments on government debt, and that inflation reduces the real value of that government debt. Although, particularly in the era of high inflation of the 1970s and 1980s, arguments were heard for calculating budget deficit in real terms, this has rarely been taken up. Further arguments suggest that government and budget deficits are misleading. Eisner and Pieper (1984, p. 23), for example, argued that:

> official measures of the federal debt and budget deficits are misleading by any of several reasonable standards. Gross public debt figures ignore financial asset accumulation as well as the real assets, which have contributed to a growing government net worth. Budget flows have failed to distinguish between current and capital accounts, and measures of surplus and deficit have been inconsistent with changes in the real value of net debt.

Further, in the context of the US during the 1970s and early 1980s, the same authors argued that 'an appropriately adjusted high-employment budget turns out to have been not in deficit in recent years, as usually supposed, but in considerable surplus. The view that fiscal policy has generally been too easy and overstimulatory is contradicted' (p. 23).

Although the general rate of inflation is significantly lower now than during say the 1980s when concerns over measuring the real value of the budget deficit were to the fore, it is still the case that some allowance should be made for inflation. Even with the present target rate of inflation in the euro area of 'near 2 per cent but from below', and with a debt to GDP ratio of over 60 per cent, then around 1.2 per cent of the debt to GDP ratio could be ascribed to inflation (perhaps somewhat less when allowance is made for the taxation of bond interest).

Notional and actual decisions

At the level of the individual, it may seem reasonable to impose a constraint of the form that over a life time expenditure is less than or equal to income. The absence of such a constraint leads to the outcome that each individual would spend an infinite amount through the insatiability assumption. Some individuals may be able to effectively 'escape' the constraint through deception etc. but in general such a constraint could well hold. But an important question is what assumption is made on the determinants of the income of the individual. Specifically is it to be assumed that the income of the individual corresponds to the individual being able to supply labour as he or she wishes (in light of the prevailing real wage), or does the income of the individual take into account periods when they are unemployed and hence quantity constrained?

The distinction drawn by Clower (1965) between notional (*ex ante*) and actual (*ex post*) is relevant here. In the lifetime optimization analysis no distinction between notional, intended and actual has been made, presumably on the basis that they coincide. The budget constraint could be applied to notional or planned income and planned expenditure (over a life time), where the notional income is derived from labour and other supply decisions with respect to relative prices where those decisions can be carried through, and similarly planned expenditure is derived from consumption decisions with respect to relative prices. But the budget constraint could be applied in terms of actual income and actual expenditure, which in effect it is equivalent to a term such as anticipated time path of received income and incurred expenditure. Actual income over a lifetime would fall short of notional income over the same period to the extent that the individual anticipates periods of unemployment and failure to effect the planned labour supply. The intertemporal budget constraint (as will any single period constraint of a similar form), expressed in notional terms, is essentially that – notional. The binding constraint comes when it is expressed in terms of outcomes. In this context what was referred to as actual income is still (in general) future expected income, but it is intended to reflect that there will be periods during which not all individuals will be able to fulfil their supply of labour plans (in other words, be unemployed).

The private sector budget constraint in notional terms cannot be impacted by fiscal policy, simply because that constraint is defined along a full employment path. But the private sector budget constraint in outcome terms can be eased through the application of fiscal policy. The issue can also be posed in the following manner. In a single period the constraint could be expressed as $sY_f - I >= 0$ (and it could be argued that the upper limit on investment comes from sY_f). But, of course, $sY_a = I$, and $Y_a = I/s <= Y_f$; running a budget deficit in these circumstances would lead to $Y'_a = (I + BD)/s$ which could reach Y_f. If, for whatever reason, the private sector collectively decided to operate within its budget constraint as in A, then income would fall short of Y_f.

Along a path given by the equality $sY_a = I$ it would of course be the case that the budget constraint would be satisfied. But path given by $Y'_a = (I + BD)/s$ also involves the budget constraint being satisfied, and leads to superior outcomes. This leads back now to the sustainability issue. Suppose $sY_a = I$ is the typical case, and a budget deficit is run; then debts and interest payments build up. However if we write $sY'_a = (I + BD)$ it is evident that the government debt is willingly acquired by the private sector.

Budget deficits and the business cycle

The intertemporal budget constraint is stated as a general constraint, and there is no immediate indication on the time path along which the economy moves, and specifically nothing about the level of income at each point in time. It has been argued above that if there is an intertemporal budget constraint for the public sector, then there has to be a corresponding constraint on the private sector. If these intertemporal budget constraints hold along the full employment path of the economy, and hence for the private sector (*ex ante*) savings and investment are equal, then there is no deficient aggregate demand problem by assumption, and hence no requirement for a budget deficit. The 'purposeful fiscal policy' approach would have strong doubts as to whether that would be the case, but if it were then there would be no need for a budget deficit.

However, in a more realistic case, the constraint may hold for a low level of economic activity. This would presumably mean that at a high level of economic activity, savings would generally exceed investment, and that a high level of economic activity could only be achieved through a budget deficit. As previously argued, the availability of net savings enables a budget deficit to be funded, and we would argue that would mean that the intertemporal budget constraint does not in fact apply.

The intertemporal budget constraint clearly is intended to apply over an infinite time horizon, and it does not indicate anything on the year to year budget position. From the perspective of the constraint, a fiscal policy rule that sought to balance the budget each year would be equivalent to a rule that sought to balance the budget over the business cycle, and equivalent to one that sought to balance the budget over an indefinite time horizon. Now if the time path of savings and investment are viewed as arising from optimizing calculations then it could be argued that an appropriate interest rate would balance savings and investment in each time period at a high level of economic activity. In effect, if a Wicksellian natural rate of interest applied in each period, again there would be no insufficiency of aggregate demand. The equality between savings and investment would be addressed through interest rate (monetary) policy.

However, if either the rate of interest cannot be adjusted to ensure the perpetual balance between savings and investment (say because the relevant rate would be negative) or because savings and investment are not based on full information optimizing calculations (whether because of the impossibility of full information in an uncertain world or considerations of bounded rationality), then *ex ante* savings and investment in general differ. Fiscal policy again has a role to play in absorbing the difference between savings and investment (and preventing the adjustment of the level of economic activity to bring about the equality of savings and investment as in the Keynesian multiplier story). The use of fiscal policy then raises the level of economic activity (above what it would have otherwise been) in those years where *ex ante* savings exceed investment. However, a higher level of economic activity in one year can have effects on the future course of the economy, most notably through the effect which economic activity and capacity utilization have on investment decisions.

The budget deficit in one period alters the level of savings and investment in that period (as compared with a balanced budget position). In the absence of the budget deficit, some of the planned savings would have been aborted. The level of economic activity is thereby higher than it would have been, and the level of savings and perhaps the level of investment higher than they would otherwise have been. The achieved levels of savings and investment would influence future behaviour and the time path of the economy. Thus, even if the intertemporal budget constraint holds, there are varying time paths within that constraint, and the nature of the constraint changes as the time path chosen varies.

Summary and conclusions

In this chapter we have examined two objections to the use of budget deficits as a means of promoting economic activity. One that arises from the idea that the government faces an intertemporal budget constraint such that, in effect, the net wealth position of the government is constrained to be zero, and hence that the sum of initial outstanding debt plus discounted future budget positions sum to zero. For a government with outstanding debt, this requires that at some stage (primary) budget surpluses would have to be run. The other objection we have dealt with relates to the idea that a continuing budget deficit would be unsustainable. The borrowing adds to the government debt with debt and interest payments rising over time without limit.

We have outlined the intertemporal budget constraint, and indeed we have shown that these objections have been overstated. We have argued that the sustainability of a budget deficit has to be considered from the perspective of the purpose for which a budget deficit is incurred and the effects of the public expenditure that is undertaken.

Notes

1. In exploring the intertemporal household utility optimization, we follow the presentation of Blanchard and Fischer (1989).
2. The notion of 'purposeful fiscal policy' referred to in the text, needs to be defined. It is a term used to refer to the general presumption that private aggregate demand is likely to be insufficient rather than excessive, and hence that there would be budget deficits rather than budget surpluses. The key notion of the 'purposeful fiscal policy' approach is that the budget position should be used to secure the desired level of economic activity, and from that perspective a budget surplus would arise when private aggregate demand was deemed excessive (or equivalently when *ex ante* private savings are less than *ex ante* private investment).
3. Let the outstanding public sector debt be D, and then the budget deficit is dD/dt and is equal to $G + rD - T$ where r is the post-tax rate of interest on public debt, G is government expenditure (other than interest payments) and T is taxation (other than that based on receipt of interest from government). With Y as national income, we have: $d(D/Y)/dt = (1/Y)dD/dt - (D/Y)(1/Y).dY/dt = (G + rDT)/Y - (D/Y)g$, where g is the growth of national income. The debt to income ratio rises (falls) if $(G - T)/Y > (<)(D/Y)(g - r)$.

References

Ackley, G. (1951) 'The wealth–saving relationship', *Journal of Political Economy*, 59(2), 154–61.

Arestis, P. and Sawyer, M. (2003) 'Reinstating fiscal policy', *Journal of Post Keynesian Economics*, 26(1), 4–25.

Arestis, P. and Sawyer, M. (2004a) 'On the effectiveness of monetary and fiscal policy', *Review of Social Economics*, 62(4), 441–63.

Arestis, P. and Sawyer, M. (2004b) 'On fiscal policy and budget deficits', *Intervention, Journal of Economics*, 1(2), 61–74.

Arestis, P. and Sawyer, M. (2006) 'Fiscal Policy matters', *Public Finance*, 54(3), 1–15.

Aschauer, D.A. (1989) 'Does public capital crowd out private capital?', *Journal of Monetary Economics*, 24, 171–88.

Blanchard, O. and Fischer, S. (1989) *Lectures on Macroeconomics*, Cambridge, MA: MIT Press.

Blinder, A. and Solow, R. (1973) 'Does fiscal policy matter', *Journal of Public Economics*, 2(3), 319–38.

Buiter, W.H. (2001) 'Notes on "A code for fiscal stability"', *Oxford Economic Papers*, 53(1), 1–19.

Christ, C. (1968) 'A simple macroeconomic model with a government budget restraint', *The Journal of Political Economy*, 76(1), (Jan–Feb), 53–67.

Clower, R.W. (1965) 'The Keynesian counter-revolution: A theoretical appraisal' in F. Hahn and F. Brechling (eds), *The Theory of Interest Rates*, London: Macmillan.

Domar, E.D. (1944) 'The "burden of the debt" and the national income', *American Economic Review*, 34(4), 798–827.

Easterly, W. and Rebelo, S. (1993) 'Fiscal Policy and economic growth: An empirical investigation', *Journal of Monetary Economics*, 32, 458–93.

Eisner, R. and Hwang, S.-I. (1993), 'Self-correcting real deficits: A new lesson in functional finance' in Harrie A.A. Verbon and Frans A.A.M. Van Winder (eds), *The Political Economy of Government Debt*, Amsterdam: North Holland, 255–94.

Eisner, R. and Pieper, P.J. (1984) 'A new view of the Federal debt and budget deficits', *American Economic Review*, 74(1), 11–29.

Erenburg, S.J. and Wohar, M.E. (1995) 'Public and private investment: Are there causal linkages?', *Journal of Macroeconomics*, 17, 1–30.

Godley, W. and Rowthorn, R. (1994) 'The dynamics of public sector deficits and debts', in J. Michie and J. Grieve Smith (eds), *Unemployment in Europe*, London: Academic Press.

Kalecki, M. (1944) 'Three ways fo full employment', in Oxford University Institute of Statistics, *The Economics of Full Employment*, Oxford: Blackwell.

Lerner, A. (1948) 'The burden of the national debt', in L.A. Metzler (ed.), *Income, Employment and Public Policy: Essays in Honor of Alvin H. Hansen* (New York: W.W. Norton), p. 264.

Martinez Lopez, D. (2006) 'Linking public investment to private investment: The case of Spanish regions', *International Review of Applied Economics*, 20(4), 411–24.

Treasury (2005), *Britain Meeting the Global Challenge: Enterprise, fairness and responsibility*, Pre-Budget Report, December 2005 CM 6701.

Turnovsky, S.J. (1977) *Macroeconomic Analysis and Stabilization Policy*, Cambridge: Cambridge University Press.

7
Automatic Stabilization, Discretionary Policy and the Stability Pact

Jérôme Creel and Francesco Saraceno

Introduction

The economic institutions of the Economic and Monetary Union in their actual design stem from two main sources. The first is the founding Treaty signed in Maastricht in 1991, and the second is the Amsterdam Treaty of 1997, which completed the setup with the Stability and Growth Pact (hereafter SGP).

The Maastricht Treaty defined the convergence criteria that countries had to fulfil in order to be admitted to the single currency area. In particular, it required a deficit to GDP ratio of no more than 3 per cent, and a public debt below 60 per cent of GDP, or approaching that level at a satisfactory pace.

The Amsterdam Treaty contains further provisions regarding fiscal policy that have the objective of increasing transparency and control on public finances. The Stability and Convergence Programme that each year Member States present to the Commission has to contain a medium-term objective for the budgetary position of close to balance or in surplus, together with an account of the adjustment path towards the objective. The Excessive Deficit Procedure states what deviations from the 3 per cent budget deficit ceiling are acceptable and describes the sanctions for the violators. As of December 2007, no country has been fined, although disapproval of budget positions in some countries has been expressed.

The prolonged period of low growth experienced by most Euro area countries (especially the largest ones), and the increasing number of countries struggling to maintain their deficits within the limits set by the Stability and Growth Pact (SGP), have triggered a debate on the flaws of the current fiscal framework, and on possible reforms aimed at a

112

better functioning of fiscal policy in Europe.[1] The reform adopted by the European Council in March 2005 relaxes somewhat the medium-term objective of a zero structural deficit for countries with low debt and/or with high potential growth; furthermore, it contemplates a number of circumstances (e.g. a strong engagement in costly structural reforms) allowing temporary deviations from the deficit ceiling, and longer delays for correcting them.

The requirement to attain a position of close to balance or surplus in the medium term is an important innovation of the SGP with respect to the Maastricht Treaty, and it was left substantially unchanged by the reform of 2005. In fact, it implies the strong consequence that public debt as a ratio to GDP should tend asymptotically to zero, a position hard to justify *per se* (De Grauwe, 2003).

Even after the reform of 2005, the focus of the Stability and Growth Pact has been on the full operation of automatic stabilizers that would allow the implementation of a counter-cyclical short-run fiscal policy. However, recent assessments of fiscal policies in the EU-15 have either pointed to their a-cyclicality (Gali and Perotti, 2003) or to their pro-cyclicality (Farina and Ricciuti, 2006). This raises doubts about the effectiveness of automatic stabilizers all over Europe. In the first part of this chapter, we support this conclusion with a variety of stylized facts related either to the tax and benefit systems or to the sensitivity of unemployment public expenditures to unemployment and GDP growth rates. We then argue that a contradiction has arisen in Europe between the fact that the SGP advocates the use of automatic stabilizers and the reality of their declining effectiveness.

A subsequent step will consist in analysing possible solutions to the contradiction. Two situations are possible: further reducing the scope of fiscal policy and making the EU economy depend even more on markets and their flexibility; or making room in the European fiscal framework for discretionary and counter-cyclical fiscal policies to compensate for the reduction in the efficiency of automatic stabilizers.[2] We argue in favour of the latter solution.

The standard textbook consensus on which the European economic institutions rest is that monetary policy is assigned the task of reacting to area-wide shocks, while national fiscal policy is left in charge of country-specific shocks.[3] Within this framework, fiscal policy has to be limited to automatic stabilization, banning discretionary intervention from the toolbox of policy interventions. The standard argument maintains that the limit of total deficit to 3 per cent, coupled with the requirement of structural balance, could avoid fiscal indiscipline (thus protecting central bank independence), while letting enough room for automatic stabilization to take care of country-specific shocks. (Brunila *et al.*, 2002). Nevertheless, some empirical studies (see, e.g., Barrell and Pina, 2004) discussed the fact that the initial levels of debt-to-GDP ratios and cyclically-adjusted deficits in some Euro area Member States might be too high to permit the automatic stabilizers to operate freely within the constraints of the SGP.

The decreasing effectiveness of automatic stabilizers in the EU-15

The European framework for fiscal policy has tended to privilege the operation of automatic stabilizers at the expense of discretionary policy changes. Distinguishing between the cyclical and the structural parts of a public deficit is not an easy task. Even abstracting from the difficulties involved in the measurement of the output gap and potential output, automatic stabilizers depend on a variety of factors from the macro and the micro spheres that are often country specific. The effectiveness of automatic stabilizers depends on the sensitivity of government revenues and spending to economic fluctuations and on the sensitivity of economic activity to cyclical changes in government revenues and spending. Among the factors affecting budgetary sensitivity, the literature highlights the size of the public sector, the progressivity of the tax and benefit system, the sensitivity of tax bases to economic fluctuations, the institutional time profile of the tax system,[4] the level of unemployment benefits and the sensitivity of unemployment to fluctuations in economic activity. Other determinants that have an influence on the effectiveness of automatic stabilizers are the nature and size of shocks. Finally, the overall flexibility of the economy may also dampen the shocks and automatic stabilizers may seem more effective than they are in reality.

Despite the difficulty of identifying the relative smoothing properties of automatic stabilizers and economic flexibility, the picture in the European context shows some key elements whose incidence on the effectiveness of automatic stabilizers presents no ambiguity: budgetary sensitivity has undoubtedly been on a downward trend for many years and recent reforms (e.g. the recent fiscal package approved by the newly elected French government) are not such that one can expect a reverse trend in the near future. This long lasting change therefore questions the exclusive reliance of European fiscal policies on automatic stabilization.

Table 7.1 Effectiveness of automatic stabilizers across EU countries (in %)

	Bundesbank model (1)	QUEST model (2)	NiGEM model (3)	INTERLINK model (4)
France	19	23	7	14
Italy	14	21	5	23
Netherlands	14	20	6	36
UK	24	18	n.a.	30
Germany	23	17	18	31
Unweighted average	18.8	19.8	9.0	26.8
Std error	4.8	2.4	6.1	8.5

Note: percentage of fluctuations in output which are smoothed by automatic stabilizers
Sources: (1) Scharnagl and Tödter (2004); (2) European Commission (2001); Barrel and Pina (2004); (3) van den Noord (2000)

Automatic stabilizers: macro evidence

We begin with a summary, in Table 7.1, of the main conclusions of different macroeconometric models that estimate the percentage of fluctuations in output which are smoothed by automatic stabilizers. The most striking result is the heterogeneity of countries in terms of the sensitivity of economic activity to the cyclical changes in government revenue and spending. The standard error across countries goes from 2 to 8 per cent, for an average smoothing of 19 per cent across models and countries. Moreover, the extent of automatic stabilizers smoothing for a country is quite different from one model to the other and the standard errors across models are large, ranging from 6 per cent for Germany to 12 per cent for the Netherlands.[5] Overall, Table 7.1 tells us that the scope of automatic stabilizers in the EU is low: at best, they smoothed a maximum of 36 per cent of economic fluctuations and at worst only 5 per cent of them.

To complement the studies mentioned in Table 7.1 we give our own preliminary assessment of the size of automatic stabilizers in five countries between 1971 and 2005. These countries are representative of the size heterogeneity of the Euro area Member States and they will also be shown later to have behaved distinctly with respect to the progressivity of the tax and benefit system. We focus on the sensitivity of public deficit (our endogenous variable) with respect to economic fluctuations (one-quarter lagged GDP growth). We report two different OLS specifications: one with a lag in fiscal policy and one without (columns 2 and 1 of Table 7.2 respectively), the former giving a better fit. A first noteworthy pattern is the heterogeneity across countries, which confirms the

Table 7.2   Automatic stabilizers

	Italy		France		UK		Netherlands		Sweden	
	(1)	(2)	(1)	(2)	(1)	(2)	(1)	(2)	(1)	(2)
Δ GDP$_{-1}$	−0.28	−0.26	0.79	0.28	0.52	0.25	0.53	0.34	1.32	0.75
	(0.9)	(1.9)	(5.4)	(1.9)	(2.6)	(1.7)	(2.8)	(2.5)	(3.3)	(2.7)
Gvt net	–	0.89	–	0.64	–	0.68	–	0.68	–	0.69
lend.$_{-1}$		(11.6)		(5.1)		(5.3)		(6.7)		(6.5)
Const	−7.0	−0.19	−4.3	−1.6	−4.3	−1.5	−4.0	−1.9	−3.1	−1.7
	(7.5)	(0.3)	(10.5)	(2.6)	(6.9)	(2.3)	(7.1)	(3.5)	(2.8)	(2.3)
$\bar{R}^2$	0.00	0.81	0.46	0.70	0.14	0.55	0.17	0.64	0.22	0.66

Notes: Dependent variable: government net lending in percent of GDP, 1971–2005; *t*-stats in parentheses
Source: OECD, *Economic Outlook*

findings of Table 7.1. Crossing the results of the two tables we are able to obtain additional information, most notably about the comparison between the UK and France. While Table 7.1 displayed a relatively high smoothing of economic fluctuations in the UK, Table 7.2 shows that the overall sensitivity of public deficit to economic fluctuations is similar. This may lead one to conclude that automatic stabilizers are more efficient in the UK than in France.

Table 7.2 also shows that cyclical sensitivity of the public deficit is very strong in Sweden, mild in the Netherlands and weak in France and the UK. In Italy, GDP growth shows the wrong sign whatever the specification used. In this country fiscal policy is highly inertial: one explanation may be related to the high level of debt and to the ensuing burden of interest payments on Italian public finances. Another explanation is the very low level of unemployment-related expenditure, which in Italy has always been largely below 1 per cent of GDP (see Figure 7.1). In the other four countries, the inertial component is comparable. Lastly, the cyclically-adjusted deficits, captured by the constant term, are also very comparable across countries except Italy.

To assess the stability of specification (2), we performed a CUSUM test (Brown *et al.*, 1975) on the cumulative sum of the recursive residuals. The test finds parameter instability of the regression if the cumulative sum goes outside the area between the two 5 per cent critical lines. Figure 7.2 displays the results. Italy and France witnessed some instability in the coefficients, between 1985 and 1991 in the former and between 1993 and 1995 in the latter. For both countries, the improvement in the specification which occurred after these respective phases came to

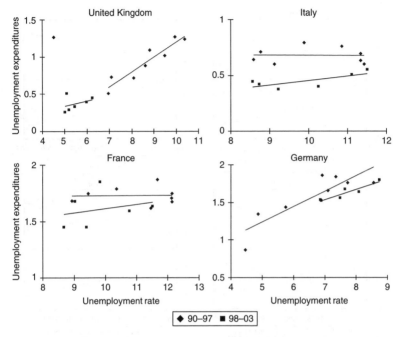

Figure 7.1 Relationships between unemployment public expenditures (expressed in percentage points of GDP) and unemployment rate, 4 main EU-15 countries, 1991–97 and 1998–2003
Source: OECD data

an end soon afterwards, although instability was not significant. In the Netherlands and the UK, the macro evidence reported in specification (2) was never significantly unstable, although the fit was continuously deteriorating from 1975 to 1990. For the UK, a new deterioration occurred between 1995 and 2000, around the implementation of the new fiscal rules. Finally, the specification for Sweden seems fairly stable.

These results confirm that macro evidence regarding automatic stabilizers is fairly robust across the time sample and it is possible to conclude that the homogeneity of imposed fiscal rules within the EU is contradictory to the heterogeneity of empirical rules since the 1970s.

Recent changes in revenue and expenditure trends: micro evidence

The working of automatic stabilizers rests predominantly on the size of the public sector, on the structure of the tax and benefit systems

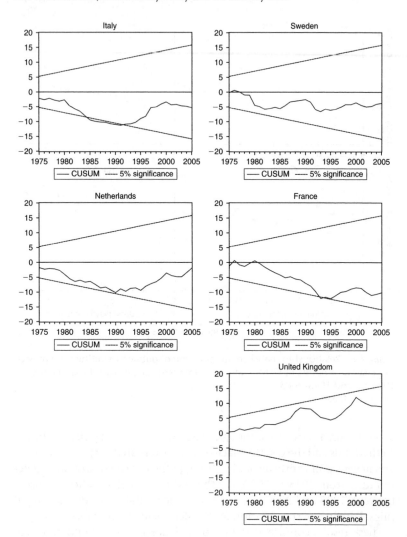

Figure 7.2   Stability of automatic stabilizers
Source: OECD data

and on the level of unemployment benefits and their sensitivity to economic fluctuations. The evolution of these factors is described in the next subsections.

The size of the public sector

With a sample of 20 OECD countries, Fatas and Mihov (2001) showed that government size and the volatility of the business cycle were

Table 7.3 General government size in the EU (in % of GDP)

		1980	1990	2000	2006
France	Total expenditure	45.6	49.6	51.6	53.5
	Total revenue	45.7	47.2	50.2	50.8
Italy	Total expenditure	40.8	52.9	46.2	49.5
	Total revenue	33.8	41.5	45.3	44.9
Netherlands	Total expenditure	55.4	54.2	44.2	46.6
	Total revenue	51.5	48.9	46.1	46.5
UK	Total expenditure	47.4	41.5	36.9	44.6
	Total revenue	41.7	39.9	40.8	41.7
Sweden	Total expenditure		72.4[1]	56.8	55.6
	Total revenue		61.1[1]	61.8	58.4
Germany	Total expenditure	47.9	44.5	45.1	45.8
	Total revenue	45.0	42.5	46.4	43.5

Note: [1] 1993
Source: European Commission, *Economic Forecasts,* Autumn 2006

negatively correlated; they concluded that larger governments had more efficient automatic stabilizers: the fact that expenditures or taxes were independent of the economic cycle was in itself a stabilizer because it was reducing volatility in the economy. Government size was measured by the ratio of public expenditures or tax revenues to GDP.

Table 7.3 displays the level and evolution of government size in 6 EU countries. A first striking result is the decrease in the discrepancy across countries, measured by the standard error: between 1980 and 2006 it was reduced by 32 per cent for total expenditures, and by 47 per cent for total revenues. The second important result is that the Netherlands, UK, Sweden and Germany have rather substantially reduced the size of their governments. For these countries, and following Fatas and Mihov (2001), it can be concluded that automatic stabilizers are today less effective than in the past. An opposite conclusion holds for France and Italy, for which government size has been on an upward trend.

The progressivity of the tax and benefit system

The progressivity of the tax and benefit system is meant to help an economy tackle ups and downs. A progressive tax system, including a generous transfer system, dampens the cycle: during the upturns, an increase of average income increases the average tax rate, thus reducing disposable income and cooling off aggregate demand. Symmetrically, during a slump, the decrease of income will entail a lower average tax rate, and hence a less than proportional decrease in disposable income, thus sustaining demand.

If, in addition, the cycle impacts differently on different income brackets (in particular, if expansions benefit the wealthiest the most), a progressive tax rate both reduces income inequalities and improves economic stabilization: during an upswing, the wealthiest pay relatively high taxes whose revenues help to reduce possible past deficits; they also improve future fiscal leeway. Meanwhile, the poorest pay relatively low taxes that help their disposable income converge towards that of the wealthiest. During a downswing, the more progressive the tax system, the higher the decrease in taxes paid by the wealthiest and the more the tax system helps to counterbalance the crisis. We can broadly speaking attribute two distinct (even if often related) objectives to a tax and benefit system: improving the situation of the poorest, on the one hand; and making the wealthiest contribute more to welfare and social expenditure, on the other hand.

Since the end of the 1990s, there has been a sharp modification in the tax and benefit systems of the EU-15 countries: In many of them the redistributive role of the system has been attenuated, while at the same time top marginal tax rates were reduced.

Aggregate data at the EU-15 level tell a mixed story. Between 1998 and 2001 (comparable data are not available for other years), the distribution of disposable income[6] remained constant, the three first deciles receiving 14 per cent of total disposable income, the next four 35 per cent, and the highest income groups more than 50 per cent. A comparison of interdecile ratios for disposable and pre-tax incomes shows instead that the EU-15 underwent a small change between 1998 and 2001: Table 7.4 shows that the benefit and tax systems permitted a reduction in inequality between Decile 5 and Decile 1 of 43.7 per cent[7] in 1998, but only of 42.0 per cent in 2001. In the meantime, redistribution between Decile 10 and Decile 5 was more substantial in 2001 than in 1998.

Here we are confronted with a specific feature of some European tax and benefit systems: For the EU-15 as a whole, the capacity of the system to redistribute between the wealthiest and the middle income deciles has increased, while redistribution between the latter and the poorest income earners has been reduced. Figure 7.3 can be illustrative in this respect. On the x-axis, a positive value means that the relative situation of households from Decile 1 has deteriorated *vis-à-vis* that of Decile 5 between 1998 and 2001. On the y-axis, a positive value means that the relative situation of households from Decile 5 has deteriorated *vis-à-vis* that of Decile 10 during the same time span. If the two above-mentioned

Table 7.4 Reduction of interdecile inequality after fiscal and social transfers, in percentage points

	D5/D1		D10/D5	
	1998	2001	1998	2001
EU-15*	−43.7	−42.0	−31.1	−32.4
France	−40.1	−37.6	−29.0	−29.4
Germany	−59.5	−63.7	−30.4	−30.6
Italy	−16.7	−17.2	−25.7	−28.7
Netherlands	−59.3	−58.4	−28.1	−23.1
Spain	−27.9	−40.8	−41.2	−30.8
Ireland	−91.7	−90.2	−33.0	−41.7
UK*	−76.4	−76.0	−35.1	−35.2

Note: * euros adjusted for PPP
Source: EUROMOD statistics on Distribution and Decomposition of Disposable Income, accessed at www.iser.essex.ac.uk/msu/emodstats/DecompStats.pdf on 1998 and 2001 using EUROMOD version 31A

objectives are reached by a country (we label it Regime 1), both values should be negative. In the case where one out of the two is reached, one value is negative whereas the other is positive: Regime 2 holds when the poorest and the wealthiest are favoured at the expense of middle-income earners; Regime 4 holds when the situation of middle-income earners improves *vis-à-vis* the poorest and the wealthiest. Finally, Regime 3 holds when the situation of the wealthiest improves *vis-à-vis* low-income and middle-income earners.

Data for EU-15 countries show that few of them have actually reached both objectives over this short period; Denmark, France, Ireland and the UK are in the same quadrant as the average of EU-15 (Regime 4), favouring middle-income earners.[8] On the opposite, Luxembourg, Spain, Sweden and, to a lesser extent, Belgium, have improved the relative situation of the poorest households, and substantially so, at the expense of middle-income earners whose relative position with respect to the wealthiest households decreased (Regime 2). Finland, the Netherlands and Portugal are all in Regime 3, witnessing a deterioration in the situations of low-income and middle-income earners, at the benefit of the wealthiest. Among the countries of the EU-15 only Austria, Germany and Italy were able to reduce both types of income inequality. However, the latter two are far from the 45° line for which the improvements in the two objectives would be comparable: Germany made more efforts for the poorest than it did to increase the contribution of the wealthiest to the tax and benefit system; the reverse is true for Italy.

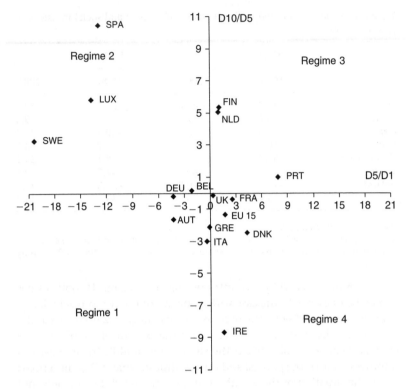

Figure 7.3   Evolution of interdecile disposable income between 1998 and 2001, EU 15

Notes: *Regime 1*: improvement in the two objectives; *Regime 2*: improvement in objective 1, deterioration in objective 2; *Regime 3*: deterioration in the two objectives; *Regime 4*: improvement in objective 2, deterioration in objective 1; *Objective 1*: reducing inequality for low-income earners; *Objective 2*: increasing the contribution effort of high-income earners
Source: EUROMOD (see Table 7.4)

To sum up, countries are quite evenly distributed across the four regimes and, except in Austria, Germany and Italy, the progressivity of the tax system decreased between 1998 and 2001 and with it, the efficiency of automatic stabilizers on the side of public receipts.

One can also assess progressivity by looking at marginal tax rates. Table 7.5 reports marginal tax rates for top-wage earners in a few European countries in 2000 and 2003. The decrease was sharp in Belgium, France, Luxembourg and Spain. A smoother decrease occurred in Germany and Italy. Table 7.6 displays corporate tax rates in EU-15 countries in 1990, 2000 and 2005. Except in Spain, corporate tax rates

Table 7.5   Marginal tax rates for top-wage earners,* in percentage points

	2000	2003		2000	2003
Belgium	60.5	53.5	Spain	48.0	45.0
France	61.2	56.1	Luxembourg	47.1	38.9
Germany	53.8	51.2	Ireland	44.0	42.0
Italy	46.4	45.9	UK	40.0	40.0

Note: * top wages are at least equal to 12 times (in 2000) and 10 times (in 2003) the average production wage
Source: OECD, *Recent Tax Policy Trends and Reforms in OECD countries*, 2004, reproduced from Saint-Etienne and Le Cacheux (2005, p. 21)

Table 7.6   Corporate tax rates, in percentage points

	1990	2000*	2005		1990	2000*	2005
Austria	30		25.0	Ireland	43 (10: industry)	24.0	12.5
Belgium	43	40.2	35.5	Italy	36	37.0	33.0
Denmark	50		28.0	Luxembourg	34	37.5	30.4
Finland	33		26.0	Netherlands	35		31.5
France	42 (distributed profit) 37 (retained profit)	37.8	34.9	Portugal	34		27.5
Germany	36 (distributed profit) 50 (retained profit)	52.0	39.3	Spain	35	35.0	35.0
Greece	46 (40: industry)		32.0	Sweden	52		28.0
EU-15	41.8		34.1	UK	35	30.0	30.0

Sources: *European Tax Handbook*, reproduced from Sterdyniak (2005, p. 24), except year 2000, reproduced from Saint-Etienne and Le Cacheux (2005, p. 22)

have decreased since 1990 or 2000. These reductions are generally meant, in a language that would not hurt the European Commission, to enhance production, incentives and entrepreneurship. In the short run, lower corporate tax rates may induce higher profitability that may fuel investment and employment. Nevertheless, they may also induce corporations to distribute more profits which may then be invested elsewhere in the world economy and which may be then missing for financing the benefit system. The decreasing size of the government may thus impair economic stability, as Fatas and Mihov (2001) argued (see earlier), but it may also fuel social unrest. This may be all the more true if marginal

Table 7.7   Marginal tax rates for dividends, in percentage points

	2000	2003		2000	2003
Belgium	49.1	43.9	Spain	52.7	50.0
France	63.2	57.0	Luxembourg	52.3	44.0
Germany	53.8	55.5	Ireland	57.4	49.3
Italy	45.9	46.1	UK	47.5	47.5

Source: OECD, *Recent Tax Policy Trends and Reforms in OECD countries*, 2004, reproduced from Saint-Etienne and Le Cacheux (2005, p. 23)

tax rates on dividends are also reduced and this is what occurred between 2000 and 2003 in Belgium, France, Spain, Luxembourg and Ireland (Table 7.7). Moreover, if lower corporate taxes do not succeed in fuelling production and growth, the consequent rise in public deficits in Europe may push governments to reduce transfers and other public expenditures; in this sense, lower taxes may have as a side effect the reduction of automatic stabilization.

Possible tensions on public finances because of lower taxes do not come exclusively from corporate tax rates: taxes on labour incomes have also decreased in the recent past (Table 7.8). Only Denmark and, to a lesser extent, Finland, Greece and Sweden, have not witnessed such a decrease. Apart from these countries, tax cuts are general and they may have a bad influence on the efficiency of future automatic stabilizers. The latter are also currently hurt by the implementation of the OECD Employment Strategy: Belgium, Denmark, Germany, Ireland, the Netherlands and UK all experienced declining replacement rates and/or shortened benefit duration.

After describing the revenue side of automatic stabilization, in the next subsection we turn to the expenditure side, more precisely to the analysis of unemployment benefits.

Unemployment expenditures

Some items of public spending, in particular those linked to the support of the unemployed, help to balance the consequences of shocks. A negative shock on aggregate demand is partly dampened by generous unemployment benefits which sustain consumption of those most dramatically hit by the shock. More active unemployment public expenditures – those labelled under the heading of active labour market policies (ALMP), mostly training – also reduce the costs of unemployment for the unemployed, promoting their employability and improving their probability of finding a new job, thus shortening unemployment

Table 7.8 Structural reforms on the labour markets, 1994–2004

	Replacement rate	Benefit duration	Taxes on labour incomes
Austria	[+, −]		+
Belgium		+	+
Denmark	+	+	−
Finland	[+, −]		[+, −]
France	−	+	+
Germany	[+, −]	+	+
Greece			[+, −]
Ireland	+		+
Italy	−		+
Luxembourg			+
Netherlands		+	+
Portugal			+
Spain	+	−	+
Sweden	[+, −]		[+, −]
UK		+	+

Notes: + reforms have been implemented in the direction of the OECD Employment Strategy; − reforms have been implemented counter to the OECD Employment Strategy; [+, −] reforms have gone in both directions
Source: OECD, *Employment Outlook*, 2006

duration. Expenditure aimed at fighting unemployment can help to maintain economic stability through a combination of supportive measures for the demand for labour and enhancing the effective supply of labour.

Consequently, we use the sum of passive *and* active unemployment public expenditures although the different choices between the two types of expenditures by EU countries may produce different lags in the stabilization properties of unemployment expenditures: passive expenditures like benefits undoubtedly impinge quicker on the aggregate demand than active expenditures which are meant to reduce the duration of unemployment for those unemployed. However, in some EU countries, the decrease of unemployment benefits cannot be separated from the increase of ALMP.

In general, the responsiveness of unemployment expenditures to the unemployment rate has decreased, thus reducing the stabilizing properties of the system. Figure 7.4 displays pairs of yearly variations[9] in unemployment public expenditures (active and passive expenditures) and yearly variations in unemployment rates, for the EU-15 countries, distinguishing two samples: 1991–97 and 1998–2003.[10]

Within this figure, we expect pairs to be evenly distributed on an upward line whose slope would reveal the average elasticity of unemployment expenditures to the unemployment rate. There is actually a very interesting pattern in Europe: since 1998, the elasticity of unemployment public expenditures to the unemployment rate has been lower than before (0.1 rather than 0.2 on average). Stated differently, the relationship between variations in unemployment expenditures and rates was more positively sloped in the preceding period despite the Maastricht public finance criteria.

It is also noteworthy that the level of unemployment expenditures for the same rate of unemployment has decreased since 1998, in comparison with the preceding period. This latter property of the European social system appears clearly in the cases of Italy, France and Germany (Figure 7.1). The UK is an outlier in this respect: With the exception of one point in the 1998–2003 sample, the relationship between unemployment expenditures and unemployment rate has hardly changed.

The stylized facts on the reduction of tax rates, the reduction in the progressivity of the tax and benefit systems, and the reduction in the generosity of the unemployment insurance system, all seem to point unequivocally towards a decrease of the effectiveness of automatic stabilization in European countries.

Therefore, public deficits may be less and less cyclical, or less and less able to dampen fluctuations. In the literature, usual assessments

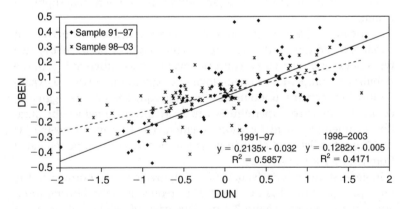

Figure 7.4   Relationships between the variation in unemployment public expenditures (expressed in percentage points of GDP) and the variation in unemployment rate, both stated in %, EU 15, 1991–97 and 1998–2003
Source: OECD data

(e.g., Girouard and André, 2005) report elasticities of taxes, transfer payments and other expenditures to GDP growth which have generally remained constant over time. Looking at unemployment expenditures only, it is however possible to suggest that for most of the EU countries their relationship with GDP growth rate has changed substantially since the end of the 1990s.

Figure 7.5 shows a dramatic change in the slope and the level of unemployment expenditures (in percentage points of GDP) versus the

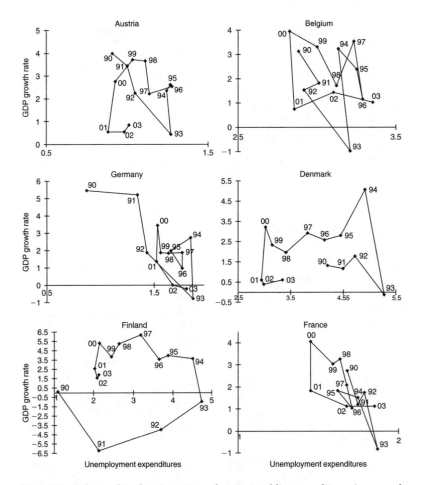

Figure 7.5 Relationships between unemployment public expenditures (expressed in percentage points of GDP) and GDP growth rate
Source: OECD data

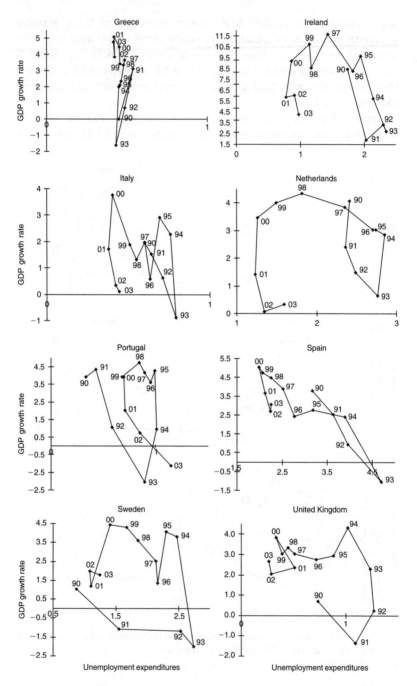

Figure 7.5 Continued

rate of economic growth.[11] In Austria, Denmark, Finland, Ireland, the Netherlands and Sweden, a positive slope emerged at the end of the 1990s: unemployment expenditures became procyclical. Moreover, for a given GDP growth rate, expenditures are substantially inferior to their level of the early 1990s, ranging from a loss of 0.5 percentage point of GDP (Austria, between 1993 and 2002), to a loss of 1.5 point (the Netherlands, between 1996 and 2000). In Germany and Spain, the negative slope has increased since 1999: the effect at the margin of the changes on the rate of economic growth on unemployment expenditures has decreased. Moreover, in Spain, for a given GDP growth rate, expenditures were 1 percentage point lower between 1990 and 2001. Exceptions are France whose negative slope has been decreasing since 2001, Greece whose a-cyclicity is obvious, Italy whose negative slope has been maintained but the level of unemployment expenditures for a given GDP growth rate has been lowered, and Portugal and the UK for which the deterioration of the automatic stabilizers occurred between 1993 and 1999 for the former and between 1991 and 1996 for the latter.

How to substitute for automatic stabilization?

If the effectiveness of automatic stabilizers has decreased, as we documented in the previous section, we need to ask whether something else could allow the system to adjust. In fact, it may be argued; e.g. by the promoters of the Classical School, that in a competitive world, where markets (for labour, goods and services or finance) are highly flexible, prices adjust rapidly to bring output fluctuations under control. The operation of automatic stabilizers could thus turn out to be less necessary than in the past.

Although the above-mentioned argument is common among economists who promote more flexibility and 'structural reforms' in Europe (see, e.g., Sapir *et al.*, 2003), it needs to be supported by identifiable empirical facts. In the vein of McConnell and Perez-Quiros (2000), who documented the decline of US output volatility, we study output volatility in Euro area countries taken as a whole, and in some EU-15 countries taken individually. We remove the mean of GDP growth from yearly GDP growth rates; we then fit a constant and a linear trend to the ensuing gap; and we perform a CUSUM and CUSUM of squares test on the cumulative sum of the recursive residuals.[12] The CUSUM of squares test reports possible instability in the variance of the parameters.

For the Euro area taken as a whole, parameter instability occurs only around the German reunification years. Nevertheless, although not

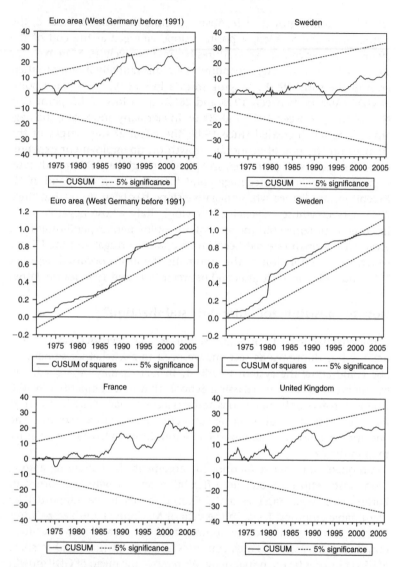

Figure 7.6   Real GDP growth rates, 1970:1–2006:2
Source: OECD data

statistically significant, parameter instability had been on an upward slope since 1985 and until 1991. The CUSUM of squares test for the Euro area detects statistically significant instability in the variance during the crisis of 1993. Movements outside the critical lines, which are suggestive

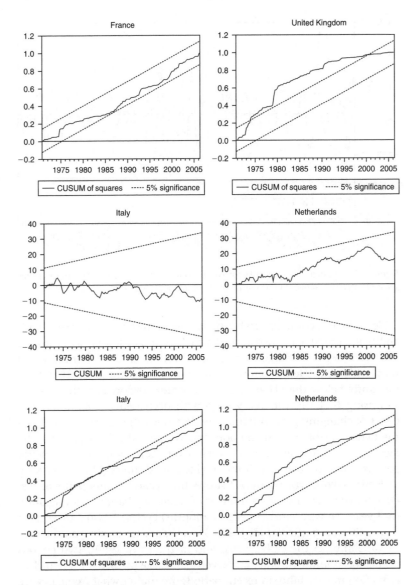

Figure 7.6 Continued

of variance instability, are also revealed in the UK from 1975 to 2000, in Italy from 1978 to 1986, in the Netherlands from 1980 to 1997, and in Sweden from 1981 to 1998 (Figure 7.6). Over the recent years, like the US, Europe seems to have experienced a decline in output volatility.

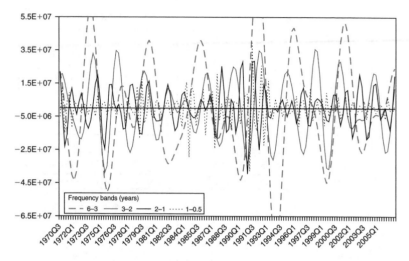

Figure 7.7   Cyclical components for the Euro area real GDP; selected frequencies
Source: OECD data; series obtained using the Iacobucci and Noullez (2005) filter

Nevertheless, contrary to what happened in the US, the decreased variability in Europe happened against a background of soft growth through
the 1990s, with the largest European countries, notably Germany and
Italy, which experienced growth rates close to zero (in 2002–3) and significantly below the EU average. In a context of low growth, it is not
surprising that the variability of growth decreased. To eliminate the
effect of changing growth trends, we detrended the series and analysed
the behaviour of cyclical components. We used the filter proposed by
Iacobucci and Noullez (2005), which, over short samples, has a better
performance compared with more widely used filters (like Baxter-King
or Hodrick-Prescott). Figure 7.7 shows the cyclical components of real
GDP for the Euro area for a number of frequency bands, from medium
(6–3 years) to very short (1 year – 6 months) cycles. A visual inspection
shows that, in particular for the 6–3 year band, we observe an increase
in variability in the early 1970s, and in the early 1990s, two periods
of macroeconomic turbulence. Nevertheless, the picture shows no clear
reduction in variability in recent periods, no matter what frequency we
examine. To obtain a less impressionist assessment, we computed, for
each of the frequency bands, the standard errors of two subperiods of
equal length (1970Q3 to 1988Q2, and 1988Q3 to 2006Q2). The results,
reported in Figure 7.8, show that for all the frequencies (except the very
long cycles 18–6 years) the variability in the second period is slightly

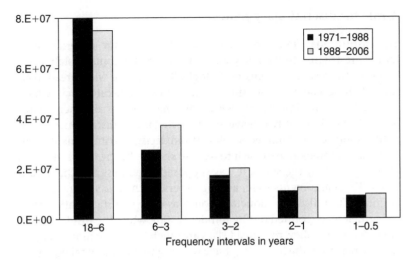

Figure 7.8 Standard error of the filtered series at different frequencies: two subsamples of equal length
Source: OECD data; series obtained using the Iacobucci and Noullez (2005) filter

larger than in the first. Using a cut-off between the periods linked to institutional changes (for example, the Single European Act of 1986, or the Maastricht Treaty of 1992), does not alter significantly our findings, which are also robust to detrending the series with the HP filter. Furthermore, this cyclical pattern is confirmed for most individual countries, with the exception of the UK.[13]

Finally, we may notice that, contrary to the US, the EU countries are confronted with a very specific policy architecture which leaves monetary and fiscal policy uncoordinated, which fetters domestic fiscal policies and whose federal budget is both small (1 percentage point of EU-25 GNP) and not allowed to contribute to stabilizing the economies.

Thus, we can conclude that the likely occurrence of asymmetric shocks in the EU and the institutional framework question the belief that increasing flexibility will be sufficient to assure income stabilization (especially when average growth will go back to more standard levels). In the next section we argue that in light of a number of recent articles on the subject, and of the decreased efficiency of automatic stabilization described above, discretionary fiscal policy should be reconsidered as a possible tool for economic stabilization, either to dampen output fluctuations or to sustain potential output through public investment expenditures.

A role for discretionary policy

The institutional framework that rules the economic governance of Europe, restricting fiscal policy to the working of automatic stabilizers, is not fortuitous, as it stems quite logically from the widespread aversion of the academic profession for discretionary fiscal policy, which emerged over the 1980s and 1990s. Four main sets of arguments have been advanced to justify this aversion: the first is that discretionary fiscal policy is subject to a number of delays (from decision to implementation) that make it impossible to use it to react to shocks. By the time the effects of policy are felt, the shock it was supposed to address may have vanished. These arguments were, among others, at the roots of the shift of attention from fiscal to monetary policy as the main stabilization tool. Nevertheless, as pointed out by Blinder (2006), while the inside lags are larger for fiscal policy, the outside lags are much longer for monetary policy. Furthermore, the inside lags have nothing to do with fiscal policy *per se*, but rather with institutions that are not always well adapted. Arestis and Sawyer (2003) made a slightly different point: they recalled that monetary policy 'being less subject to democratic decision making', it does not need Parliamentary approval. For this reason, monetary policy can be decided and implemented quickly whereas expenditure changes generally take much longer. Blinder (2006) notes that the arguments on implementation or inside lags do not hold for particular items of fiscal policy, like temporary tax cuts, that proved very effective in changing the intertemporal allocation of resources by the private sector. Arestis and Sawyer (2003) further point out that the adoption of a fiscal policy rule in the vein of the monetary 'Taylor rule', that is, with reference to deviations of economic activity from the desired level, would contribute to reducing inside lags.

The second set of arguments against discretionary fiscal policy deals with its effectiveness, originating from the rational expectations revolution, and the Lucas' Critique (Lucas, 1976). First, a fiscal expansion may crowd out private expenditure (in particular investment) up to a point at which the overall increase in income becomes negligible. This may happen because the deficit is financed through borrowing, thus increasing interest rates and the cost of investment; or because public spending is aimed at moving the economy away from some sort of optimal or 'natural' position, so that rational consumers react in order to bring the system back to its natural level. A weaker version of this argument focuses on the intertemporal budget constraint of rational consumers, who anticipate future tax increases to repay for current deficits, and hence react by increasing their current savings and reducing their expenditure (the Ricardian equivalence, see Barro, 1974).[14]

A third argument against fiscal policy discretion, made popular by the recent experience in the US, is the *twin deficits* hypothesis; based on the national accounting identity it is possible to show that an increase in budget deficit may create an equivalent deficit of the current account, so that total domestic income may not increase, and the expansionary effect may benefit other countries through increased imports.[15]

Finally, fiscal policy may be inflationary, if it succeeds in improving economic activity (thus increasing imports and putting downward pressure on the exchange rate) and reduce unemployment. In a globalized world, financial markets may react by withdrawing funds from the economy and causing a financial crisis.

Theoretical counter arguments or empirical weaknesses may be found for each of these reasons against the use of discretionary fiscal policy as a tool for stabilization. As a general first point, we can observe that these arguments are not necessarily coherent with each other: If there is crowding out then neither inflation nor twin deficits will appear.

Going more into detail, it does not seem that the link deficit-interest rate-private spending is as robust as it would seem at first sight. First, a good policy mix can allow an increase in borrowing without significant increases in interest rates. This may explain why past evidence that increases in the public debt were correlated with rises in interest rates is weak (see, e.g., Heilbroner and Bernstein, 1989). Furthermore, the empirical link between interest rates and private spending (in particular investment) is also weak (see, e.g., Ducoudré, 2005; Fazzari, 1994–95).

Another reason for the empirical weakness of the crowding out argument is the extremely restrictive set of assumptions on which Ricardian equivalence builds. If consumers for whatever reason do not discount the future perfectly, or if public expenditure is productive, and increases the future tax base, then there is no *a priori* reason for crowding out. A very simple model can also precisely highlight two other shortcomings of the Ricardian argument: it also assumes public spending irresponsibility and very few liquidity-constrained households.

Take an economy in which a proportion μ of households are liquidity constrained. As in Hayashi (1982) and Campbell and Mankiw (1990), liquidity-constrained individuals cannot borrow or lend, so that they consume all their disposable income in each period. The economy lasts 2 periods. In the first ('Keynesian'), demand drives production, while in the second ('Classical') the contrary holds. Without investment, the usual demand equations hold:

$$y_1 = c_1 + G_1 \tag{7.1}$$

$$y_2 = \bar{y} \tag{7.2}$$

where subscripts refer to time periods, y is production or demand, c is private consumption and G are public expenditures.

Unconstrained individuals smooth consumption over their entire horizon: their consumption depends on their permanent income. They maximize their intertemporal utility function subject to the usual intertemporal budget constraint:

$$Max\, u = \ln(c_1) + \beta\ln(c_2) \quad s.t.\, c_1 + c_2 = R \tag{7.3}$$

where $R = y_1 + y_2 - (T_1 + T_2)$ is lifetime income, defined as the sum of disposable incomes, β is the discount factor, and T is total taxes on individuals. To simplify the exposition and without loss of generality, a zero interest rate on savings and a constant intertemporal price of consumption are assumed. Under perfect foresight, the solution gives:

$$c_1 = \frac{1}{1+\beta}R$$

$$c_2 = \frac{\beta}{1+\beta}R \tag{7.4}$$

Aggregate consumption of liquidity-constrained and unconstrained individuals in period 1 thus writes:

$$c_1 = \mu(y_1 - T_1) + (1 - \mu)\frac{1}{1+\beta}R \tag{7.5}$$

The government has an intertemporal budget constraint (BC): $B_0 + G_1 + G_2 = T_1 + T_2$, where B_0 represents the initial level of public debt in the economy.

Following Perotti (1999), present and future public expenditures are assumed to be correlated; i.e. they follow an inertial process whose strength depends on the value of ρ:

$$G_2 = \bar{G} + \rho G_1 \tag{7.6}$$

where $\bar{G}$ are discretionary expenditures in period 2.

Defining $B_0 + \bar{G} = \Gamma$, the BC becomes:

$$\Gamma + (1 + \rho)G_1 = T_1 + T_2 \tag{7.7}$$

At equilibrium, production writes:

$$y_1 = G_1 + c_1 \tag{7.8}$$

Substituting (7.4) in (7.7) gives:

$$y_1 = G_1 + \mu(y_1 - T_1) + \frac{(1 - \mu)}{1 + \beta}(y_1 + y_2 - \Gamma - (1 + \rho)G_1)$$

$$= \frac{\beta + \mu - \rho(1 - \mu)}{\beta(1 - \mu)}G_1 - \mu\frac{1 + \beta}{\beta(1 - \mu)}T_1 + \frac{1}{\beta}(y_2 - \Gamma) \tag{7.9}$$

from which the multiplier effect of public spending on short-run GDP can be computed: $\partial y_1/\partial G_1 < 0 \Leftrightarrow \rho(1 - \mu) > \beta + \mu$. It is then straightforward to show that non-Keynesian (NK) effects occur if and only if:

$$\mu < \frac{\rho - \beta}{1 + \rho} \tag{7.10}$$

Intuitively, in this extreme framework, if an increase in expenditure today is perceived as permanent, and consumers are not patient enough, then G crowds out private expenditure and has negative effects on income. NK effects would thus appear if the degree of persistence of fiscal policy is larger than the discount factor: long-lasting expenditure cuts would improve permanent income as individuals would expect lower taxes in period 2. There are a number of reasons for considering that condition (7.10) cannot be met. First, it is really tricky to obtain: with a share of liquidity-constrained households (μ) equal to one-third, and a discount factor (β) equal to 0.95, the degree of persistence in public expenditures necessary to yield NK effect would have to be extremely high ($\rho \geq 1.95$). Second, as the fraction of liquidity-constrained agents approaches to 1, the area of NK effects decreases. Therefore, assuming NK effects is equivalent to assuming the existence of Ricardian consumers; however, the empirical validity of the second assumption is very disputable (see Ricciuti, 2003, for a recent assessment and survey of the literature). Third, a necessary, though not sufficient, condition to satisfy inequality (7.10) is $\rho > \beta$. This condition would become sufficient only if there were perfect consumption smoothing ($\mu = 0$), but again the literature holds that this is rather implausible.

If crowding out is not an automatic consequence of running a deficit, then the current account argument has to be reconsidered as well. Twin deficits are not an empirical regularity, and in fact seem to be more of a long run national accounting phenomenon, than a property that holds over the cycle when the *ex ante* equality between investment and savings is not necessarily guaranteed. Moreover, the US current account imbalances started in 1992–93, at a time when public deficits were sharply declining. Finally, there is no convincing evidence that financial markets react to 'normal' rates of inflation, and at the same time, in a situation of financial distress contractionary fiscal policies do not seem a viable solution, as proven recently by Argentina.

Beyond the 'critique to the critique', there are two prominent reasons for defending discretionary fiscal policy: First, a recent strand of literature, started by Blanchard and Perotti (2002), confirms that the empirical evidence is unable to rule out a positive role for discretionary fiscal policy. If anything, it generally shows significant short term effects and also, in some studies, a significant effect in the long-run (the multiplier values for some of these papers are reported in Table 7.9). Second, Taylor (2000) has shown that lower efficiency of automatic stabilizers in the US, assessed by the estimated response of the cyclical surplus to the output gap, has been compensated by a 'rather sizeable countercyclical' discretionary stance.

Table 7.9   Fiscal multipliers in the recent literature

	Country	Multiplier of ...	
Blanchard and Perotti (2002)	USA	expenditure	= [0.9;1.3] (short run)
Perotti (2004)	USA	expenditure	= [0.1;0.7] (short run)
			= [−1.3;1.0] (long run)
	Germany	expenditure	= [0.8;1.3] (short run)
			= [−0.7;1.1] (long run)
	UK	expenditure	= [−0.2;0.5] (short run)
			= [−1.1;0.8] (long run)
	Canada	expenditure	= [0.1;0.6] (short run)
			= [−2.2;0.9] (long run)
	Australia	expenditure	= [0.0;0.6] (short run)
			= [0.2;0.6] (long run)
Biau and Girard (2005)	France	expenditure	= 1.4 (short run)
			= 1.8 (long run)
Giordano *et al.* (2006)	Italy	expenditure	= 1.7 (short run)
Creel *et al.* (2007a)	France	primary balance	= 0.8 (short run)
			= 2.0 (long run)
Creel *et al.* (2007b)	UK	investment	= 3.1 (long run)

A similar exercise was conducted by Farvaque *et al.* (2006) on EU countries, but results in terms of countercyclical discretionary stance were much less pronounced than in the US case.

The papers in the vein of Blanchard and Perotti (2002) borrow from the structural VAR methodology. Very simple reduced form VAR models are estimated, and then the identification is obtained by imposing to the contemporaneous residual correlation matrix a number of constraints that originate in the institutional system, in estimated elasticities, and so on. Contrary to Taylor's methodology, Blanchard and Perotti (2002) have attempted to extract purely discretionary fiscal components. They did not use computed structural deficits which rely on estimations of the output gap and the biases they are associated with. Moreover, the discretionary stance has been corrected for interest payments.

The impulse response functions for these exercises usually show short-term Keynesian effects across countries (Biau and Girard, 2005; Blanchard and Perotti, 2002; Giordano *et al.*, 2006; Perotti, 2004). Perotti (2004) is an exception in this respect: he found low and even negative fiscal spending multipliers in the short run in the UK, Australia and Canada, depending on the sample (1960–2000, 1960–79, 1980–2000). Creel *et al.* (2007a, b) recently extended this methodology by imposing longer-run constraints (namely through the introduction of a debt accumulation equation); neglecting these constraints, as done in the existing literature did not seem justified, especially when trying to assess the effect of public investment. They show that, if the long-term interaction between debt, fiscal policy and monetary policy is not artificially shut off, the long-run multiplier remains significantly positive and equal to 2 in France after a discretionary shock on the primary deficit and to 3 in the UK after a discretionary shock on public investment.

It is, therefore, possible to conclude that, on empirical grounds, a discretionary fiscal policy has a positive and persistent impact on output. From a short-run perspective, it also means that this policy has an impact on long-run economic growth, hence it has an impact on potential output. This empirical conclusion is consistent with a strand of the literature that argues that the natural rate of growth is sensitive to aggregate demand (see, e.g., Leon-Ledesma and Thirlwall, 2002) or with papers that argue that fiscal contractions impinge negatively on potential output, since 'the failure to use expansionary fiscal policy when slack resources exist could lead to a prolonged period of wasted economic potential' (Fazzari, 1994–95, p. 245).

Concluding remarks

In this chapter we highlighted a contradiction between the spirit of the Stability and Growth Pact, and the actual behaviour of fiscal policies in Europe. On the one hand the former is designed with the objective to rule out any discretion in the conduct of fiscal policy, thus leaving to automatic stabilization the exclusive burden of countercyclical policy; on the other hand, though, a number of stylized facts that we reported in the chapter point to a significant decrease of the role of automatic stabilization. Progressivity of the tax system and the size of the public sector have been reduced in most European countries, and structural breaks in the sensitivity of public spending to GDP changes appeared in the 1990s.

Thus, even if we were to adhere to the principles behind the setting chosen by European countries to rule economic policy, and we gave importance only to automatic stabilization, we would be forced to admit that nowadays fiscal policy in the EMU is mostly dysfunctional.[16]

We believe that this moment of crisis may actually be an opportunity. The debate opened at the beginning of this decade on the flaws of the Stability Pact has been closed by the reform of 2005 that took it out of the political agenda. Maybe that reform was too hasty, and what is needed is a more radical rethinking of the framework for fiscal policy. This chapter and the small illustrative model that we have presented suggest that a reformed fiscal rule for Europe should leave some room for discretionary policy. In particular we believe that the countries of the Euro area should learn from the successful experience of the UK (see Creel *et al.*, 2007b), and implement some form of 'golden rule' to encourage long-term public spending (investment, but also expenditure on crucial items like public health and education), without hampering the long-term sustainability of public finances.

Acknowledgements

The chapter is based on a paper prepared for the conference on 'Current Thinking on Fiscal Policy', OFCE/Sciences Po, Paris, 15 June 2007. We are grateful for the comments by the participants. We also wish to gratefully acknowledge comments by and discussion with Philip Arestis, Gerard Cornilleau, Giuseppe Fontana, Malcolm Sawyer, and Henri Sterdyniak. Alessandra Iacobucci has been very helpful in explaining her filtering method. Correspondence should be sent to Jérôme Creel, OFCE, 69 Quai d'Orsay, 75007 Paris. +33-1-44185456, jerome.creel@sciences-po.fr.

Notes

1. For detailed accounts of the debate on reforming the Pact, see, e.g., Arestis *et al.* (2001), Buti *et al.* (2003), Creel *et al.* (2002), Farina and Tamborini (2007), Fitoussi and Le Cacheux (2007), Mathieu and Sterdyniak (2003) and Monperrus-Veroni and Saraceno (2005).
2. A third proposition could be to rebuild the effectiveness of the automatic stabilizers (Solow, 2004), but their effectiveness has been deteriorating so much over the years in Europe that a dramatic U-turn is needed to compensate. Moreover, time elapsed before automatic stabilizers become effective again will be very long. Implementing discretionary fiscal policies may give quicker results.
3. While it is not the main subject of this chapter, it is nevertheless worth mentioning the inconsistency of the framework, which leaves to monetary policy the task of reacting to common output shocks, while at the same time explicitly limiting its mandate to inflation targeting (article 4.2 of the Treaty). This leaves in fact an objective (reaction to common output shocks) without assigned instruments.
4. By this we mean that automatic stabilizers are more effective if, e.g., main tax revenues come from taxes which are very sensitive to economic fluctuations and whose lags are short. For example, corporate taxes have generally been very sensitive to the economic cycle but delays in collection have reduced the overall effectiveness of this tax as a prominent automatic stabilizer.
5. Contrary to the other studies, the one based upon NiGEM introduces rational expectations by households on future fiscal policy. In this context, which draws heavily on some sort of Ricardian equivalence, it is normal that the effectiveness of fiscal policy is small.
6. Disposable income is original income (from employment, investment, private pension) minus taxes plus received benefits, from maternity allowances to public pensions.
7. In 1998, for the EU-15 countries on average, the ratio of Decile 5 to Decile 1 original income was equal to 473 per cent; with disposable income data, it was equal to 266 per cent. Thus, we have a variation of minus 43.7 per cent.
8. The situation of the 'middle-class' in these societies is well beyond the scope of this chapter, which intends to give some macroeconomic and microeconomic clues on the efficiency of automatic stabilizers. By 'middle-income earners', we only refer to Decile 5. It is possible that the 'middle-class' starts at, say, Decile 4 or 6 and, were it the case, conclusions related to the possible improvement or deterioration *vis-à-vis* the 'upper-class' (also to be strictly defined) might be different.
9. With a short sample it is not possible to perform a panel test with fixed effects, so that we chose the specification in first differences to remove country effects.
10. The Amsterdam Treaty in 1997 made clear that the transition period towards the adoption of the Euro would not be followed by a benign-neglect attitude towards public deficits: the convergence criterion of a public deficit below 3 percentage points of GDP was soon to become a rule of conduct within the newly constituted Euro area.

11. Here we assume that the relationship between the unemployment rate and economic growth has remained unchanged.
12. A well-known drawback with a CUSUM test based upon recursive residuals is that a shift late in a sample is likely to go relatively unnoticed. A CUSUM test using OLS residuals gives better results for late-sample data, but none of the tests can be considered significantly superior to the other (Ploberger and Krämer, 1992).
13. Figures are not reported. They are available from the authors upon request.
14. A strand of the literature, that on 'expansionary fiscal contractions', has largely stemmed from a mix of this equivalence and credibility issues influencing risk premia (see Hemming *et al.*, 2002, for a general survey; and Creel *et al.*, 2004, for a critical one).
15. It must be acknowledged that though twin deficit is an accounting identity (under the assumption of constant net private savings), at another level it tends to be seen as 'budget deficits cause current account deficits'. It is worth distinguishing between the formal accounting position and the causal relationship which is often postulated. We discuss below that empirical evidence on the causal relationships has not been convincing so far.
16. Andres *et al.* (2008) show that government size and the volatility of output are negatively correlated, arguing then that this stylized fact cannot be replicated in a real-business cycle model. They conclude that 'models with Keynesian features can better replicate the empirical evidence on the effects of fiscal policy on the volatility of output fluctuations'. Nevertheless, they do not conclude that a fiscal framework where automatic stabilizers are made less and less efficient is dysfunctional.

References

Andres, J., Domenech, R. and Fatas, A. (2008) 'The stabilizing role of government size', *Journal of Economic Dynamics and Control*, 32, 571–93.

Arestis, P. and Sawyer, M. (2003) 'Reinventing fiscal policy', *Journal of Post-Keynesian Economics*, 26(1), 3–25.

Arestis, P., McCauley, K. and Sawyer, M. (2001) 'An alternative stability pact for the European Union', *Cambridge Journal of Economics*, 25(1), 113–30.

Barrell, R. and Pina, A.M. (2004) 'How important are automatic stabilisers in Europe? A stochastic simulation assessment', *Economic Modelling*, 21(1), 1–35.

Barro, R.J. (1974) 'Are government bonds net wealth?', *Journal of Political Economy*, 82(6), 1095–117.

Biau, O. and Girard, E. (2005) 'Politique budgétaire et dynamique économique en France: l'approche VAR Structurel', *Revue économique*, 56(3), 755–64.

Blanchard, O. and Perotti, R. (2002) 'An empirical characterization of the dynamic effects of changes in government spending and taxes on output', *Quarterly Journal of Economics*, 117(4), 1329–68.

Blinder, A.S. (2006) 'The case against the case against discretionary fiscal policy', in R.W. Kopcke, G.M.B. Tootell and R.K. Triest (eds), *The Macroeconomics of Fiscal Policy*, Cambridge and London: MIT Press, pp. 25–61.

Brown, R.L., Durbin, J. and Evans, J.M. (1975) 'Techniques for testing the constancy of regression relationships over time', *Journal of the Royal Statistical Society*, Series B, 37n, 149–92.

Brunila, A., Buti, M. and Veld, J. In't (2002) 'Fiscal policy in Europe: How effective are automatic stabilisers?', *European Economy, Economic Papers*, 1, no. 77-2002.

Buti, M., Eijffinger, S.C.W. and Franco, D. (2003) 'Revisiting the SGP: Grand design or internal adjustment?', *CEPR Discussion Paper*, no.3692, January.

Campbell, J.Y. and Mankiw, N.G. (1990) 'Permanent income, current income, and consumption', *Journal of Business and Economic Statistics*, 8(3), 265–79.

Creel, J., Ducoudré, B., Mathieu, C., Saraceno, F. and Sterdyniak, H. (2004) 'Should we forget fiscal stabilisation policies? A critical survey of the new anti-Keynesian view of public finances', paper presented at the 1st Euroframe Conference, Paris, June.

Creel, J., Latreille, T. and Le Cacheux, J. (2002) 'Le Pacte de Stabilité et les politiques budgétaires dans l'Union européenne', *Revue de l'OFCE*, 245–97.

Creel, J., Monperrus-Veroni, P. and Saraceno, F. (2007a) 'Politique budgétaire discrétionnaire en France: Les effets à court et à long terme', *Revue économique*, 58(5), 1035–53.

Creel, J., Monperrus-Veroni, P. and Saraceno, F. (2007b) 'Has the Golden Rule of public finance made a difference in the United Kingdom?', *OFCE Working Papers*, 2007–13.

De Grauwe, P. (2003) 'The Stability and Growth Pact in need of reform', *mimeo*, University of Leuven.

Ducoudré, B. (2005) 'Fiscal policy and interest rates', *OFCE Working Paper*, 2005–08.

European Commission (2001) 'Public finances in EMU – 2001', *European Economy*, 3.

Farina, F. and Ricciuti, R. (2006) 'L'évaluation des politiques budgétaires en Europe', *Revue de l'OFCE*, 99, 275–301.

Farina, F. and Tamborini, R. (eds) (2007) *Economic Policy in the EMU. From the Old to the New Stability and Growth Pact*, London: Routledge.

Farvaque, E., Huart, F. and Vaneecloo, C. (2006) 'Taylor's fiscal rule: An exit to the Stability and Growth Pact dead-end?', *Acta Oeconomica*, 56(3), 323–40.

Fatas, A. and Mihov, I. (2001) 'Government size and automatic stabilisers: International and intranational evidence', *Journal of International Economics*, 56(1), 3–28.

Fazzari, S.M. (1994–95) 'Why doubt the effectiveness of Keynesian fiscal policy?', *Journal of Post-Keynesian Economics*, 17(2), 231–48.

Fitoussi, J.-P. and Le Cacheux, J. (eds) (2007) *Report on the State of the European Union*, Vol. 2. Basingstoke: Palgrave Macmillan.

Gali, J. and Perotti, R. (2003) 'Fiscal policy and monetary integration in Europe', *Economic Policy*, 18(37), 533–72.

Giordano, R., Momigliano, S., Neri, S. and Perotti, R. (2006) 'The effects on the economy of shocks to different government expenditures items: Estimates with a SVAR model', *Proceedings of the Workshop on Public Expenditure 2005*, Roma: Banca d'Italia.

Girouard, N. and André, C. (2005) 'Measuring cyclically-adjusted budget balances for OECD countries', *OECD Economics Department Working Paper*, 434.

Hayashi, F. (1982) 'The permanent income hypothesis: Estimation and testing by instrumental variables', *Journal of Political Economy*, 90(5), 895–916.

Hemming, R., Kell, M. and Mahfouz, S. (2002) 'The effectiveness of fiscal policy in stimulating economic activity – a review of the literature', *IMF Working Paper*, 208.

Heilbroner, R.L. and Bernstein, P.L. (1989) *The Debt and the Deficit: False Alarms/Real Possibilities*, New York: Norton.

Iacobucci, A. and Noullez, A. (2005) 'A frequency selective filter for short-length time series,' *Computational Economics*, 25(1–2), 75–102.

Leon-Ledesma, M.A. and Thirlwall, A.P. (2002) 'The endogeneity of the natural rate of growth', *Cambridge Journal of Economics*, 26(4), 441–59.

Lucas, R.E. Jr. (1976) 'Econometric policy evaluation: A critique', in K. Brunner and A.H. Meltzer (eds), *The Phillips Curve and Labor Markets, Carnegie-Rochester Conference Series on Public Policy*, 1, 19–46.

Mathieu, C. and Sterdyniak, H. (2003) 'Réformer le Pacte de Stabilité: l'état du débat', *Revue de l'OFCE*, 84, 145–79.

McConnell, M.M. and Perez-Quiros, G. (2000) 'Output fluctuations in the US: What has changed since the early 1980s?', *American Economic Review*, 90(5), 1464–76.

Monperrus-Veroni, P. and Saraceno, F. (2005) 'Reform of the Stability and Growth Pact: Reducing or increasing the nuisance?', *OFCE Working Paper*, 2005–01.

Perotti, R. (1999) 'Fiscal policy in good times and bad', *Quarterly Journal of Economics*, 114(4), 1399–436.

Perotti, R. (2004) 'Estimating the effects of fiscal policy in OECD countries', *IGIER Working Paper*, 276.

Ploberger, W. and Krämer, W. (1992) 'The CUSUM test with OLS residuals', *Econometrica*, 60(2), 271–85.

Ricciuti, R. (2003) 'Assessing Ricardian equivalence', *Journal of Economic Surveys*, 17(1) (February), 55–78.

Saint-Etienne, C. and Le Cacheux, J. (2005) 'Croissance équitable et concurrence fiscale', *Rapport du Conseil d'analyse économique*, 56, La Documentation française, October.

Sapir, A., Aghion, P., Bertola, G., Hellwig, M., Pisani-Ferry, J., Rosati, D., Vinals, J. and Wallace, H. (2003) *An Agenda for a Growing Europe*, Oxford: Oxford University Press.

Scharnagl, M. and K-H. Tödter (2004) 'How effective are automatic stabilisers? Theory and empirical results for Germany and other OECD countries', *Deutsche Bundesbank Discussion Paper*, 21.

Solow, R.M. (2004) 'Is fiscal policy possible? Is it desirable?', in *Structural Reform and Economic Policy*, International Economic Association Conference Vol. 139. Basingstoke, UK and New York: Palgrave Macmillan, pp. 23–39.

Sterdyniak, H. (2005) 'Taxation in Europe: Towards more competition or more co-ordination', *OFCE Working Paper*, 2005–19.

Taylor, J.B. (2000) 'Reassessing discretionary fiscal policy', *Journal of Economic Perspectives*, 14(3), 21–36.

Van den Noord, P. (2000) 'The size and role of automatic stabilisers in the 1990s and beyond', *OECD Economics Department Working Paper*, 230.

8
Fiscal and Monetary Policies in a Keynesian Stock-Flow Consistent Model

Edwin Le Heron

Following the New Classical Macroeconomics (NCM) and the New Keynesian Macroeconomics (NKM), the independence of central banks significantly increased after 1990, which could preclude coordination between the fiscal and the monetary policies. The purpose of this chapter is to consider the stabilizing effects of fiscal policy within the framework of the new monetary policies implemented by independent central banks. We contrast a rule on public expenditures with a rule on public deficits. In order to do so, we develop a two-country model. In the first country, the government implements a fiscal policy with automatic stabilizers and a central bank, like the Fed, has a dual mandate: inflation and growth. There is a coordination between fiscal and monetary policies. The second country respects the Maastricht treaty of the European Union. The government implements an orthodox fiscal policy (balanced budget) and a fully independent central bank, like the ECB, has a unique objective: inflation.

In the first part of the chapter, we build a Post-Keynesian stock-flow consistent (SFC) model (Dos Santos and Zezza, 2004; Godley and Lavoie, 2007; Lavoie and Godley, 2001; Mouakil, 2006) with a private bank sector introducing more realistic features. We introduce the borrower's and the lender's risks from the Minskian approach. New Keynesian Macroeconomics replaces the three equations of the Keynesian synthesis by three new equations of the new consensus: an IS relation, a Taylor Rule (TR) (Taylor, 1993) and a New Keynesian Phillips Curve (NKPC) (Taylor, 1979). the IS-LM-Phillips Curve has been changed into IS-TR-NKPC. Our Post Keynesian SFC model (59 equations) replaces the IS relation. Then, we add two of the three equations of the new consensus in macroeconomics: a Taylor rule and a NKPC. IS-TR-NKPC is changed in SFC-TR-NKPC.

In the second part, we simulate the model to study the stabilizing effects of fiscal policy. The aim is to analyse the consequences of a supply shock within our two assumptions on the policy mix. If the society seeks three aims: stability of prices, full employment and stability on the financial markets, we can measure the welfare performance of our policy mix by their welfare cost deduced from the loss function of the society. We make a comparison for the two countries.

A Post-Keynesian stock-flow consistent growth model with a full banking sector, a Taylor rule and a new Keynesian Phillips curve

Building a stock-flow consistent model requires three steps: writing the matrices, counting the variables and the accounting identities issued from the matrices, and defining each unknown with an equation (accounting identity or behavioural equation).

Matrices

Five sectors form our economy: government; firms; households; private banks and central bank. All production must be financed. However, current production is financed by the working capital of entrepreneurs (retained earnings) and by contracted revolving funds granted by banks at the current rate of interest. These two factors constitute a shock absorber to possible monetary rationing by banks. We are essentially limiting our study to the effects that monetary policy might have on new financing for investment and growth of production.

Let us proceed to examine the gross supply (φ) and the net supply (ΔF) of finance by banks – that is to say, the new flow of money, as opposed to the existing stock of money (D). Also, there is a stock of money demand equal to transaction, precaution, finance and speculative motives, whereas the desired gross finance demand (φ^d) represents the new flow of financing required by firms (I^d) plus the redemption of the debt (amortization = amort) minus the undistributed profits (P^u). Thus the internal funds of firms (IF) represent the undistributed profits (P^u) minus the redemption of the debt (amort). Assuming a closed economy, demand for money can be satisfied by banks, either by the stock markets or by credit. At the end of the period, net financing demand (ΔF_D) can be constrained by net money supply from banks (ΔF) (granted financing – paid off financing – amortization). ΔF determines monetary creation in the period.

We discuss here a closed economy. Firms issue equities, bonds with fixed rates of interest and commercial papers, and borrow money from banks to finance investments but never hold money balances. They have excess capacity but no inventories.[1] Two factors are involved in producing goods (fixed capital and labour), but we deal with a vertically integrated sector and hence ignore all intermediate goods. Banks have no operating costs and they don't make loans to households. Contrary to Lavoie and Godley (2001), private banks own a net wealth and retain all their profits.

The central bank has neither operating costs nor net worth. The central bank pays all its profits to the government, which collects taxes from households and finances its deficit by issuing Treasury bills. Government expenditures are only final sales of consumption goods: there is neither operating costs (like wages for state employees) nor transfers between households. The financial behaviour of households is simplified: they hold only banking deposit accounts (current accounts and time deposits).

SFC modelling is based on two tables: a balance sheet matrix (stocks) and a transactions matrix (flows). Table 8.1 gives the transactions matrix that describes monetary flows between the five sectors of the economy. Every row represents a monetary transaction, and every column corresponds to a sector, which is fragmented in a current and a capital account, except in basic cases such as the government and that of households. Sources of funds appear with plus signs and uses of funds with negative signs, so every row must sum to zero seeing that each transaction corresponds always simultaneously to a source and a use of funds. The sum of each column must also be zero since each account (or sub-account) is balanced.

Table 8.2 gives the balance sheet matrix of our economy. Symbols with plus describe assets and negative signs indicate liabilities. The sum of every row is again zero except in the case of accumulated capital in the industrial sector. The last row presents the net wealth of each sector.

Variables and accounting identities

Building a model that describes the monetary economy of production discussed above in a consistent way requires that the transactions matrix should be properly translated into equations. First, the model must contain the 26 variables of the matrix. Each of these 26 variables can be associated with the behaviour of one of the five sectors of our economy.

Table 8.1 Transactions matrix

Sector / Operation	Govt	Firms Current	Firms Capital	Households	Private banks Current	Private banks Capital	Central Bank (CB) Current	Central Bank (CB) Capital	Σ
Consumption		$+C$		$-C$					0
Government expenditures	$-G$	$+G$							0
Net investment		$+I$	$-I$						0
Wages		$-W$		$+W$					0
Taxes	$+T$			$-T$					0
Interest on Treasury Bills	$-i_{b-1} \cdot B_{-1}$				$+i_{b-1} \cdot B_{-1}$				0
Interest on loans		$-i_{l-1} \cdot L_{-1}$			$+i_{l-1} \cdot L_{-1}$				0
Interest on comm. paper		$-i_{cp-1} \cdot CP_{-1}$			$+i_{cp-1} \cdot CP_{-1}$				0
Interest on bonds		$-i_{of} \cdot of_{-1}$			$+i_{of} \cdot of_{-1}$				0
Interest on bank deposits				$+i_{d-1} \cdot D_{-1}$	$-i_{d-1} \cdot D_{-1}$				0
Interest on CB advances					$-i_{cb-1} \cdot REF_{-1}$		$+i_{cb-1} \cdot REF_{-1}$		0
Profits of firms		$-P$	$+P^u$	$+P^d$					0
Profits of banks					$-P_b$	$+P_b$			0
Profits of CB	$+P_{cb}$						$-P_{cb}$		0
Δ HPM						$-\Delta H$		$+\Delta H$	0
Δ T Bills	$+\Delta B$					$-\Delta B$			0
Δ equities			$+\Delta e \cdot p_e$			$-\Delta e \cdot p_e$			0
Δ loans			$+\Delta L$			$-\Delta L$			0
Δ commercial paper			$+\Delta CP$			$-\Delta CP$			0
Δ bonds			$+\Delta of \cdot p_{of}$			$-\Delta of \cdot p_{of}$			0
Δ bank deposits				$-\Delta D$		$+\Delta D$			0
Δ CB advances						$+\Delta REF$		$-\Delta REF$	0
Σ	0	0	0	0	0	0	0	0	0

148

Table 8.2 Balance sheet matrix

Sector Assets	Government	Firms	Households	Private banks	Central Bank	Σ
Capital		$+K$				$+K$
HPM high powered money				$+H$	$-H$	0
Treasury Bills	$-B$			$+B$		0
Equities		$-e \cdot p_e$		$+e \cdot p_e$		0
Loans		$-L$		$+L$		0
Commercial paper		$-CP$		$+CP$		0
Bonds (fixed-yield)		$-of \cdot p_{of}$		$+of \cdot p_{of}$		0
Bank deposits			$+D$	$-D$		0
CB advances				$-REF$	$+REF$	0
Net wealth	$-B$	$+V_f$	$+D$	$+V_b$	0	$+K$

Government: G, T, B, i_b
Firms: I, W, P, P^u, P^d, e
Households: C, D
Private banks: i_l, L, i_{cp}, CP, i_{of}, p_{of}, of, p_e, i_d, P_b
Central Bank: H, i_{cb}, REF, P_{cb}

Second, we must use the accounting identities resulting from each row and each column sum to zero. We have nine accounting identities corresponding to the eight columns of the transactions matrix and to the non-ordinary row.[2] To start we transcribe the identities (uses of funds on the left side, sources of funds on the right side) without being precise how we will use them in the model:

(i) $G + (i_{b-1} \cdot B_{-1}) \equiv T + P_{cb} + \Delta B$

(ii) $W + (i_{l-1} \cdot L_{-1}) + (i_{cp-1} \cdot CP_{-1}) + (i_{of} \cdot of_{-1}) + P \equiv C + I + G$

(iii) $I \equiv P^u + (\Delta e \cdot p_e) + \Delta L + \Delta CP + (\Delta of \cdot p_{of}) \equiv \varphi + P^u - amort$

(iv) $C + T + \Delta D \equiv W + (i_{d-1} \cdot D_{-1})$

(v) $(i_{d-1} \cdot D_{-1}) + (i_{cb-1} \cdot REF_{-1}) + P_b \equiv (i_{b-1} \cdot B_{-1}) + (i_{l-1} \cdot L_{-1}) + (i_{cp-1} \cdot CP_{-1}) + (i_{of} \cdot of_{-1}) + P^d$

(vi) $\Delta H + \Delta B + (\Delta e \cdot p_e) + \Delta L + \Delta CP + (\Delta of \cdot p_{of}) \equiv P_b + \Delta D + \Delta REF$

(vii) $P_{cb} \equiv i_{cb-1} \cdot REF_{-1}$

(viii) $\Delta REF \equiv \Delta H$

(ix) $P \equiv P^u + P^d$

A feature of SFC models is that if there are M columns and N non ordinary rows in the transactions matrix, then there are only $(M+N-1)$ independent accounting identities in the model. Because of this one equation must be dropped: we shall use exactly eight accounting identities in the model. Concerning the balance sheet matrix, it is simpler: we just make sure that initial values of stocks are consistent with the matrix. In the following periods, stocks will stay consistent since our eight identities will generate consistent flows. Now we must define every variable relative to the five sectors using an accounting identity[3] or a behavioural equation. When we introduce new unknowns in a behavioural equation we define them immediately so that our model should have the same number of equations as unknowns.

The national income (Y) adds the household consumption (C), investment of the firms (I) and the public expenditure (G). The rate of growth of the national income is gr_y:

$$Y = C + I + G \tag{8.1}$$

$$gr_y = \Delta Y / Y_{-1} \tag{8.2}$$

Two fiscal policies for the government: G, T, B, i_b

The government collects only taxes from households (on wages):

$$T = \tau \cdot W_{-1} \quad \text{with } \tau \text{ constant} \tag{8.3}$$

The government finances any deficit by issuing bills, so that the supply of treasury bills (B) in the economy is identical to the stock of government debt. In other words, it is given by the pre-existing stock of debt plus its current deficit (GD). The current deficit of the government includes the redemption of the National debt. We assume that private banks give limitless credit to the government at the long-term rate of interest:

$$B = B_{-1} + GD \tag{8.4}$$

$$i_b = i_l \tag{8.5}$$

To analyse the consequences of a supply shock, we assume two different assumptions for the fiscal policy. We contrast a rule on public expenditures (F1) with a rule on public deficits (F2).

Assumption 1 (F1): A stabilizing effect of the fiscal policy

First, we assume that public expenditure (G) is always growing at the same rate (gr_y) as the national income (Y). With F1, public expenditure is pro-cyclical, because G falls with the GDP. But the final effect of the fiscal policy is measured by the government deficit (GD). Tax revenue is proportional to income and hence varies in line with the public expenditure. But with a contractionary monetary policy and its higher interest rate, the financial costs of the national debt increase. The global impact is linked to the key interest rate and, then, to the monetary policy. It looks like a coordination between the monetary and the fiscal policies. With F1, the economy has a self-stabilizing tendency due to the fiscal policy, though the fiscal policy effect comes through the effects of interest rate on the budget deficit:

$$G = G_{-1} \cdot (1 + gr_{y-1}) \qquad (8.6\text{-F1})$$

$$GD = G + (i_{b-1} \cdot B_{-1}) - T - P_{cb} \qquad (8.7\text{-i-F1})$$

Assumption 2 (F2): a 'neutral' fiscal policy as in the European Union

Second, we assume that a 'neutral' fiscal policy corresponds to a constant ratio (r_{GD}) of government deficit-to-the last national income: DB/Y_{-1}. This is more or less the case of the Maastricht treaty of the European Union. The stability and growth pact of the Treaty decrees that 'Member States shall avoid excessive government deficits'. Compliance with this requirement is assessed on the basis of a maximum value for the government deficit-to-GDP ratio of 3%, and a maximum value for the government debt-to-GDP ratio of 60%. Then we use the first accounting identity to calculate the adequate public expenditure. In experiences, we shall take the ratio (r_{GD}) equal to zero as is required by the Maastricht treaty. Contrary to the previous assumption, the public debt is zero, since the budget is balanced. As the interest rate does not act on fiscal policy, there is no coordination between the fiscal and the monetary policies:

$$GD = r_{GD} \cdot Y_{-1} \qquad \text{with } r_{GD} \text{ constant} \qquad (8.6\text{-F2})$$

$$G \equiv GD - (i_{b-1} \cdot B_{-1}) + T + P_{cb} \qquad (8.7\text{-i-F2})$$

With these assumptions, we should better understand the links between monetary policy and fiscal policy (Figure 8.1). In all the figures (except Figure 8.4) values on the vertical axis are such that the steady state equals one.

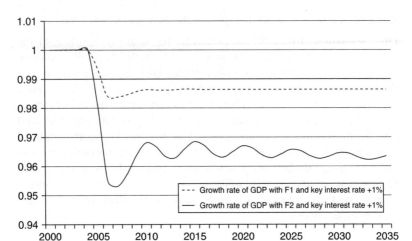

Figure 8.1   Higher key interest rate (from 2 to 3% after 2005): effects on the growth rate of the economy with F1 and F2

Firms: *I*, *W*, *P*, P^u, P^d, *e*, *OG*

The investment function is the most important one in a growth model. The stock of capital increases with the flow of net investment (*I*) that is financed by the total of external funds from commercial banks (gross finance = φ) and by the internal funds of firms. The self-financing of firms corresponds to the retained earnings (P^u) minus the redemption of the debts of firms (amort). Amortization concerns only the debt: loans (*L*), bonds (*OF*) and commercial papers (*CP*):

$$K = K_{-1} + I \tag{8.8}$$

$$I \equiv \varphi + IF \tag{8.9-iii}$$

$$IF = P^u - \text{amort} \tag{8.10}$$

$$\text{amort} = (a_l \cdot L_{-1}) + (a_{of} \cdot of_{-1}) + (a_{cp} \cdot CP_{-1}) \tag{8.11}$$

In our model, we focus on the difference between actual investment (*I*) and the desired investment of firms (I_D). The banks agree to finance totally or in part, the latter according to their lender's risk (*LR*) (see equations 8.32, 8.33 and 8.35). A monetary rationing on investment can exist

$(\varphi < \varphi^d$ or $I < I_D)$. The desired rate of accumulation (gr_{kD}) is a function of an exogenous state of confidence (γ_0), the capacity utilization rate (u) and of the borrower's risk (BR), which is measured by the rate of cash flow (r_{cf}) and by the financial condition index (FCI). The rate of cash flow is the ratio of retained earnings to capital and the financial condition index captures the sensitivity of investment to the long-term interest rate, to the short-term interest rate and to the financial capitalization ratio. The lender's risk and the borrower's risk come from the analysis of Minsky:

$$I_D = gr_{kD} \cdot K - 1 \tag{8.12}$$

$$\varphi^d = I^d - IF \tag{8.13}$$

$$gr_{kD} = \gamma_0 + (\gamma_1 \cdot r_{cf-1}) + (\gamma_2 \cdot u_{-1}) - (\gamma_3 \cdot FCI_{-1}) \quad \text{with } \gamma_i \text{ constant} \tag{8.14}$$

where the rate of capacity utilization is defined as the ratio of output to full capacity output (Y_{fc}):

$$r_{cf} = P^u / K_{-1} \tag{8.15}$$

$$u = Y / Y_{fc} \tag{8.16}$$

The capital-to-full capacity ratio (σ) is defined as a constant:

$$Y_{fc} = K_{-1} \cdot \sigma \quad \text{with } \sigma \text{ constant} \tag{8.17}$$

$$FCI = (\mu_1 \cdot i_l \cdot L/K) + (\mu_2 \cdot i_{cb} \cdot CP/K) - (\mu_3 \cdot E/Y) \quad \text{with } \mu_i \text{ constants} \tag{8.18}$$

Concerning wages, they can be decomposed into a unit wage (w) times the level of employment (N):

$$W = w \cdot N \tag{8.19a}$$

where employment is determined by sales given productivity (σ_2):

$$N = Y / \sigma_2 \quad \text{with } \sigma_2 \text{ constant} \tag{8.19b}$$

The full employment (N_{fe}) is:

$$N_{fe} = Y_{fc} / \sigma_2 \quad \text{with } \sigma_2 \text{ constant} \tag{8.19c}$$

The unemployment (Un) or the output gap (OG) are easily found:

$$Un = N_{fe} - N \tag{8.19d}$$

$$OG = Y - Y_{fc} \tag{8.19e}$$

The rate of unemployment r_{un} is:

$$r_{un} = Un/N_{fc} \tag{8.19f}$$

For the model, we measure the output gap in ratio:

$$OG_R = (Y - Y_{fc})/Y_{fc} \tag{8.19}$$

We assume that the ratio 'wages on output' (W/Y) is exogenous and constant:

$$W = Y/\rho \qquad \text{with } \rho \text{ constant} \tag{8.20}$$

Total profits (P) of firms are the difference between their sales and their expenditures (wages and interest payments on loans, commercial papers and bonds):

$$P \equiv Y - W - (i_{l-1} \cdot L_{-1}) - (i_{cp-1} \cdot CP_{-1}) - (i_{of} \cdot of_{-1}) \tag{8.21-ii}$$

Distributed dividends (P^d) are a fraction of profits realized in the previous period:

$$P^d = (1 - s_f) \cdot P_{-1} \qquad \text{with } s_f \text{ constant} \tag{8.22}$$

Retained earnings (P^u) are determined as the residual:

$$P^u \equiv P - P^d \tag{8.23-ix}$$

Equations concerning issues of equities by firms are usually oversimplified in SFC models. We simply assume that the stock of shares grows at the rate of the GDP with a lag of one year (gr_{y-1}): $\Delta e/e_{-1} = gr_{y-1}$. The more the economy grows, the more firms issue equities. There are two explanations. First it is easier to sell new equities when the economy, and thus the profits, grow. Second, firms need new finance to follow the growth of the GDP:

$$e = e_{-1} \cdot (1 + gr_{y-1}) \tag{8.24}$$

Households: C, D

We assume that households determine their consumption expenditure (C) on the basis of their expected disposable income and their wealth from the previous period (this consists entirely of bank deposits: current accounts and time deposits):

$$C = (\alpha_1 \cdot Y_w^a) + (\alpha_2 \cdot Y_v^a) + (\alpha_3 \cdot D_{-1}) \text{ with } \alpha_i \text{ constant } 1 > \alpha_1 > \alpha_2 > \alpha_3 > 0$$

(8.25)

$$Y_w^a = Y_{w-1} + \theta_h \cdot (Y_{w-1} - Y_{w-1}^a) \quad \text{with } \theta_h \text{ constant} \tag{8.26}$$

$$Y_v^a = Y_{v-1} + \theta_h \cdot (Y_{v-1} - Y_{v-1}^a) \tag{8.27}$$

$$Y_w = W - T \tag{8.28}$$

$$Y_v = i_{d-1} \cdot D_{-1} \tag{8.29}$$

$$Y_h = Y_w + Y_v \tag{8.30}$$

where Y_w^a is the expected disposable income of workers, Y_v^a the expected disposable financial income and each α_i is a propensity to consume. There are adaptive expectations.[4]

Following the Kaleckian tradition, we assume that wages are mostly consumed while financial income is largely devoted to saving ($1 > \alpha_1 > \alpha_2 > 0$). This class-based saving behaviour is of importance in a SFC model where interest payments play a great role. With the same high propensity to consume ($\alpha_1 = \alpha_2$), an increase of the interest rates can move the economy to a higher growth path in the long run. The consumption decision determines the amount that households will save out of their disposable income Y_h:

$$D \equiv D_{-1} + Y_h - C \tag{8.31-iv}$$

Private banks: $i_l, L, i_{cp}, CP, i_{of}, p_{of}, of, i_d, p_e, P_b$

Firms' financing is fundamental in a monetary economy of production. Firms begin by being self-financed then turn to external finance (ΔF_D). Banks only finance projects they consider profitable, but confidence in their judgement is variable and can justify various strategies. Banks examine firms' productive and financial expectations and also their financial structure. This investigation is made according to their confidence in the state of long-term expectations of yields on capital assets, influencing what Keynes referred to as 'animal spirits'. After the study of expected production and of demand of financing that integrates the firm's borrowing risk (r_b), bankers can refuse to finance. The state of confidence of banks summarizes these factors.

Banks know a lender's risk (LR) when underwriting finance[5] and creating money. Lender's risk is the sum of three fundamental risks:

- First, risk of default corresponds to the bank's perception regarding the borrower's likelihood failure to repay the claim.
- Second, risk of liquidity. Liquidity entails the ability to reverse a decision at any moment at the smallest possible cost.
- Third, market risk corresponds to unanticipated changes on the various financial markets. Market risk can be split into other risks. Fluctuations in capital asset prices modify their value and explain capital risk – which is very high for equities and fixed-yield bonds. For the fixed-yield bonds, capital risk is inversely proportional to interest rates. The risk of income mainly concerns the highly uncertain dividends of equities and the variable yield of loans. Finally, monetary policy involves a money market risk when fluctuations in the money interest rates occur.

In equations (8.32, 8.35, 8.52, 8.53), the risks of default and of liquidity are take account by the gap of the leverage ratio with a conventional leverage ratio. We also introduce Tobin's q ratio and the cost of indebtedness for the risk of default. The market risk is taken into account by the expected capital gains on equities (CG_e^a) and on fixed-yield bonds (CG_{of}^a), and also with the central bank interest rate.

When the lender's risk is at a maximum ($LR = 1$), commercial banks refuse to finance the net investment of firms: $\Delta F = 0$. Desired investment (I_D) faces a serious finance rationing. The flow of net investment is only financed by self-funding, that is the retained earnings (P^u), minus the amortization of the debt, minus the capital losses of firms (CG). Thus the money supply (in stock) can be reduced with the redemption of the debt. If the lender's risk is null ($LR = 0$), desired investment is fully financed: $\Delta F = \Delta F_D$ or $\varphi = \varphi^d$. It is the horizontalist case. The capital losses of firms are also the capital gains of banks, measured by the capital losses on equities (CG_e) and on fixed rate bonds (CG_{of}) (Equations 8.44 and 8.50):

$$\varphi = \varphi^d \cdot (1 - LR) \qquad \text{with } 0 \leq LR \leq 1 \qquad (8.32)$$

$$\Delta F = \varphi - \text{amort} + CG \qquad (8.33)$$

$$CG = CG_e + CG_{of} \qquad (8.34)$$

In the model, the lender's risk (LR) is measured by the difference between the current leverage ratio and the conventional leverage ratio (quantity of indebtedness), by the Tobin's q ratio and by the cost of indebtedness (i_{cb}). The higher current indebtedness of firms (($CP + OF + L)/K$) is over the accepted indebtedness, the more the lender's risk is. The accepted indebtedness is conventional, but this conventional indebtedness can increase during a boom and decrease during a crisis. Tobin's q ratio is measured by the financial value of the firms on the capital (K). The financial value is the value of the equities on the market:

$$LR = a_1 \cdot (\text{lev}_{-1} - \text{lev}_c) - (b_1 \cdot q_{-1}) + (c_1 \cdot i_{cb})$$

with a_1, b_1, c_1 and lev_c constant $\qquad (8.35)$

$$\text{lev} = (CP + OF + L)/K \qquad (8.36)$$

$$q = (e \cdot p_e)/K \qquad (8.37)$$

We now come to the equations defining the portfolio behaviour of banks. We follow the methodology developed by Godley and Lavoie (2007) and inspired by Tobin (1958). Banks can hold four different assets: bonds (with fixed rate of interest) $OF = of \cdot p_{of}$; equities $E = e \cdot p_e$; loans at variable long-term interest rate (L) and commercial paper (CP) at short-term interest rate. The λ_{ij} parameters follow the vertical, horizontal and symmetry constraints (Godley and Lavoie, 2007). Banks are assumed to make a certain proportion λ_{i0} of their financing in the form of asset i but this proportion is modified by the rates of return on these assets. Banks are concerned about (i_l) and (i_{cp}), the rates of interest on loans and on commercial paper to be determined at the end of the current period, but which will generate the interest payments in the following period. We have further assumed that it is the expected rates of return on equities (r_e^a) and on bonds (r_{of}^a) that enter into the determination of portfolio choice. The four assets demand functions described with matrix algebra are thus:

$$OF = (\lambda_{10} + \lambda_{11} \cdot r_{of}^a - \lambda_{12} \cdot r_e^a - \lambda_{13} \cdot i_l - \lambda_{14} \cdot i_{cp}) \cdot F \qquad (8.38)$$

$$E = (\lambda_{20} - \lambda_{21} \cdot r_{of}^a + \lambda_{22} \cdot r_e^a - \lambda_{23} \cdot i_l - \lambda_{24} \cdot i_{cp}) \cdot F \qquad (8.39)$$

$$L = (\lambda_{30} - \lambda_{31} \cdot r_{of}^a - \lambda_{32} \cdot r_e^a + \lambda_{33} \cdot i_l - \lambda_{34} \cdot i_{cp}) \cdot F \tag{8.40}$$

$$CP = (\lambda_{40} - \lambda_{41} \cdot r_{of}^a - \lambda_{42} \cdot r_e^a - \lambda_{43} \cdot i_l - \lambda_{44} \cdot i_{cp}) \cdot F \tag{8.41a}$$

As it is the case with every matrix, we cannot keep all these equations in the model because each one of them is a logical implication of the others. We model commercial paper as the residual equation:

$$CP = F - OF - E - L \tag{8.41}$$

For the bonds, the expected rate of yield (r_{of}^a) is the fixed interest rate plus the expected capital gains on the market value of the previous period of these bonds (OF_{-1}). The market value of the bonds is the number of bonds (of) times their prices (p_{of}). The interest rate (i_{of}) is always the long-term interest rate of the first period applied to the initial price (in t_0, $p_{of} = 1$). But after the first period, the prices of the old and of the new fixed-yield bonds (p_{of}) is inversely proportional to the changes in the long-term interest rates (i_l).

The expected value of capital gains on bonds (CG_{of}^a) and on equities (CG_e^a) for the current period depends on its value from the previous period plus an error correction mechanism where (θ) represents the speed of adjustment in expectations. The capital gains (CG_{of} and CG_e) correspond to the variations in the price times the quantity of the previous period:

$$r_{of}^a = i_{of} + CG_{of}^a/OF_{-1} \qquad \text{with } i_{of} \text{ constant} \tag{8.42}$$

$$CG_{of}^a = CG_{of-1} + \theta_b \cdot (CG_{of-1} - CG_{of-1}^a) \tag{8.43}$$

$$CG_{of} = \Delta p_{of} \cdot of_{-1} \tag{8.44}$$

$$of = OF/p_{of} \tag{8.45}$$

$$p_{of} = p_{of-1} \cdot (1 + i_{of})/(1 + i_l) \tag{8.46}$$

For the equities, the expected rate of yield (r_e^a) is the sum of the expected distributed profits (P^{da}) and the expected capital gains (CG_e^a), on the market value of the previous period of these equities (E_{-1}). As usual, the expected distributed profits (P^{da}) for current period depends on its value of the previous period plus an error correction mechanism where θ represents the speed of adjustment in expectations. The only price clearing mechanism of this model occurs in the equity market. The price of equities (p_e) will allow the equilibrium between the *number* of equities (e; see Equation 8.22) that has been issued by firms (the supply) and the *amount* of equities (E) that private banks want to hold (the demand):

$$r_e^a = (P^{da} + CG_e^a)/E_{-1} \tag{8.47}$$

$$P^{da} = P_{-1}^d + \theta_b \cdot (P_{-1}^d - P_{-1}^{da}) \tag{8.48}$$

$$CG_e^a = CG_{e-1} + \theta_b \cdot (CG_{e-1} - CG_{e-1}^a) \tag{8.49}$$

$$CGe = \Delta p_e \cdot e_{-1} \tag{8.50}$$

$$p_e = E/e \tag{8.51}$$

Monetary authorities determine exogenously the key rate on the money market (i_{cb}). In 1936, Keynes asserts that this rate is widely conventional. While central banks fix the short-term rates, private banks' liquidity preference determines banking rates (short-, medium- and long-term interest rates). Significant rates for growth and financing (loan) are the long-term interest rates (i_l). The link between short-term and long-term interest rates is complex. Macroeconomic banking interest rates (i_l) are the production costs of money plus a risk premium. The first element corresponds to functioning costs (wages, investment, immobilization); payment costs for monetary liabilities (subjected to the firms competition for households savings) and the cost of high powered money determined by the central bank; and to a rate of margin (χ) corresponding to standard profits of banks. The production costs of money are equal to (i_{cb}) plus a relatively constant mark up (χ).

Risk premiums are not constant because they are the fruits of the banks' liquidity preference. Risk premiums cover lender's risk (lr). Five expectations strongly influence risk premiums: anticipations about productivity, economic evolution (growth, employment) and budget; expected inflation; the level of future short-term rates of interest; financial markets' evolution and capital assets' prices; foreign long-term rates present. In the model, we use the same lender's risk as the one seen previously (Equation 8.35), that is a mix of leverage ratio and Tobin's q ratio. But with the different coefficients (a_2) and (b_2), (lr) can be negative and reduces the mark up. Therefore the long-term interest rate becomes endogenous and the spread between (i_{cb}) and (i_l) is not constant. Contrary to the horizontalist view, we introduce an endogenous curve of the interest rates.

To explain the short-term interest rates (i_b or i_{cp}), i_{cb} and χ are sufficient. On the contrary, lr is the primary variable in order to explain long-term interest rates (i_l, i_{of}). Banks apply a spread (χ_3) between the key rate and the rate on deposits in order to realize profits:

$$i_l = i_{cb} + lr + \chi_1 \qquad \text{with } \chi_1 \text{ constant } \chi_1 > \chi_2 \qquad (8.52)$$

$$lr = a_2 \cdot (\text{lev}_{-1} - \text{lev}_c) - b_2 \cdot q_{-1} \qquad (8.53)$$

With a_2, b_2, lev_c constant and c = convention on the 'normal' debt ratio:

$$i_{cp} = i_{cb} + \chi_2 \qquad \text{with } \chi_2 \text{ constant } \chi_1 > \chi_2 \qquad (8.54)$$

$$i_d = i_{cb} - \chi_3 \qquad (8.55)$$

The initial structure of interest rates is as follows: $i_l > i_{of} > i_{cp} > i_b = i_{cb} > i_d$.

Banks try to maximize their net income. To make a profit, they finance the economy and agree to become less liquid. By making the almost irreversible decisions of financing, they are subjected to the lender's risk. They can hope for big profits only by lowering their LP_B. Economic activity also depends on the animal spirits of banks. Finance scarcity can only be the consequence of a deliberate choice. 'Desired scarcity' of financing is the sign of banks' liquidity preference. From an optimal structure of their balance sheet, we can measure the profits of commercial banks (P_b) obtained by monetary financing:

$$P_b \equiv i_{b-1} \cdot B_{-1} + i_{l-1} \cdot L_{-1} + i_{cp-1} \cdot CP_{-1} + i_{of} \cdot of_{-1} + P^d$$
$$- i_{d-1} \cdot D_{-1} - i_{cb-1} \cdot REF_{-1} \qquad (8.56\text{-v})$$

Central Bank: H, i_{cb}, REF, i_b, P_{cb}, Π, LF

It is assumed that banks are obliged by the government to hold reserve requirements (H) in high-powered money that do not generate interest payments and that must always be a fixed share (the compulsory ratio η) of deposits:

$$H = \eta \cdot D \qquad (8.57)$$

Since the central bank is collecting interest payments advances while paying out no interest on the notes, it is also making profits P_{cb}:

$$P_{cb} \equiv i_{cb-1} \cdot REF_{-1} \qquad (8.58\text{-vii})$$

It is assumed, in line with current practice, that any profits realized by the central bank revert to the government. Following the theory of endogenous money, we assume that the central bank is fully accommodating. First the central bank fixes the key rate of interest (i_{cb}) using a Taylor rule and second it provides whatever advances (*REF*) demanded by banks at this rate.

Taylor propounded his first rule in 1993, modelling the dual mandate of the Fed. It was founded on the output gap and on the inflation gap. But the output gap generates a theoretical problem to the RBC models (Goodfriend-King [Goodfriend and King, 2001] or Rotenberg-Woodford [Rotenberg and Woodford, 1997]) and creates an implementation problem for inflation targeting. Inflation targeting is more a hierarchical mandate than a dual mandate. A truncated rule (without the output gap) appeared as a theoretical answer (Batini and Haldane, 1999), but this solution does not characterize well the practice of central banking. The development of the DGSE models and of the New Macroeconomic Consensus (NCM) around three equations (IS, TR and NKPC) explains the numerous papers on the status of the output gap.

In our model, we use two of three equations from the NCM: a Taylor rule and a New Keynesian Phillips Curve. But we replace the IS equation by our Post-Keynesian SFC model. We take two sorts of Taylor rule: a standard one and a truncated one.

The first hypothesis (M1) is that central bank uses a standard Taylor rule, modelling the dual mandate of the Fed. The key interest rate (i_{cb}) is a negative function of the output gap and a positive function of the inflation gap. Output gap is the difference between the full capacity output (Y_{fc}) and the current output (Y). Output gap in ratio (see Equation 8.19 for OG_R) is output over the output gap. Inflation gap is the difference between current inflation and the target of inflation (Π^*). As in a standard Taylor rule, we add a neutral interest rate, exogenously fixed at 2%. The inflation target is 1%. At the steady state, the key interest rate is equal to 3%, so the real key interest rate is equal to the neutral interest rate ($i_{cb} - \Pi^* = i^* = 2\%$). In this case, the three gaps (output, inflation and interest rate) are equal to zero. The monetary rule M1 is:

$$i_{cb} = i^* + \Pi + \alpha_4 \cdot OG_R + \alpha_6(\Pi - \Pi^*) \qquad (8.59\text{-M1})$$

The second hypothesis (M2) is a truncated Taylor rule similar to the unique mandate of the ECB. A truncated Taylor rule only contains the inflation gap. When the central bank has a unique mandate, the fear of inflation is higher. We should have: $\alpha_5 > \alpha_6$. We put $\alpha_6 = 0.5$ and $\alpha_5 > 1$. The monetary rule (M2) is:

$$i_{cb} = i^* + \alpha_5(\Pi - \Pi^*) \qquad \text{(8.59-M2)}$$

$$REF \equiv REF_{-1} + \Delta H + \Delta B + \Delta F - CG - P_b - \Delta D \qquad \text{(8.60-vi)}$$

a kind of New Keynesian Phillips Curve models inflation (Taylor, 1979).

When inflation is low and close to its target, we consider that the anticipations of inflation are anchored on the target. In this case, inflation does not react to the variations of output gap (OG_R). Inflation depends only on the anticipated inflation (Π^a) that is anchored on the target: $\Pi^a = \Pi^*$. This leads to a horizontal NKPC. But if the variations in output are too important (for instance, close to full capacity output) or, if an exogenous supply shock occurs (for instance, a shock in productivity or in the oil price), inflation reacts. Inflation reappears over OG_{Rmini} and disinflation under OG_{Rmaxi}. The idea that for small disturbances the inflation rate is stable while for large disturbances it is unstable was coined by Leijonhufvud (1981, p. 112n) in the notion of a 'corridor'. The economy has stability inside the corridor, while it will lose stability outside. Such a 'corridor of stability' can provide another way of looking at Keynes's insight that the economy is not violently unstable. The shape of the curve is as shown in Figure 8.2.

We can write the equation of inflation as a sort of NKPC:

$$\Pi = \Pi^* + d_1 \cdot (OG_{Rmini} + OG_R) + d_2 \cdot (OG_{Rmaxi} + OG_R) + \text{Cost push} \qquad \text{(8.61)}$$

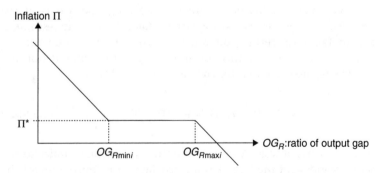

Figure 8.2   NKPC with a 'cost push' $= 0$

We can model the loss function of the society as a linear-quadratic function. It supposes that the society has a symmetric target. It is an *ad hoc* loss function because it does not have any micro-foundations. It is not a utility-based loss function based on the utility function of the representative agent (Woodford, 2003). It is connected with the final objective of the society. The society seeks to reach three objectives: price stability, full employment and financial-market stability. The price of equities is not part of governments' or central banks' policies. Society as a whole does not share the same concerns as the government or the central bank. Their reaction functions are not derived from the loss function. Asset prices in the steady state correspond to (p_e^*). We measure the volatility of the asset prices by $(p_e - p_e^*)$. We can represent the welfare performance of such policies by their welfare cost. In our model, we have: $\beta_1 = \beta_2 = \beta_3 = 1.33$:

$$LF = \beta_1(\Pi - \Pi^*)^2 + \beta_2 OG_R^2 + \beta_3(p_e - p_e^*)^2 \qquad (8.62)$$

Our model is now closed. We have defined the 26 variables of the transactions matrix introducing 37 new variables[6] and we now have the same number of equations (62) and unknowns. Furthermore, we have managed to use the $M + N - 1 = 8$ accounting identities issued from the transcription of the transactions matrix. The missing identity concerns the capital account of the central bank:

$$REF = H \qquad (8.63\text{-viii})$$

This identity reflects the fact that high-powered money is supplied through advances to private banks. Of course, this accounting identity must invariably hold. When we solve our model numerically, identity (viii) $H \equiv REF$ holds perfectly.

Experiments about a supply shock with two policy mix

We make simulations[7] by imposing exogenous supply shocks corresponding to an inflationary shock of 1% during three years, for example an increase in oil price. This cost-push increase in inflation is first reflected in the NKPC and then, the key interest rate given by the Taylor rule. The key interest rate of the central bank is endogenous. In turn, changes in the short-term rate of interest modify the long-term interest rate and the growth rate through the different channels of transmission developed by the model. Then fiscal policy acts upon the economy.

The consequences of the supply shock are examined for two kinds of policy mix[8]:

- For country (1), monetary policy is determined by a standard Taylor rule (M1) that corresponds to a dual mandate: output gap and inflation gap. The fiscal policy rule (F1) has a stabilizing effect (see Figure 8.1). But this effect is insufficient to restore the economy to the previous steady state. There is a coordination between the monetary and the fiscal policies. Country (1) describes the United States.
- For country (2), monetary policy is determined by a 'truncated' Taylor rule (M2) that corresponds to a unique mandate: inflation gap only. Fiscal Policy (F2) is neutralized, because we assume the fiscal rule that the ratio of the current deficit of the Government (GD) on the GDP is constant and equal to zero, as imposed by the Maastricht treaty. Country (2) describes the European Union.

In our economy, the steady state is not the full-employment equilibrium. The output gap is positive, with a significant rate of unemployment. Potential output corresponds to the full capacity output.

Figure 8.3 shows that country (1) resists much better than country (2) to a supply shock. The fall in the growth rate and in the desired growth rate of accumulation of capital is much lower. In addition, the emergence of economic cycles is obvious in the country (2). Without

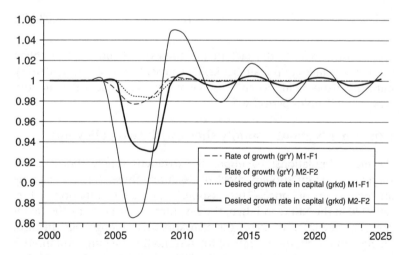

Figure 8.3 Inflationary shock of 1% during 3 years (M1–F1, M2–F2): effects on the growth rate of the economy and on the desired rate of accumulation

output gap in the Taylor rule and with the removal of the fiscal tool, the economic situation deteriorates and becomes more strongly cyclical.

The rate of utilization of productive capacity falls more in the second country than in the first (Figure 8.4). The financial behaviour of firms explains much of these developments. The borrower's risk measured by the rate of cash flow (r_{cf}) and the financial condition index (FCI) rises substantially. With higher costs of financing, the rate of cash flows ($r_{cf} = P^u/K_{-1}$) drops in the short term. Interest payments on loans and commercial papers increase, and this reduces retained profits. But then, firms reduce the issue of equities to preserve the part of undistributed profits (P^u) and the rate of cash flow rises but under its first position. The drop in the Tobin's ratio is an additional negative effect (Figure 8.5). The financial condition index increases vigorously with the fall in the financial capitalization (E/Y). With the depressed FCI and the lower cash flow ratio, the borrower's risk increases seriously.

To simplify, we introduced inflation only in the NKPC and we do not take into account the difference between real and monetary variables in the rest of the model. Inflation could be integrated into the determinants of lender's risk and borrower's risk and into the portfolio matrix, in order to better integrate the wealth effects. Monetary policy tries to neutralize expectations of inflation, but it had little impact on the shock of inflation, which is exogenous.

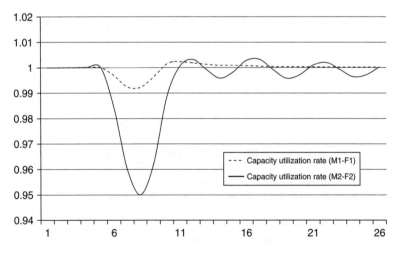

Figure 8.4 Inflationary shock of 1% during 3 years (M1–F1, M2–F2): effects on the rate of utilization capacity

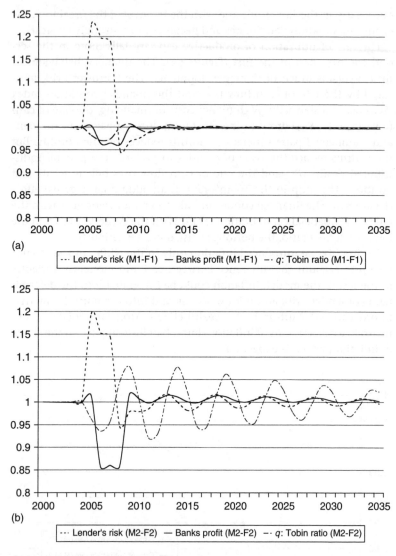

Figure 8.5 Inflationary shock of 1% during 3 years; (a) M1–F1, (b) M2–F2: effects on lender's risk, on banks profit (6%), and on Tobin's *q* ratio

Since the fear of inflation is higher in country (2), central bank rate of interest reacts more vigorously (Figure 8.6). This rise enlarges the output gap more in country (2) than in country (1). Business cycles appear (Figure 8.7). With a lower inflation rate and a higher interest rate, the real

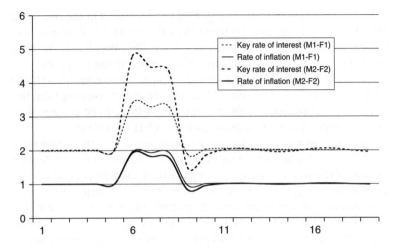

Figure 8.6 Inflationary shock of 1% during 3 years (M1–F1, M2–F2): effects on the rate of interest and on the rate of inflation

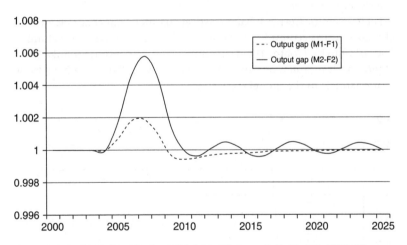

Figure 8.7 Inflationary shock of 1% during 3 years (M1–F1, M2–F2): effects on the output gap

interest rate of country (2) far exceeds that of country (1), which restricts more investment and growth.

The influence of output gap on the key interest rate is lower than that of inflation, even with the standard Taylor rule. With the sharp rise in interest rates, investment, which reacts swiftly to the interest rate, will be more affected than other components of demand. On the one hand, the fall in investment will be larger than the expansion resulting from the stabilizing policy of the country (1). On the other hand, the fiscal policy F2, which has no stabilizing effect, explains the strong negative effect on the growth of the country (2). Finally, the rise in interest rates improves the financial income of households and so consumption. But, with our Kaleckian consumption function, the benefits on consumption are very weak. This effect is insufficient to offset the others.

One key element of the experiments is the increase of the lender's risk. The fall of the Tobin's q ratio plus the lowest solvency of firms following the rise of the interest rates explain the rise of the lender's risk and the decreasing leverage ratio (Figure 8.5). Our virtual economies experience a transitory business depression, characterized by a lower rate of utilization capacity, a lower Tobin's ratio and leverage, and higher lender's and borrower's risks. The consequence is a credit rationing of the investment of firms by private banks (Figure 8.8). The credit rationing of firms explains an increasing rate of unemployment. The situation is worse in the second country.

Let us examine the bank-balance-sheet channel. Four channels are usually taken into account by literature: wealth effect (Davis and Palumbo, 2001), Tobin's q (Tobin, 1969), the financial accelerator (Bernanke *et al.*, 1999) and the capital of banks (Van den Heuvel, 2002). We have these four channels in the model (Le Heron, 2007a).

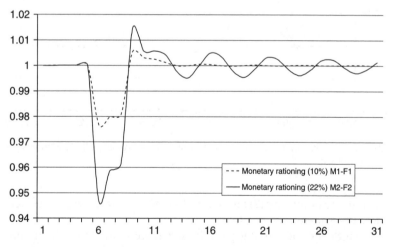

Figure 8.8 Inflationary shock of 1% during 3 years (M1–F1, M2–F2): effects on credit rationing

With country 2, we see a sharp volatility in the financial markets (stocks and bonds) and a significant fall in the profit of banks (Figures 8.5 and 8.9). These elements could explain the coming out of financial crises.

We can argue from these experiments that it is preferable to include the output gap in the Taylor rule and that the use of stabilizing fiscal

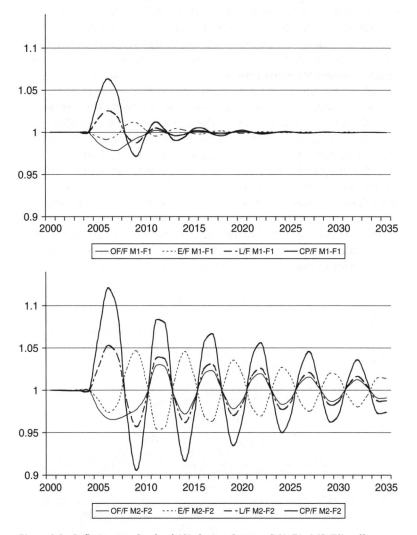

Figure 8.9 Inflationary shock of 1% during 3 years (M1–F1, M2–F2): effects on finance structure (E = 50%; OF = 23%; L = 19%; CP = 8%)

policy is beneficial. Indeed, the simulations showed a high volatility in production with the truncated rule, but also price volatility on the financial markets. Financial instability may be an unforeseen consequence. Since money is not neutral, it is difficult to consider inflation only for the monetary policy. We note that the absence of output gap accentuates the decline in the growth, and increases the volatility of, the economy. In case of supply shock, coordination with a stabilizing fiscal policy always generates better results and does not cause any business cycles. Coordination between policies, as we see in the United States, is more efficient than the total separation between fiscal and monetary policies, which is required by the Maastricht treaty.

We have modelled two kinds of institutions. We can use a welfare function of the society seeking to maximize the following three objectives with the same weight for each of them: price stability, growth and stability in financial markets. Clearly, the institutional design of the United States is far better than in the European Union (Figure 8.10).

In this chapter, we have tried to make the New Keynesian consensus in macroeconomics compatible with the Post Keynesian theories in a stock-flow consistent approach. By taking into account the behaviour of private banks, a more realistic creation of money, the stocks and the financial risks of firms and banks, we can analyze more deeply the problems of coordination between fiscal policy and monetary policy. Indeed, the intensity of these problems has increased with the full independence

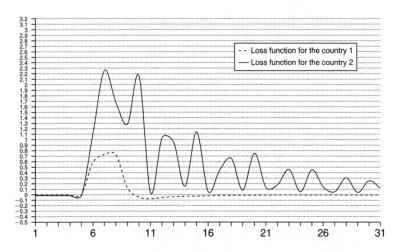

Figure 8.10 Welfare performance of the society: loss function with three equal objectives: inflation, output gap and stability of asset prices

given to some central banks. This stock-flow consistent model is a first step into this research agenda.

Acknowledgements

Our grateful thanks to Philip Arestis, Emmanuel Carré, Jérôme Creel, Wynne Godley, Mark Lavoie, Jacques Mazier, Dominique Plihon, Malcolm Sawyer, Eric Tymoigne and Gennaro Zezza for their helpful comments on the previous drafts. See Le Heron and Mouakil (2008) for the Post Keynesian SFC model.

Appendix: glossary of variables

Y	National income
Y_{fc}	Output of full capacity
gr_y	Growth rate in the national income
Π	Inflation
Π^*	Inflation target
N	Employment
N_{fe}	Full employment
OG	Output gap
OG_R	Ratio of output gap
Un	Unemployment
r_{un}	Rate of unemployment
L	Loans (variable long-term rate)
CP	Commercial paper
B	Treasury bills
E	Equities
e	Number of equities
p_e	Price of equities
OF	Bonds (Fixed rate)
of	Number of bonds
p_{of}	Price of fixed rate bonds
LF	Loss function of the society

Central Bank

P_{cb}	Central bank profits
REF	Reserve requirements (CB refunds)
H	High-powered money
i_{cb}	Central bank key interest rate
i^*	Neutral interest rate

Commercial Banks

P_b	Banks profits
V_b	Net wealth of banks
CG	Capital gains of banks (Capital losses of firms)
CGe	Capital gains on equities
CG_e^a	Expected capital gains on equities
CG_{of}	Capital gains on bonds
CG_{of}^a	Expected capital gains on bonds
i_{cp}	Interest rate on commercial paper
i_d	Interest rate on deposits
i_l	Interest rate on loans
i_b	Interest rate on treasury bills
FCI	Financial Condition Index
LR	Lender's risk
lr	Lender's risk for long-term interest rate
r_{of}^a	Expected yield of bonds
r_e^a	Expected return on equities
P^d	Expected distributed profits
lev	Leverage ratio
q	Tobin's q ratio

Firms

I	Net investment
I_D	Investment demand
W	Wages
K	Stock of capital
V_f	Net wealth of firms
u	Capacity utilization rate
gr_k	Growth rate in the stock of capital
gr_{kD}	Desired growth rate in the stock of capital
ΔF	Net finance
φ	Gross finance
φ^d	Desired gross investment
IF	Internal Funds
amort	Amortization (debt redemption)
P	Firms profits
P^d	Distributed profits
P^u	Undistributed profits
r_{cf}	Borrower's risk (ratio of cash flow)

Government

G   Government expenditure
DG   Government deficit
g_{dg} Constant ratio of government deficit
P_{cb} Central bank profits
T   Taxes

Households

C   Consumption
D   Bank deposits
Y_w^a Expected disposable income of workers
Y_v^a Expected disposable financial income
Y_w Disposable income of workers
Y_v Disposable financial income
Y_h Disposable income of household

Notes

1. Excess capacity exists because of expectations of future demand, entry barriers, cost minimization, time-taking production. For the role of inventories see Godley and Lavoie (2007, ch. 9).
2. What we call 'non-ordinary row' is the row concerning banks' profits, which includes three different variables (see ix).
3. When we use an accounting identity we often need to rewrite it so we will always include its number (using Roman numeral), to make it more easily recognizable by the reader.
4. The expected value of any variable for the current period (represented with the superscript *a*) depends on its value from the previous period plus an error correction mechanism where θ represents the speed of adjustment in expectations.
5. We will take into account the loans (*L*) (long-term), the short-term securities as treasury bills (*B*) and commercial papers (*CP*), bonds (fixed-rate (*OF*)) and equities (*E*).
6. These 37 new variables are the following:

   Government: DG
   Firms: gr_y, gr_{KD}, Y, Y_{fc}, K, I_D, r_{cf}, u, ICF, φ, φ^d, IF, amort, OG_R
   Private Banks: CG, CG_{of}, CG_{of}^a, CG_e, CG_e^a, RP, lev, q, OF, E, r_{of}^a, r_e^a, P^{da}, rp
   Households: Y_w^a, Y_v^a, Y_w, Y_v, Y_h
   Central Bank: i_{cb}, Π, LF

7. We use the E-views 5.5 software.
8. For a more precise analysis of the institutional design (European Union, United States, Japan), see Creel and Capoen (2007) and Le Heron (2007b).

References

Batini, N. and Haldane, A. (1999) 'Forward-looking rules for monetary policy', in J. Taylor (ed.), *Monetary Policy Rules*, Chicago: The University of Chicago Press, pp. 157–92.

Bernanke, B., Gertler, M. and Gilchrist, S. (1999) 'The financial accelerator in a quantitative business cycle framework', *Handbook of Macroeconomics*, vol. 1, Amsterdam: North-Holland, pp. 1341–93.

Creel, J. and Capoen, F. (2007) 'Efficiency of stability-oriented institutions: The European case', OFCE, Working paper no 2007–06, February.

Davis, M.A. and Palumbo, M.G. (2001) 'A primer on the economics and time series econometrics of wealth effects', *Fed Finance and Economics Discussion Series*, no. 2001–09.

Dos Santos, C. and Zezza, G. (2004) 'A post-Keynesian stock-flow consistent macroeconomic growth model: Preliminary results', The Levy Economics Institute, working paper no. 402, February.

Godley, W. and Lavoie, M. (2007) *Monetary Economics: An Integrated Approach to Credit, Money, Income, Production and Wealth*, Basingstoke: Palgrave Macmillan.

Goodfriend, M. and King, R. (2001) 'The case for price stability', Federal Reserve Bank of Richmond, working paper no. 01–02.

Kalecki, M. (1937) 'The principle of increasing risk', *Economica*, 4(13), 440–7.

Keynes, J.M. (1973) *The General Theory, in The Collected Writings of J.M. Keynes*, vol VII, London: Macmillan (first published 1936).

Lavoie, M. and Godley, W. (2001) 'Kaleckian growth models in a stock-flow monetary framework: A Kaldorian view', *Journal of Post-Keynesian Economics*, 24(2): 277–312.

Le Heron, E. (2007a) 'The dynamic analysis of monetary policy shock on banking behavior', in J. McCombie and C. Rodriguez (eds), *Issues in Finance and Monetary Policy*, Basingstoke: Palgrave Macmillan, pp. 79–99.

Le Heron, E. (2007b) 'The new governance in monetary policy: A critical appraisal of the Fed and the ECB', in P. Arestis, E. Hein and E. Le Heron (eds), *Aspects of Modern Monetary and Macroeconomic Policies*, Basingstoke: Palgrave Macmillan, pp. 146–71.

Le Heron, E. and Mouakil, T. (2008) 'A Post Keynesian stock-flow consistent model for the dynamic analysis of monetary policy shock on banking behavior', *Metroeconomica*, 59(3), 405–40.

Leijonhufvud, A. ([1973] 1981) 'Effective demand failures', *Swedish Journal of Economics*. Reprinted in Leijonhufvud, A. (1981) *Information and Coordination. Essays in Macroeconomic Theory*, New York: Oxford University Press.

Minsky, H. (1975) *John Maynard Keynes*, New York: Columbia University Press.

Mouakil, T. (2006) 'Instabilité financière et méthode stocks-flux: analyse critique de l'hypothèse de Minsky', PhD thesis, University Montesquieu Bordeaux 4, November.

Rotemberg, J. and Woodford, M. (1997) 'An optimisation-based econometric framework for the evaluation of monetary policy', *NBER Macroeconomics Annual*, 297–346.

Taylor, J. (1979) 'Staggered contracts in a macro model', *American Economic Review*, 68 108–13.

Taylor, J. (1993) *Discretion versus Policy Rules in Practice,* Carnegie-Rochester Conference Series on Public Policy, no. 39, pp. 195–214.

Tobin, J. (1958) 'Liquidity preference as behavior toward risk', *Review of Economic Studies*, 25(2), 65–896.

Tobin, J. (1969) 'A general equilibrium approach to monetary theory', *Journal of Money, Credit, and Banking*, 1, 15–29.

Van den Heuvel, S.J. (2002) *The Bank Capital Channel of Monetary Policy*, The Wharton School, University of Pennsylvania, mimeo.

Woodford, M. (2003) *Interest and Prices: Foundations of a Theory of Monetary Policy*, Princeton University Press.

Index